Black

Economic

Empowerment

BLACK

ECONOMIC

EMPOWERMENT

20 YEARS LATER

THE BABY AND THE BATHWATER

Phinda Mzwakhe Madi

kr
publishing

2016

First published in 2016

ISBN: 978-1-86922-585-8
eISBN: 978-1-86922-586-5 (PDF eBook)

Published by KR Publishing
P O Box 3954
Randburg
2125
Republic of South Africa

Tel: (011) 706-6009
Fax: (011) 706-1127
E-mail: orders@knowres.co.za
Website: www.kr.co.za

Printed and bound: Creda, Eliot Avenue, Epping II, Cape Town, 7460, www.creda.co.za
Typesetting, layout and design: Cia Joubert, cia@knowres.co.za
Cover design: Cia Joubert, cia@knowres.co.za
Cover photograph: Keith Groenewald, keith@cswpics.com, www.cswpics.com
Editing and proofreading: Elsa Crous, getitedited@mweb.co.za
Project management: Cia Joubert, cia@knowres.co.za

DEDICATION

This book is dedicated to all the original entrepreneuers of Soweto, but more especially my Mom, Thulisile Martha Madi, and my Dad, Petros Madi.

Pioneers from Sophiatown.

Political promise can only be validated in economic delivery... You can't sleep well in Sandton until they can eat in Soweto.

–Mark Barnes

Source: Findlay: BEE outcomes. Pie in the sky? (eNCA, September 2015)

TABLE OF CONTENTS

SECTION 2: BEE TRENDS IN A DEMOCRATIC SOUTH AFRICA

SECTION 3: SO WHERETO FROM HERE?

SECTION 4: PROMINENT VOICES ON BEE BY SOUTH AFRICAN BUSINESS LEADERS

BEE ACRONYMS AND ABBREVIATIONS

AA	affirmative action
ACHIB	African Cooperative for Hawkers and Informal Businesses
ADCH	African Development and Construction Holdings
ANC	African National Congress
ASGISA	Accelerated and Shared Growth Initiative for South Africa
BBBEE	broad-based black economic empowerment
BBC	Black Business Council
BEE	black economic empowerment
BEECom	Black Economic Empowerment Commission
BEN	black economic enablement
BMF	Black Management Forum
BOSS	Bureau of State Security
BRICS	Brazil, Russia, India, China, South Africa
Busa	Business Unity South Africa
CEO	Chief Executive Officer
CIBD	Construction Industry Development Board
Codesa	Convention for a Democratic South Africa
Cosatu	Congress of South African Trade Unions
CSBD	Centre for Small Business Development
CSI	corporate social investment
DFI	developmental funding institution
DTI	Department of Trade and Industry
EE	employment equity
EED	economic empowerment for the disadvantaged
Eskom	Electricity Supply Commission
EY	Ernst & Young
FMF	Free Market Foundation
GDP	gross domestic product
GDS	Growth and Development Summit
GEAR	Growth Employment and Redistribution
HRD	human resources development
IDC	Industrial Development Corporation
IFRS	International Financial Reporting Standards
IMF	International Monetary Fund
JIPSA	Joint Initiative on Priority Skills Acquisition
JMDP	Joint Management Development Programme
JSE	Johannesburg Stock Exchange
Nail	New Africa Investments Ltd
Nafcoc	National African Federated Chamber of Commerce

Nasasa	National Stokvels Association of South Africa
NDA	National Development Agency
NDP	National Development Plan
Nedlac	National Economic Development and Labour Council
NEF	National Empowerment Fund
Nefa	National Empowerment Funding Agency
NP	National Party
NPC	National Planning Commission
PetroSA	Petroleum, Oil and Gas Corporation of South Africa
PIC	Public Investment Corporation
PPF	Progressive Professionals Forum
Prasa	Passenger Rail Agency of South Africa
PWC	Price Waterhouse Coopers
RAIL	Real Africa Holdings
RAU	Rand Afrikaans University
RDP	Reconstruction and Development Programme
SAA	South African Airways
SAIRR	South African Institute of Race Relations
Sapo	South African Post Office
SASTA	South African Spaza and Tuck Shops Association
Saqa	South African Quality Assurance
Seta	Service Education and Training Authority
SOE	state-owned enterprise
TRC	Truth and Reconciliation Commission
UCT	University of Cape Town
UJ	University of Johannesburg
UK	United Kingdom
US	United States
Wits	University of the Witwatersrand

ABOUT THE AUTHOR

Professor Phinda Madi, a corporate lawyer by profession, is chairman of the diversified investments holding company, Madi Investments, which he founded 17 years ago. He is also majority shareholder and chairman of Allcare Medical Aid Administrators, one of South Africa's oldest privately owned medical aid administration companies. He was commissioner and founding member of the South African Black Economic Empowerment Commission (BEECom). Over the years, from time to time he has also served as advisor to various South African heads of state since democracy. He is the director of major South African public corporations like the Spar Group, Nampak Group, Illovo Sugar, Sovereign Foods Limited and the Automobile Association of South Africa, and a host of other private companies. A law graduate of the University of Zululand, in South Africa, he acquired business administration qualifications from Northwestern University Kellogg Business School in Chicago and HEC Business School in Paris. Between 2002 and 2008 he served tenure as visiting professor and lecturer at Rhodes Investec University Business School and was awarded Ad Hominem Honorary Professor at the conclusion of his tenure. This is his fourth book on economic transformation in South Africa.

He can be contacted at thanda@iafrica.com

ACKNOWLEDGEMENTS

I extend heart-felt words of thanks to the following people:

My wife, Christina (Poppy) Madi for putting up with these bouts of me withdrawing from real life and living like a zombie for three or four months as I write a book. This is the fourth time, and she's still with me!

My kids (especially my daughters, Ayanda and Thuli), who on many occasions when I had writer's block, would volunteer to write the text for me. If only that were possible, my girls! Maybe one day you'll write your own books …

My sister Mendi, for helping me reminisce on the life of our entrepreneurial and highly inspirational late parents. Thanks, Sis, their memory will live in our hearts forever.

My academic mentor at Rhodes University, Prof Gavin Staude. Thanks, Prof, for allowing me to hone my skills at your august institution.

Gaby Magomola. Wow, where do I start? You are probably the only boss I have ever had in my life whose teachings literally changed my view of the world. If you hadn't participated in this book, Ntate, I would have abandoned the project! Thank you so much for being such a great leader and visionary.

The staff at Knowledge Resources, especially Cia Joubert, Dina Nel and many others whom I cannot mention by name, thank you for putting up with my tinkering and changing things!

Last, but certainly not least, my very deep gratitude goes to all the titans of South African industry and commerce who graciously agreed to participate in this project, either by way of granting me their valuable time so that we could have conversations on BEE-related matters, or through their written contributions. I take my hat off to you, ladies and gentlemen: you are the torchbearers of a truly empowered South Africa. This country is fortunate to have leaders of your calibre.

KEYNOTE FOREWORD by TITO MBOWENI

former South African Reserve Bank Governor and director of companies

THE INCOMPLETE OR INCOMPLETABLE
REVOLUTION: ARE WE GOING THERE YET?

The struggle for freedom in South Africa was always summarised as one for political, social and economic emancipation. Adult suffrage has been achieved, allowing for a democratically elected government that is representative of the aspirations of all South Africans, regardless of race, gender or creed. We have held regular elections since 1994 – all of them deemed free and fair – and can thus be happy that we are a functioning democracy. This is a significant achievement, given where this country was prior to 1994. Many people tend to take this for granted, but we who suffered so much under white minority governments dare not forget even for a moment. However, predictable and stable political processes do not guarantee an automatic translation of political values into material experience. This is the challenge that we now grapple with, and it is most evident in the social and economic spheres. The challenge is that although aspects of the social justice imperative can be legislated, no government can enforce behavioural change and, above all, no government has all the material resources required to realise immediate benefit for all. That is why the pact between government, business and society is such a crucial one.

For example, when we built Cosmo City, we idealistically hoped that black, white, rich and poor would live next to each other in harmony. It did not work that way, sadly, and the lesson there is that social cohesion cannot be driven entirely through state constructs. More importantly, the lessons of Cosmo City should not detract from our continuous striving for a common South African identity, exchanging and enjoying our cultural diversity, the fostering of national pride, and simply being happy to be South African and part of the great continent of Africa. In other words, we need to refocus our attention on the national question, knowing that we cannot harness the power of our unified strength if we continue to tolerate, in any shape or form, racism, sexism, tribalism and any persistent manifestations of bigotry. Leadership is critical in this regard. Intellectuals; priests and pastors; shop owners; teachers and principals; trade unionists; business executives and management; farmers; football, netball and any other sports team captains; policemen and –women, station commanders, army sergeants and colonels; student leaders; the chief of the defence force and all politicians, regardless of party affiliations, must cross this rubicon. They must lead us away from the self-imposed yoke that results from viewing our fellow brothers and sisters as inferior others. This is truly what transformation is – a tangible social and economic outcome that reflects a deeper (dare I say) psychological and spiritual shift that embraces all of humanity as equally entitled to freedom, happiness and prosperity.

Needless to say, then, transformation is not about substituting white with black but about reorienting our entire society towards the genuine equality envisioned by the *Freedom Charter*. The burden of my dear brother, Phinda Madi, has always been on that third element of the national question: the economic freedom challenge. And, indeed, this remains a focus of the energies of the liberation movement. How do we, in practice, advance economic freedom? Prof Madi has, in this offering, attempted to begin the process of delving into the causes and effects of our economic powerlessness. This struggle has spawned all kinds of organisations which are attempting to resolve the issue. 'What is to be done?', to borrow Vladimir Lenin's words.

Perhaps we should start at the beginning. Govan Mbeki, one of the earlier African intellectuals, a product of the Healdtown Institution and Fort Hare University, journalist, editor, teacher, publicist, polemicist, political leader, prisoner and a good old man, wrote as follows:

> A better understanding of our past historical development is essential, a clearer interpretation of the historical facts that have led to the present position of the Africans is urgent. A clearer grasp of the problems that confront us today is impossible without a clear understanding and interpretation of the facts that made our forefathers put away their shields and spears... to seek fortunes on the diamond and gold mines. (Mbeki, 1996, p. 60)

Simply, we need to understand how it is that we got here, in order to generate relevant pathways for our future. Prof Madi has tried to delve a little bit into this by discussing, albeit briefly, the instruments the apartheid state used to disempower the African people. This is very important to understand and continuously interrogate if we are to construct an accurate explanation for why we are where we are today, as Africans. Let nobody tell you that this is just history in an attempt to distract you from understanding yourself in relation to the world. No! We are where we are today because of these 'historical facts' that Oom Gov writes about, when he states:

> Where do we, the present generation stand? We stand on the shattered ruins of a once African social structure. We are living in chaotic times where it becomes, daily, exceedingly difficult to grasp the problem in its wholeness. We are inclined to see it (the problem) in dissociated parts, and that makes it impossible for us to find a solution. This is the thing, we cannot isolate the lack of economic empowerment from all other 'historical facts'. (Mbeki, 1996, p. 61)

And so we trudge from one point to the next in search of black economic empowerment (BEE). And the problem here is that most of us actually want to 'receive' a share (or shares) from existing companies. That's the truth, sad as it is! We have come to see empowerment as this or that percentage of Anglo-American given to me, the African. And when that happens, wow! Anglo-American has now attained a level 2 BEE rating, let's go for a black-tie dinner! In this book, Prof Madi has written systematically about the caricature of black people: from lazy to the lowering of standards – the typical anti-African thing. He forgot to write about how people used to say that 'they will come here, bare feet, and jump into our swimming pools'. I am afraid that the prevalent attitude is actually that 'they will occupy our boardrooms, take way our shares and offer no value in return'.

These fears exist not solely from a place of prejudice, but also because – and this we must take responsibility for – we have constructed transformation as a system of wealth transfer, rather than wealth generation. Let's go back a bit in trying to learn from history about economic empowerment. Again, here I want to apply Oom Gov's methodology. He writes:

> In this paper we seek to initiate, hopefully, an in-depth study on the rise and growth of Afrikaner capital... Why that of the Afrikaner and not any other white ethnic group? ... In the course of the study we hope to be able to uncover some unique aspects in the process, of capital accumulation by the Afrikaner operating consciously as a group... in this country. (Mbeki, 1991, p. 1)

He goes on to say:

> The problem we are setting out to study is wide and complex. Failure to grasp its essentials can and does lead to a great deal of confusion among the populace. (Mbeki, 1991, p. 1)

So what did the Afrikaners do? Three things: They

1. organised into the Dutch Reformed Church (DRC), the Broederbond, die Suid-Afrikaanse Buro vir Rasse-Aangeleenthede (Sabra), die Federasie van Afrikaanse Kultuurvereniginge (FAK), die Afrikaanse Handelsinstituut (AHI), die Afrikaanse Studentebond (ASB), die Reddingsdaadbond, die Instituut vir Christelike Nasionale Onderwys, die Onderwysers Unie en die Federasie van Vakbonde;

2. focused attention on the economic front by creating an insurance company, Sanlam; a bank, Volkskas; then Gencor;

3. finally assumed political power.

Aha! The role of the state in empowering its historically disadvantaged immediately becomes apparent. We therefore have to rebuff the notion, told to us every day via radio and the print media, in boardrooms and at schools and universities, that the state has no role to play in the economy. It does, always had and always will have a role – in South Africa, in China and, most certainly, in the hyper-capitalist United States. And so that is the economic empowerment of the Afrikaners, a classic case of state-led capitalism that made millionaires of a once poor grouping. Millionnaires. Another thing we ought not to fear. The accumulation of capital is necessary, but must be accompanied by redistribution to ensure that gains are fairly shared and reinvested. So whereto for today's Africans? That is one of the burdens of this book.

Apart from an obvious appreciation of the central questions that Prof Madi grapples with, I must also stress that I enjoy the passion with which this book has been researched and written. I therefore strongly recommend this publication. We should be thankful that one amongst us has taken the time and made the effort to do this. We are the 'masters of our destinies and the captains of our ships'. But we have to go the extra mile: we must organise, act in solidarity and stop pulling each other down. We must be focused and precise, start a bank, mobilise ourselves into top-class education (even better than Healdtown Institution), groom top-class politicians and civil servants, and rotate private sector and public sector brains (cross-pollination). Critically, let's deal with failure courageously, for it grants us the opportunity to learn. Economic transformation must now move beyond wealth sharing to grapple with the complex question of supporting the innovation that will lead to new wealth creation. This can be done. Let us be strategic.

REFERENCES

Bundy, C. (2012). *A Jacana pocket biography: Govan Mbeki.* Johannesburg: Jacana Media.

Bundy, C. (1992[2015]). *Govan Mbeki, 'Learning from Robben Island'.* Cape Town: Kwela Books.

Magubane, B.M. (1979). *The political economy of race and class in South Africa.* London and New York: Monthly Review Press.

Mbeki, G. (1996). *Sunset at midday*: *Latshon'ilang'emini.* Braamfontein: Nolwazi Educational Publishers.

Mbeki, G. (1991). *Learning from Robben Island: the prison writings of Govan Mbeki.* London, J. Currey.

O'Meara, D. (1983). *Volkskapitalisme: Class, capital and ideology in the development of Afrikaner Nationalism, 1934–1948.* Johannesburg: Ravan Press.

SUPPLEMENTARY FOREWORD
by REUEL KHOZA
prominent business leader and director of companies

The years leading to the advent of democracy in South Africa and those shortly thereafter constituted an ideal national transformation crucible, with political leadership and economic or business leadership as necessary catalytic agents.

Political leadership has in large measure played its catalytic role by, inter alia, establishing political institutions and processes which, viewed individually or collectively, match (if not exceed) those of the best democracies; crafting a constitution with commitment to freedom, justice, equality, accountability and transparency regarded as second to none; and coming out strongly and publicly against the continued racial monopoly of sectors of our economy. Political leadership has initiated a policy and introduced a government procurement system designed to draw blacks into the economic mainstream and attendant benefits from which they were previously excluded. This is by no means exhaustive, nor am I suggesting that the politicos have had unqualified successes.

The point is that, in terms of establishing a foundation for black economic emancipation, political leadership has come to the party; they have by and large established their bona fides. Their task now is to deepen and consolidate the political framework for the economic empowerment and emancipation of blacks.

What is sorely needed, 20 years after the advent of democracy, is for similar initiatives to be undertaken in the economic field, to support and nourish the cardinal object of economic emancipation. This is where those of us (like Phinda Madi) who are involved in economic leadership should come to the table, where we as business demonstrate our bona fides and pay our dues. The black business intelligentsia have a historical responsibility to help create and shape the economic process, systems and institutions which support and nourish the cause of economic emancipation.

The task for black business is simple and easy, yet also profoundly difficult. In the economic sphere our contribution as businesspeople is to begin doing those things that most fundamentally reflect African values and interests; those things that help define Africa and its people as competent, successful and with a profound sense of dignity and self-worth.

It is easy and simple because it is straightforward and it is a natural desire of any people, individually and collectively. It is difficult because we have not sufficiently developed the vision, the courage, the honesty, the consistency and the discipline to make those decisions consistently and to do those things, in the course of BEE deals, that could be seen to be contributing to an African Renaissance.

Many of our decisions and activities are characterised more by short-sightedness, expediency, greed and vanity. In many instances where our hearts are in the right place and we are trying to do the right things, we seem to lack the intellectual framework or the self-belief to stay the course and prevail when challenges arise.

As thought leader and author, Phinda Madi's role can best be described as that of a catalyst. Catalysts are what leaders need to be if they are to inspire their followers to undertake the work at hand. A catalyst for a chemical reaction may be a small element within the entire mix, but it speeds up the rate of molecular exchange and bonding, having a pervasive effect on the entire process. Those few words of encouragement that a corporate leader offers to hard-pressed technology managers and laboratory boffins can inspire the confidence needed for breakthroughs. A catalyst is one who shows enthusiasm, personal commitment and intelligence in tackling the job, while infecting others with the same spirit.

According to John C. Maxwell, in his book on teamwork, "[c]atalysts are not consultants. They don't recommend a course of action. They take responsibility for making it happen." There is one significant difference between the chemistry example and catalytic leadership in real life. The human catalyst is changed by his or her engagement with followers, whereas the chemical catalyst, by definition, emerges unchanged from the reaction. A true leader can never escape the moral introspection that forms part of serving the greater community. For good or ill, one bears responsibility for what happens.

Madi effectively urges us to be economic catalysts in empowering blacks, by first comprehending what handicapped and hampered BEE for 20 years, and then developing more effective models.

In order for South Africa's true transformation to eventuate, the politics of liberation and its consequence as well as its economics of emancipation must be in near perfect tandem: politics in consonance with economics. This is the only sure way to slay that pervasive and venomous apartheid hydra. Apartheid was, at its core, sinister social engineering characterised by politics of oppression and economics of exclusion and exploitation. The political head of this hydra has virtually been severed. Beheading the economic one is proving a lot more challenging; as legend has it, each time it is beheaded it regrows. Madi's persistent writing about BEE and now his admonition against throwing out the baby with the bathwater, make an earnest contribution towards severing the hydra's economic head.

A crowning feature of Madi's authorship is his collaborative approach. The book is, in essence, his brainchild, but commendably buttressed by contributions from fellow black intellects of unassailable stature.

From Madi's latest monumental contribution, and on reflection, one gleans the following among other ideas:

- Government should lead by articulating a clear vision and providing a conducive regulatory framework for empowerment, while demonstrating the firm resolve to employ the instruments and organs of the state, which it has at its disposal, to achieve this;

- Black business primarily faces a business challenge, and only part of that is the transformation of the political economy of the country. It is and should not be the 'end all' of broad economic transformation, but must be seen as distinctive despite being connected to other transformation challenges facing the nation;

- There is no single solution or even a set of solutions to ensure effective, sustainable empowerment. It would be naïve to expect a definitive solution for the empowerment challenge. Comprehensive, durable strategies are called for;

- Durable companies are not built in four to five years, they are built over decades and require generational investment;

- Black business has compromised the achievement of empowerment in several material ways. Black business must learn to look in on itself as much as it looks to external impediments to empowerment.

In a moving and compelling way, Madi's book, *Black economic empowerment, 20 years later – the baby and the bathwater*, exhorts us to face stark choices:

- We could choose to pursue an illusion, or we could choose to invest in the development and employment of the necessary strategic and technical capabilities and in the intellectual capacity to understand cause and effect;

- We could choose to be like parasitic weeds, sprouting opportunistically at any and all instances, striving for instant growth and flowering, or we could choose to be like oak trees, independently rooted, sturdy and designed for the next millennium;

- We could choose to follow blindly in the paths of those who have gone before us, and to follow the dictates and agendas of others, or we could choose to develop our own compelling vision and agenda, being confident and courageous enough to follow our dreams no matter how long it takes, no matter what obstacles we face;

- We could choose to invest in the development of a mirage of appearances, through fancy ownership and financing structures and courtiers who make the critical decisions behind the scenes, or we could choose to invest in the development of the real thing, of blacks as unquestionable principals of their own ventures, through the development of our only true asset, black intellectual capital;

- We could choose to perpetuate the stereotype of the African as a dependent, servile, parasitic citizen of the world, or we could choose to create a new prototype of the African as a proud, productive and independent citizen of the world, equal to his compatriots and commanding unconditional global respect.

Yes, indeed, beware – there is a baby in the BEE bathwater. The baby is crucial to economic prosperity, and for posterity not to reinvent the wheel. A complementary African proverb admonishes: *A kulahlwa mbeleko ngokufelwa* (The loss of a child is no cause to jettison the cradle).

SUPPLEMENTARY FOREWORD

by BONANG MOHALE

President, Black Management Forum and Chairman, Shell South Africa

This book could not have come at a more appropriate time. After 20 years of democracy, it is time for all of us to take stock. As we reflect, we need to recognise that the massive legacy, not just of 48 years of apartheid rule but also 350 years of colonialism in our land, continues to make its presence felt. That is why we have to keep talking about black economic empowerment (BEE) and employment equity (EE), even today.

To drill a bit further, it remains a common experience for me to sit with senior African managers and executives who, when they are for instance studying for their BSc (or any other) degree, are also doubling up as petrol attendants in order to generate the income needed to fund their university studies and, in some cases, to supplement the family income. I still interview people for senior positions who relate stories of their ambition to go to university, their studies having been interrupted because they had to drop out and seek menial jobs due to financial pressures from their homes and families. The experience of being employed as a menial labourer lasted a number of years for many of them, while they continued to supplement the family's income and studied part time. It is therefore no exaggeration to say that the average black professional today is likely to have dealt with incredible odds to get where he or she is, mainly because the legacy of apartheid and colonialism continues to stare us in the face.

My personal story, as someone who grew up in a black township at the height of apartheid, is not particularly different from these kinds of stories. Swimming against the tide has been the hallmark of the current crop of black professionals, and is likely to be the case for some time to come. And their stories of making it against incredible odds continue to inspire all of us. So, for black executives this is a common experience. However, things are different and become somewhat complicated when you try to share these stories with your white counterparts in the professional world. They just cannot relate to this. Some may have empathy, but many tend to be bewildered by these tales.

I would even go so far as to say the majority of white executives in this country simply have neither an understanding of, nor an appreciation for, these stories. To them, it sounds as if you are describing life on a different planet. As a black executive who has virtually your entire extended family continuing to live in the same areas where apartheid planted them, with largely the same economic challenges, this is still substantially your world. You may have achieved a noticeable degree of financial success yourself, but by and large the legacy of the rest of your extended family still casts a dark shadow over your own individual success. And that is why, later on in this book, many readers will be surprised and perhaps even bewildered by the great degree of frustration that black leaders express. Surely they are the 'elite', the best and brightest amongst us. So, why are they so overwhelmingly unhappy with the pace of change and transformation? Well, it is because by and large the world from whence they come remains untransformed. As individuals they have done exceptional things, but the world of their past weighs heavily on their shoulders. These are the challenges we have to deal with at the Black Management Forum: highly qualified and successful people but who still feel their own individual success is hollow, because the rest of their folk remain locked out of opportunities.

These achievers operate in a reality of gross income inequality, and it haunts them. For instance, a 2014 study by Duke University and the Centre for Global Policy Solutions, a Washington-based consultancy, found that the median amount of liquid wealth (assets that can easily be turned into cash) held by African households was about $200, for coloured households it was about $340 and for white households $23 000. It is therefore no exaggeration to say that the average African family remains mired in relative poverty. More importantly, the world of black folk in South Africa remains starkly different from the world of white folk. For instance, when you describe hunger to a white colleague, it sounds esoteric to him or her. The white colleague's conception of hunger may have resulted from an experience of being grounded, confined to their room by their parents for a couple of hours, as punishment for some misbehaviour, while your conception of hunger as a black professional may be going without food for a day or two. This is a challenge faced by many of us, who are still advocating for economic transformation. The retort from the white world is likely to be: 'But it's been 21 years of democracy! Can we please move on from this transformation talk, please!' It can be excruciatingly frustrating for us black executives to convey this message to the rest of corporate South Africa that, for our people, our families, hunger is still an issue, as is a lack of amenities, resources and opportunities. It remains a significant issue, and I can't divorce myself from that simply because I, as an individual, have broken through the glass ceiling. What a white colleague sees in me is not representative of the current black experience.

As business leaders generally, you find that white business leadership and black business leadership do not share a common South African experience. Sometimes, as a black business leader, you get so animated defining experiences that are completely alien to your white colleagues that it becomes very difficult to develop shared visions or common programmes. For me it is important that, in an attempt to address especially issues of economic transformation, there is first an unequivocal and wholehearted admission by the business leadership in this country that our points of departure are so starkly different, that we truly come from different worlds. Of course we as blacks have had a much better and greater exposure to the white world because, for decades, we entered it as gardeners, domestic servants and other types of labourers. We had a glimpse and a fairly good understanding of how that world operates. But when it comes to white South Africans, by far the majority have never had any exposure to the black world. Except for minor snippets which they see on TV, the black world is as alien to them as the planet Pluto. And here I am talking about today, not 20 or 50 years ago. No, today, in the year 2015.

There are people in Cape Town, for instance, who have never been to any other part of South Africa. I can confidently say the majority of white people here in Gauteng have never been to Soweto, which is just 30km from the 'white world'. It is not uncommon to find a situation where a 38-year-old black domestic helper, who may have been hired 20 years ago by the parents of her current employer and actually raised her current employers when they were children themselves, is now raising their children too. Surely this domestic helper is, for all intents and purposes, a member of that family – or at least is supposed to be. But chances are that, other than a vague understanding that she stays somewhere in Soweto with a husband and three children, they probably have never been to her four-roomed house to see how she lives.

I am also mindful of the fact that, due to apartheid having kept black and white people apart, there has been a tendency by many of my white compatriots to complain of 'lowered standards' with regard to public amenities since the dawn of democracy. This complaint has unfortunately led to many of them retreating further into their enclaves and almost, once again, creating their own private world of privilege – private schools, private security, private hospitals, private gated communities – thereby perpetuating the divisions of apartheid which we had hoped to eradicate with the advent of our democracy. Many of my white compatriots, in my view, had assumed that, post-apartheid, they would continue to have exclusive access to South Africa's best public amenities (top schools, hospitals, etc.) where, because of their population size and exclusive access, they had grown used to receiving speedy, top-class service. They had grown used to going to a hospital, for instance, where there were plenty of doctors at their beck and call, using specialised equipment. They could be in and out of there in two hours. Meanwhile, at Baragwanath Hospital in Soweto, which was a single hospital serving all the four or five million people of Soweto, it would have taken a black patient up to four days to eventually be seen to. Nowadays, a white patient who goes to hospital will no longer be in and out of there in two hours; he may be there for four hours, because the hospital is now available to all citizens, not just white citizens only. But similarly, for a black patient, it no longer takes four days to see a doctor, perhaps he will see one within a day. These are the experiences that have characterised the new South Africa. Obviously it would have defeated the purpose of the anti-apartheid struggle to maintain the grossly discriminatory allocation of state resources. The new democratic state has to take care of everybody.

Such disparate experiences have led some white citizens to contend that the new South Africa is failing. But they don't take into account the totality of experiences of the citizenry.

In my mind I like to characterise the post-election collision between the black and white worlds as follows: the black world was like a cold well of water feeding the multitudes, whereas the white world of middle-class privilege was but a single glass of warm 'cozy' water that had been exclusively available to them for all these years. When, as a nation, we were born anew in 1994, and earnest attempts began to merge these two worlds, in a way that glass of warm water had to be poured into the well of cold water, in order to enable all South Africans, irrespective of colour, to access the water. Inevitably, that could only create shock and discomfort for our white compatriots. They had grown used to having warm water available to them alone, all these years, but that was no longer the case.

In order to develop a South Africa where there is economic justice for all, we as business leaders, both black and white, have to find ways to transcend the barriers that continue to be a reality. First, we have to acknowledge that we come from different worlds and experiences, because paper-coating over them has cost us dearly over the past 20 years, thereby stunting transformative economic programmes like BEE and affirmative action (AA). Once we have acknowledged this, we can begin to earnestly and determinedly tackle issues related to the economic marginalisation of black people. But if we keep denying these barriers and different experiences, we will continue to run in circles. We will exhaust our energy trying to duck and dive and second-guess one another – something which has unfortunately accounted for the poor progress on BEE and EE over the past two decades.

Looking ahead, we as South Africans have to begin to internalise the transformation imperative, and not just regard it as an institutional imposition, as has been the case to date. Many of us previously held the view that, 'Ah well, I have to do this transformation thing because it is part of the law and the government will levy penalties on me if I don't.' The time has now come for each of us, as individuals, to ask ourselves tough questions about economic justice and say: Am I comfortable with the fact that the legacy of apartheid continues to hobble millions of my fellow citizens on a day-to-day basis? Does it matter to me that many of my fellow citizens are still mired in poverty and deprivation, or am I just going to look the other way and enjoy my lavish lifestyle? At the end of the day, stripped of its emotionality, that is what the transformation issue is all about: it is about economic justice. Any change and realisation has to come from deep down within each one of us. I know that the minute you utter the word 'transformation', people begin to bring down the shutters and say: 'Oh, here comes this nasty word again.' The tendency is therefore to institutionalise this imperative and, consequently, externalise it.

The cry for economic justice is really a cry to complete the unfinished project of a South Africa that offers opportunity for all, not just some. How do we give effect to the South Africa of Nelson Rolihlahla Mandela? How do we ensure that this economy grows so that it can accommodate all of us? How do we ensure that all the country's resources and amenities are accessible to the entire population, not just 20 per cent of it, knowing of course that our resources are limited? Also, how do we temper our expectations to realistic levels, knowing that it is not possible to reverse the legacy of apartheid and colonialism in a few decades, when it actually was in place for centuries? In a way, we need to take a leaf from the book of those Asian countries which tend to have long-term national development plans.

One thing that would be remiss of me not to mention as a major concern (and here I have to criticise our democratic government from a perspective of tough love) is the goings-on within our state-owned enterprises (SOEs). Ordinarily, these being major corporations (eight of them are actually bigger in economic terms than some countries on our continent), have become the burial ground of the reputations and careers of black executives. Given that these entities are 100 per cent owned by our own democratic government, I would have expected them to become the natural home of, and skills-honing grounds for, our executives, yet they have become arenas of their destruction. As a result of unclear policy guidelines and continuous violations of the tenets of good governance by principally the shareholder, many a towering reputation (of black executives) has emerged in tatters at the end of the day. By way of an example, at Eskom we recently saw a highly qualified black executive with an impeccable track record in the public sector being strangely replaced within six months of taking office. Just how brutal can one be as a shareholder? This, in our view as the Black Management Forum, has almost made us conclude that our government is doing similar (if not worse) damage to the standing of black executives as the apartheid government sought to do. We are traumatised by these events. We are almost at the stage where many of us believe that no self-respecting black executive would want to have anything to do with SOEs, either as executives or by serving on their boards. This constitutes a monumental tragedy. Indeed, many amongst us are beginning to believe that the government which we love so much, through various inexplicable acts and omissions, is doing as much damage to black enterprise as the apartheid regime inflicted. This is dealt with at such length in the book, by the author and by the other contributing black business leaders and entrepreneurs, that I won't go into detail here.

We need our government to draw closer to black enterprise and black executives, so that we can have frank yet constructive engagements, realising that our successes (and failures) are inextricably intertwined. Black executives and black entrepreneurs are so keen to become part of the economic engine of this country that our energy, expertise and unique experience remain available to government. We just wish it could be used more often, and fairly.

SUPPLEMENTARY FOREWORD
by ROY ANDERSON
director of companies

At the time I was President of the Johannesburg Stock Exchange (JSE) some 20 years ago, our attention was focused on the total restructuring of the equities market, to make it world class. We replaced the trading floor with electronic trading, opened membership to the banks and foreign entities and updated the listing requirements. At the same time, however, we were grappling with the concepts of reconstruction and development, transformation, AA) and BEE. The best ways for the JSE to contribute to the economic future of South Africa and to provide access to capital were vigorously debated. We realised that this was even more important than the other restructuring we were embarking on.

There was consensus that BEE was vital and that the listings requirements in particular should allow for the issuing of shares to new black shareholders, without having to make an offer to existing shareholders. We also supported the aspirations of what was then King I, a predecessor to King III.

The question now, however, is how well BEE has been implemented.

This book by Prof Madi goes a long way to answering the question. It is clear that the goal of BEE was (and still is) laudable. There have been a few successes but the scorecard is, at best, mixed. There has been some progress in terms of AA, limited progress in broad-based equity ownership (although the figures are disputed) and little progress in enterprise development.

Many participants in our economy are cynical about BEE and hold widely differing views. There are also signs of high levels of frustration on all sides.

We find ourselves in a situation where many of our companies have excess cash for which they are seeking a home, often in the rest of Africa, while local entrepreneurs are struggling to access capital. At the same time we have high levels of unemployment, a large differential in the distribution of wealth, accompanied by poor levels of education.

Prof Madi and his contributors provide an excellent analysis of why we have not succeeded and, more importantly, they provide thoughts on what we should do now. Their ideas on black economic enablement are worthy of serious consideration. We certainly should not 'throw the baby out with the bathwater'.

I trust that this book will stimulate thought and provide a platform for business, government and labour to rethink BEE, and spread the wealth and opportunity in South Africa.

SUPPLEMENTARY FOREWORD
by LITHA NYHONYHA

**Chartered Accountant, Executive Chairman and
founding member of Regiments Capital**

The title of this publication captures the essence of the book, *Black economic empowerment 20 years later – the baby and the bathwater.* Debate has been raging for quite some time about the state of BEE in South Africa. Have we as a nation achieved the stated objectives of embarking on this road to broaden the participation in the economy by those who were previously (deliberately and systematically) excluded from it?

In embarking on this critical self-analysis, what learnings can we derive from this? What do we change, and why? Who has benefited and who has not, and why? Who are (or were) the key role players? What roles have they played or should they have played? What role (if any) has society at large played in the BEE space? What about rural communities and other vulnerable communities?

These and many other questions are the ones we need to be asking ourselves, 20 years post the implementation of BEE. As a market participant over the entire period when BEE was implemented, I felt honoured to be invited to pen a supplementary foreword on such an important subject. This is a topic that I remain very passionate about.

At the heart of BEE is the aim to reverse the imbalances created by previous policies of exclusion. Because that legislation was implemented over many decades, it is by definition going to take a very long time to reverse those policies and their devastating effects. South Africa remains among the most unequal societies in the world, with a Gini coefficient closely approaching 1.

This book will give the reader a critical analysis of what BEE is all about. What has been achieved, what has worked and what has not. In our critical review of the BEE journey we must not throw out the proverbial baby with the bathwater. The author and other contributors to this book will make recommendations about what should be taken forward, so as to inform future policy choices around the subject.

I congratulate Professor Phinda Madi for undertaking the task of writing a book of this nature, the final instalment in his trilogy of books on economic advancement. First came *Affirmative action in corporate South Africa* (1993) and then *Black economic empowerment in the new South Africa* (1997). It is indeed incumbent on us, as black professionals, to begin to write our own story, both for ourselves and for posterity. Our failure to do so, may end up creating a vacuum which will allow others to take ownership of the discourse on issues pertaining to our people.

SUPPLEMENTARY FOREWORD
by TREVOR MUNDAY
prominent business leader and director of companies

It has been clear for 20 years that a foremost priority of our country, needed to secure our long-term socio-economic stability and sustainability, has been to grow our economy and thereby to create jobs (required in their millions) to ensure meaningful participation in our economy for all our people. Many pundits have remarked that our progress has been poor, and that this poses a risk to our future.

In recent years, various views have suggested that our economic policy has been both fragmented and obfuscated across government ministries, and led by people who are not experienced proponents of a free market economy that has growth as a primary objective. This has resulted in confusion. The National Development Plan, which under government supervision was interactively developed by esteemed people from multiple constituencies, led by the accomplished duo of Cyril Ramaphosa and Trevor Manuel, has seemingly lost its gravitas and been upended by uncoordinated policy decisions. Sadly, it seems to receive only occasional utterings of support from our political leadership, usually to appease specific audiences.

Together with other influences, this has resulted in low economic and related jobs growth that has caused us as a nation to compare poorly with the strong growth performances of many of our African neighbours. Certainly, electricity shortages, ongoing industrial instability (with unions at war with themselves) and the clumsy application of trade and competition laws have also helped lower the confidence of business and curtailed our economic progress.

The view provided by Professor Madi in this, his third book about our progress (or otherwise) with BEE, is insightful and thought-provoking. In the quest to advance share ownership, EE and board membership demographics, it is apparent that the challenge of enterprise development has received lower priority. And yet it can address the true meaning of empowerment in a manner that will surely be more beneficial to our people. In a version of the age-old axiom, it will result in our people fishing for themselves and their families, rather than being given fish from time to time. We are reminded that more people in South Africa today receive social grants than pay tax.

What is not needed now to rectify the shortfall in our progress since democracy (which Madi so eloquently exposes) are more ill-considered and populist decisions by politicians or government bureaucrats. Enterprise development needs firm foundations to enable it to sustain itself. We need an inspired and inclusive restart that addresses the foundation of empowerment and the status of any nation, for instance, its education system, where today in South Africa a 30 per cent matric pass rate for our children is considered acceptable.

We need to revive training institutions and colleges in which respected standards are restored and in which, for example, expedient three-week artisan certificates are banished for the trash they are. We need to rebuild the true ethos and dedication of our teaching fraternity and rid it of negative union influence. We need to cast aside any encumbrances to the entrepreneurial spirit and remove laws that inhibit rapid free-market expansion. We need to find ways of empowering people economically through enterprise development that is fair to all and respects the fact that some are job-creators and others are job-holders. We need to be fearless in removing barriers in our quest as a nation to establish and foster a process of empowerment that will nurture self-esteem and provide a respectable life for all.

If we succeed in addressing these challenges, then enterprise development will have the foundation it needs to sustain itself as the true driving force behind an empowered nation. The views of Professor Madi in this regard are courageous, insightful and illuminating. Not only do they need to influence our national discourse, they should be a prescribed reference in the restart required. But this much is clear: they cannot be ignored.

INTRODUCTION: Why this book? Why now?

Early in the 90s I happened to be one of the very few black executives who were slowly and surely climbing the corporate ladder in South Africa as a trainee manager in one of the country's top four banks. While working in the corporate banking division, I also happened to be one of the beneficiaries of that particular bank's AA policy. Of course, like many corporate institutions in the Republic at the time, that particular bank was taking tentative and exploratory steps around the very sensitive issue of black upward mobility. I was fortunate that my then boss was genuinely passionate about the issue of black advancement in established South African entities.

One Friday afternoon, while enjoying drinks in the company bar, my boss, perhaps having acquired some Dutch courage, said to me: 'Phinda, would you mind doing a special project for me? You know that as an institution, like many others in this country, we are quite hesitant about this AA issue. However, we know that it's inevitable. Rather than having cottage industries around this organisation, perhaps the time has come to develop a programme that will be implemented with uniformity across our entire organisation. Would you mind developing a programme of that nature?'

I was both intrigued and fascinated by this request, especially because I realised that, at least at the time, it was quite lonely for a black executive in the corridors of corporate South Africa. I have to confess that it was with a measure of self-interest that I took the educated risk and enthusiastically embraced my new task. Together with a few other black executives, we then formed a committee and began earnestly working on developing a programme for that particular organisation.

For me, this exercise was something of an eye-opener, in that for the very first time since joining the bank, I had an opportunity to interact with the top (and almost exclusively white) upper echelons. While this was a truly enlightening process, it would be disingenuous of me not to admit that we experienced many painful moments. It was indeed a rude awakening.

The hallowed halls of corporate power were resplendent with a sanitised, clinical politeness. Many senior executives held onto their prejudices, earnestly (albeit quietly) keeping their thoughts and feelings close to their chest. Although I cannot recall any particular racist incident happening to either myself or anybody I knew, many of us who were up and coming black executives knew we would have to navigate our way through any deep-seated prejudice with both dexterity and alacrity. While to us as black executives it appeared obvious why any organisation needed to embark on an AA programme, I learnt much later that, with the exception of a very few, most top executives at the time thought AA was a nuisance, a grand political gesture which had to be undertaken in order to appease the African National Congress (ANC) government, which was widely expected to win South Africa's first democratic elections in the not-too-distant future.

No sooner had my black colleagues and I begun earnestly tackling the vexed issue of AA, when the dreaded prejudices of some of those 'polite' top executives started to rear their ugly heads. It was almost as if we had kicked a hornet's nest. Perhaps it was a cathartic experience for them, but it hit us right in the face. I recall one senior executive saying to me: 'This AA initiative of yours isn't really relevant to me, because I mainly deal with senior government officials. And you know that there are hardly any blacks there.' (Incidentally, the man who voiced this opinion was amongst the first cohort to be hastily retired after the 1994 elections!) This comment clearly illustrates how insular and out of touch some very bright, senior executives were at the time. Nonetheless, my team and I eventually succeeded in getting our programme approved by the board, and that particular bank today benefits from the pool of black talent that was nurtured as a result of our initiative. The irony is that all the members of my 'crack AA squad', as we called ourselves, were so bruised by this experience that soon after delivering the programme and having it approved, we left the institution (and the corporate world) and set off to start up our own ventures. Perhaps we needed therapy after this gruelling period? In effect, we never really tasted the fruits of our labour, despite having enthusiastically embraced the project in the hope of benefitting from it ourselves!

After that harrowing yet enlightening experience, my head was bursting with lessons learned and insights waiting to be shared. I then began dabbling in what was to eventually become the manuscript of my first book. The book was published in 1993 – a year before this country's first multiracial elections. Published by Juta, the title was *Affirmative action in corporate South Africa – surviving in the jungle*. Trite as its title may sound now, the book actually advocated to the rest of corporate southern Africa to take AA seriously. The prevailing view at that time within corporate South Africa was that there was absolutely no business rationale for embarking on AA: it was widely believed that black people in general had neither had the aptitude nor the inclination to become *effective executives* in an established organisation. Admittedly, the sub-title of my book may seem cringe-worthy, but a great deal of effort went into painstakingly disproving commonly held myths and prejudices about blacks in the corporate jungle. It was my view then, as it is now, that unless such prejudices were confronted head-on, there would be no progress in dealing with issues around (and impediments to) black advancement in the corporate world. Some of the myths that I attempted to debunk, in a chapter-by-chapter format in my book, include the following:

1. Standards will have to be lowered (in order to accommodate new black entrants);

2. White education is the perfect education (therefore blacks, with their Bantu Education background, had little to offer established white business beyond low-level and intellectually undemanding forms of work);

3. Blacks are by nature inclined to communism rather than free enterprise, therefore the basic tenets of business will be inimical to their DNA;

4. Black people's cultural values are incompatible with Western culture in general and corporate culture in particular (the fallacy is that blacks have no conception of time and deadlines, etc.);

5. Black people simply do not have a work ethic and therefore stand no chance in the frenetic corporate world;

6. Blacks will run established white businesses (and other institutions) into the ground: just look at the rest of Africa!

7. Blacks in general (especially the educated ones) have unreasonably high and unrealistic expectations (they will have no patience when it comes to paying their dues and climbing the corporate ladder rung by rung. They will expect to be parachuted to the very top, right from the start);

8. Black executives lack initiative and drive (I found this a bizarre notion, but it was repeated so often in the surveys we did, that I had to concede and give it some attention);

9. Black executives do not think of themselves as managers (they are not assertive enough).

The abovementioned myths were identified during the numerous climate surveys I carried out. Quite frankly, many of them sounded simply outlandish to me. However, it became increasingly clear that in order to make progress, I would have to tackle these issues head-on. While writing the manuscript of my first book, I simply reflected on these findings in as raw and uncensored a manner as I could. Tragically, today, more than 20 years later, there appears to be a resurgence of many of these fallacious assumptions. In fact, I would argue that the true tragedy lies in the fact that, in many respects, we seem to have come full circle as a nation. It is not uncommon to hear these myths being peddled about today as justification for pessimism around our country's performance. Indeed, there may well be some who feel that the current state of affairs vindicates their negative assumptions.

For me, it is a bittersweet moment that it is precisely the aforementioned myths that have compelled me to once again pick up the pen (or open my laptop, in this instance). In corporate South Africa today, although the gloom and doom may be couched in polite terms, in essence the widely held views of the late 80s appear to be gaining traction once again.

In 1997 I wrote a follow-up book entitled *Black economic empowerment in the new South Africa: The rights and wrongs*. At that time, organisations were looking not only at issues around AA, but there was already discourse about black players needing to be accommodated as shareholders within established white business. However, this being a novel process, a variety of practices was being developed, and improvisation was rife. It was indeed a free-for-all which somewhat resembled a Wild West scenario, in that rules were 'made up along the way'. My book advocated that unless the fledgling BEE initiative was codified, all sorts of practices would thrive in the name of this process. In the book I voiced the concern that, noble as the initiative was, it was open to serious abuse, which made it imperative to codify good practice.

The following year a BEE commission was constituted under the chairmanship of South Africa's current Deputy President, Cyril Ramaphosa. I was invited to serve as a commissioner in this body, which eventually produced the first BEE policy framework in a democratic South Africa. That document was a precursor to the now widely known BEE Codes of Good Practice.

Not withstanding the existence of clear and well-considered guiding documentation, my fear is that, despite BEE-related issues being of concern to the general populace, the current debate has over the years become very elitist in character. My intention this time around is, amongst other key objectives, to migrate the debate from the confines of the intelligentsia and policy-makers, toward those ordinary folk who feel either let down by or left out of the process altogether.

It is no exaggeration to say that to the average South African, BEE has virtually become a swearword. In some instances it is regarded as a euphemism, enabling the political elite (or those who are connected to such an elite) to enrich themselves, their associates or their families, to the exclusion of the man in the street.

With the benefit of hindsight and all the lessons I have learned over the past 20 years on issues of black economic advancement in general, it is my view that the time has come to reflect and refine our way forward. A frank, clinical, yet balanced assessment of where we are and where we need to go, must be undertaken. While the process may have its naysayers, it is my contention that BEE remains as important and necessary today as it was two decades ago. The challenge we all face is to separate the baby from the (sometimes murky) bathwater. But the baby must not only be spared, it must survive and thrive.

Many discussions around BEE are today carried out amidst resurgent prejudices. Instead of a surgical and dispassionate analysis of where BEE may have gone wrong in the past, and how such a wrong can be corrected, the tendency now is simply to throw the baby out with the bathwater, to scrap everything that went before and to begin afresh. And that is precisely what this book argues against.

The second section of this book features the voices of prominent South Africans who, over the years, have been very vocal and active in this arena. These are people who have distinguished themselves not only in their areas of expertise and skill, but who are patriotic South Africans. If, at times, they disagree, they do so amicably. They help us to reflect on the road we have travelled so far as a nation as they share their experiences with us, but, more importantly, also set out their vision for the future, insofar as it relates to the integration of blacks into the South African economy. Many of these individuals are pioneers who were successful in their own right, long before BEE became official policy in this country. Indeed, many of them braved the tough days of apartheid to become torchbearers of black economic success.

In conclusion, when all is said and done, there will never be peace and stability in this country as long as large swathes of black people feel excluded from meaningful economic activity. BEE is fast becoming a national security and social stability issue, period. White economic security is inextricably intertwined with black economic advancement: the more black people are economically engaged and viable, the more peacefully each of us will sleep at night.

Throwing the baby out with the bathwater is simply NOT an option.

SECTION 1

AT THE DAWN OF DEMOCRACY

Chapter One

The state of black economic disempowerment at the dawn of democracy and the conundrums facing the new government

I t is imperative for all of us to remind ourselves what the state of black economic activity was at the dawn of democracy in this country. We need to cast our minds back to the euphoria of what was widely regarded as a miracle. Indeed, it was miraculous because the birth of our democracy was preceded by unprecedented bloodshed, and many of us tend to forget that. Ours was not a sterile and uneventful birth into political freedom – it was in fact very violent. More people died prior to our elections than did during the ten years preceding the elections (Nelson Mandela Centre of Memory, by Padraig O'Malley, 1990-1994). So, the international community's expectations of doom and gloom were not entirely unjustified. Indeed, we now know that these incidents were neither random acts of violence nor 'black-on-black' violence as was widely reported by state media at the time (TRC Report, volume five). State-sponsored terrorists unleashed mayhem in black communities around the country, ostensibly to intimidate them from expressing and providing support to the then recently unbanned black political organisations. These revelations were subsequently confirmed at the Truth and Reconciliation Commission (TRC), chaired by Archbishop Desmond Tutu, where high-ranking apartheid security forces revealed how they orchestrated these acts of terror. Elements within the apartheid security forces were determined to ensure that the new South Africa would, at the very least, be stillborn. We now have testimony from former members of the security forces (like Eugene de Kock), who confirmed in their testimony to the TRC that many of those in government at the time – even those in the highest office in the land – turned a blind eye to the violence and chose to ignore hotspots as the country burned.

There was the Boipatong Massacre (South African History Online, 1992) (an armed attack carried out by residents of a nearby migrant workers' hostel who, escorted by security forces, went on to mercilessly kill 47 civilians, including infants, on 17 June 1992) and other similarly brutal attacks that occurred in particularly the urban areas of South Africa.

This mayhem created the impression amongst the international community that South Africa was on the verge of imploding and self-destructing, that the country that was not merely teetering on the brink of collapse, but had started collapsing already. International analysts were almost unanimous in their conclusion that the country was doomed. Global news agencies deployed senior staff to come and witness Armageddon unfolding in South Africa. When the elections finally took place, the country was surprisingly peaceful – a true miracle. My understanding of a miracle is that it is an occurrence that cannot be scientifically or logically explained. In other words, it is a turn of events that defies common human experience.

The peaceful elections and the eventual handing over of the reins of government, from the National Party (NP) to the ANC, were indeed miraculous events. Of course we were blessed with certain powerful leaders who saw to it that the miracle did occur. In fact, some have argued that the reason why other trouble spots around the world appear not to be getting anywhere in terms of transitioning towards peaceful settlement is because, unlike South Africa, they are not blessed with larger-than-life characters like Nelson Mandela and F.W. de Klerk. It is now the stuff of legend that the ANC's Cyril Ramaphosa and the NP's Roelf Meyer, acting almost as mavericks, literally jump-started negotiations after relations between the elders from their respective parties had collapsed. Of course many other leading lights were present at the birth of the new South Africa, but the influence of these titans (and young mavericks) is something that cannot be logically explained. Amidst despair, mayhem and violence, a new, peaceful democracy was being established. It was almost as if the gods were determined to see to a peaceful political settlement in this country. South Africa was indeed blessed.

Sadly, while in the world of white South Africans, by and large, the social fabric was strong and economic activity was blooming, in black communities the cumulative effect of both colonialism and apartheid had inflicted serious social and economic devastation. This is the harsh reality that confronted the new democratic government, which had to move beyond the euphoria of the dawn of democracy to get down to the business of improving the lives of the black citizenry.

During its election campaign, the ANC used the slogan "A better life for all". It would have been remiss of the government to be completely oblivious to the deprivation inflicted on black communities, on various levels. With their political aspirations having been realised, black South Africans now began looking to ameliorate their economic condition. The legacy of the past was stark indeed:

from hopelessly underdeveloped rural areas to townships where meaningful social and economic activity had virtually ground to a halt, for the black populace, having the right to vote was simply never going to be enough. Indeed, people had voted not merely as an expression of their political aspirations, but also in the hope of finding a path to better their personal circumstances.

This is the stark reality that faced the new ANC-led government. Something had to be done to redress the economic imbalances initially unleashed by colonisation and entrenched through various laws, like the 1913 *Land Act*, which deprived black communities of the right to own land in virtually 97 per cent of the country, as well as many other Acts that had been passed over the years to ensure that blacks were not just kept on the periphery of economic activity, but were completely excluded.

Chapter Two

One big 'miracle' should beget many others – election euphoria and the post-election hangover

The worst thing that can happen to any society is for it to begin to believe its own PR. When Archbishop Desmond Tutu proclaimed South Africans to be the 'rainbow people of God' (Tutu & Allen, 1994), it was more of an aspirational statement than an anointment. As indicated earlier, the transition from near collapse and mayhem to peaceful elections triggered the use of the word 'miracle', which was so beloved of the popular media at the time. While there truly was justification for references to a miracle, this intoxicating word creates the impression that one big miracle should beget many others. Indeed, it may even have induced some within the South African community at large to believe we were the chosen ones, and that miracles would continue post-1994. Being the 'rainbow people of God', many certainly believed the intractable problems seething beneath the surface would somehow be resolved by divine intervention. It was common at that time, in political discussions, to hear especially white community members expressing the view that now that the elections had been held peacefully and there was a new democratic government essentially led by a black president, the past must be forgotten and 'we should all just move on'. Needless to say, this was a short-sighted view because it somehow negated the horrors that colonialism and apartheid had unleashed on black communities – at a social level (in terms of disruptions through mechanisms like the migrant labour system and the splintering effect it had on families) and legally through a slew of laws (that, essentially since 1910, had all conspired to consign blacks to the periphery of political and economic activity in South Africa). For so long, black communities had been deprived of their political rights as citizens – and therefore of their citizenship. Certain laws had essentially made it illegal for black people to engage in any serious economic activity within what was deemed to be white South Africa, which encompassed more than 90 per cent of the territory of this land. Having been stripped of their citizenship, blacks were now consigned to so-called 'homelands' that were basically economic backwaters and labour reserves, set apart from 'mainland'

South Africa. In this context, expectations that we should all just 'move on' were a pipe dream. Clearly, the new government was compelled to rectify the situation and unify the nation. The big question was how to do so.

Chapter Three

Exploring avenues for participation

Nationalisation of the commanding heights – the *Freedom Charter*

It would be no exaggeration to say that the *Freedom Charter* (ANC, 2014) is as close to the ANC and its allies as the *Bible* is to Christians. Indeed, the Secretary-General of the ANC, Gwede Mantashe, is quoted as saying on 8 January 2015 that "every Tom, Dick and Harry claims the *Freedom Charter* as their own these days. We know its history very well. It is our own history" (News24, 2015). The *Freedom Charter* had been so central to ANC policies that it was to eventually influence the direction of South Africa's democratic constitution. It would therefore be appropriate at this stage to reflect on the history and relevance of the *Freedom Charter*, particularly as it relates to economic policy.

In the early 50s, the ANC decided it needed to craft a vision document that encapsulated the hopes and aspirations of all South Africans about what a democratic South Africa should look like (Mandela, 1994). Therefore, in 1955 the ANC sent out volunteers across the length and breadth of the country to establish, from ordinary folk, what their hopes and aspirations were for a democratic South Africa. All their hopes, dreams and opinions were eventually collated into the document that we now know as the *Freedom Charter*. These citizens' aspirations were so broad as to cover almost every aspect of life in this country. Matters that were broached ranged from social and political to economic change. The charter was officially adopted on 26 June 1955 in a township called Kliptown, just outside Soweto (South African History Online, n.d.).

Amongst many of its demands, the charter calls for land reform, labour rights and the nationalisation of the commanding heights of the economy. As a guiding document of the fledgling ANC government, there were indeed many within the Party's own alliance partners who expected nationalisation to form a natural part of the country's new economic policy.

The most telling and economically expressive section in the *Freedom Charter* is the following (see ANC, 2014):

The people shall share in the country's wealth

The national wealth of our country, the heritage of all South Africans, shall be restored to the people, wealth beneath the soil, the banks and monopoly industry shall be transferred to the ownership of the people as a whole:

- all other industry and trade shall be controlled to assist the well-being of the people,

- all people shall have equal rights to trade where they chose, to manufacture and to enter all trades, crafts and professions ...

It is clear from the above that although 'nationalisation' is not mentioned per se, it would be safe to assume that it was on the agenda when the *Freedom Charter* was drafted. (Interestingly, this issue has now been debated to the point where some argue that nationalisation was actually *not* part of the charter. Their argument is that the absence of the word 'nationalisation' is no accident, and that the intention was simply to ensure that all the resources mentioned in this section were owned by the people, not necessarily by the government, as they would be in the event that they were nationalised.

However, notwithstanding all these finer debates, there is wide consensus that, when the ANC came to power, it could have embarked on a process of nationalisation using the *Freedom Charter* as its inspiring document.

It can also be argued that the *Freedom Charter* was overtaken by unfolding events: by the time the ANC came to power, the economic theories and practices of the recently collapsed Soviet Union had been significantly discredited (Butler, 2011). On many occasions Nelson Mandela would repeat that soon after he became president of the country and was invited to the World Economic Forum held in Davos, in January 1992, when he tried to espouse the philosophy of the *Freedom Charter* as it related to economic policy, he was corrected by many who told him he was 20 years behind in his economic thinking (Mandela, 1994).

So, while there was indeed some debate and discussion after the new government came to power, it was clear that pursuing the part of the *Freedom Charter* which urged nationalisation on a vast scale, was no longer viable. Amidst these raging debates, fears and rumours of nationalisation – which had been swirling even before the ANC assumed power – reached almost irrational levels.

Former President, Thabo Mbeki, lamented this mass hysteria: "The apartheid government had succeeded in painting us to the white Establishment as an organisation that would nationalise swimming pools and nationalise wives" (*City Press*, July 7, 2015).

The ANC was to eventually decide not to embark on nationalisation (Masina in *City Press*, October 19, 2014), to the massive relief of established white business in particular. Abandoning attempts at nationalisation did not, however, go down without opposition from within the ANC ranks (Macozoma, 2003). Certain members of the ANC's tripartite alliance felt that an economic policy which was closely aligned to the *Freedom Charter*, should be adopted. To appease left-leaning members of the alliance who saw abandoning nationalisation as a betrayal, the Mandela's government adopted the Reconstruction and Development Programme (RDP).

The key point here is to note that, in an attempt to deal with black economic deprivation, the newly elected ANC government could indeed have embarked on wide-scale nationalisation. Such drastic action would have been justified on the basis that it appeared in the ANC's 'Bible'. But it opted not to, and it is rather unfortunate that many today – especially within the established business community – have chosen to forget this pivotal moment in the history of our country.

Wide-scale privatisation and putting shares in black hands

With the nationalisation option off the table, another option that was widely discussed at the time was to look at state-owned enterprises (SOEs) as a vehicle for BEE. In other words, businesses that were owned by the government would go on a wide-scale privatisation drive that would culminate in the new government handing those shares over to black citizens, as part of the process of their economic empowerment.

The most vocal proponent of this option was the late Don Caldwell, the economic libertarian who wrote a very provocative and widely discussed book in which he espoused this option forcefully (1989). The model he proposed originated in Britain, where wide-scale privatisation had been carried out by the government of Margaret Thatcher. Caldwell was an admirer of the kind of privatisation that was unfolding in the Eastern-bloc countries of the former Soviet Union, as well as in Russia itself.

In Russia in particular, numerous SOEs – be they in the mining or the resources sector – were being privatised on a grand scale, with shares given, ex gratia, to former employees of those entities as well as to citizens at large. Naturally these developments did not escape the attention of economists in South Africa. Their view was that government needed to look at SOEs such as Transnet, Iscor, Eskom and Telkom, and privatise those entities by first allocating shares to the black employees of those operations, before making them available to the rest of the black citizenry. The argument was that this would enable government to kill two birds with one stone: it would 1) improve the efficiency and service delivery of these entities, and 2) transform blacks, almost overnight, into major shareholders of vital South African business entities.

While debates raged around this possible avenue of BEE, certain disquieting aspects surrounding such an approach to wide-scale economic empowerment were beginning to emerge from countries that had already embarked on this initiative – primarily from Russia itself. In that country, a few highly entrepreneurial individuals of dubious ethics approached individuals who had just secured such shares, knowing full well that the shareholders were desperate for cash. These unscrupulous operators would then buy up shares at rock bottom prices, taking advantage of those who wanted cold, hard cash, rather than wealth on paper. Essentially, what was unfolding was a situation where a process designed to empower the many, was now enriching the few (Ellerman, n.d.).

On taking a closer look at the Russian version of mass privatisation, it transpired that citizens were each given vouchers that were the equivalent of a share certificate in an SOE. Voucher privatisation took place between 1992 and 1994, and roughly 98 per cent of the population benefited. The vouchers, each corresponding to a share in the national wealth, were distributed equally among the population, including minors, and could be exchanged for shares in enterprises which were set to be privatised. Because most people were not well informed about the nature of the programme, or were very poor, they were quick to sell their vouchers for hard cash, being either unprepared or unwilling to invest. Most vouchers (and hence, most shares) were acquired by the management of the respective enterprises. Although Russia's initial privatisation legislation attracted widespread popular support, given its promise to distribute the national wealth among the general public and ordinary employees of privatised enterprises, eventually the public felt deceived (Appel, 1997). This process marked the birth and subsequent rise of Russia's oligarchs.

It seems likely that such a sad turn of events may well have discouraged any further exploration of this avenue. Although it was widely debated, a similar strategy was never really pursued by the new democratic government. The voucher option, like nationalisation, died a slow death. The ANC government, upon observing the creation of Russian oligarchs, may have taken the view that wide-scale privatisation would not necessarily be in the interest of genuine BEE and would, instead, simply create a similar hierarchy in this country. However, I would argue that if one looks at the economic policy of the new government broadly, it was clear that the ANC still wanted to be actively involved in the economy, and that any form of privatisation, whether for BEE purposes or for the sake of broader economic transformation, was no longer on the table. Some have gone so far as to argue that, given the current state of SOEs, the ANC government may well have looked at these entities as political leverage, and vehicles for patronage and cadre deployment. This notion will be explored later on in the book.

It is my contention that failure to explore this option represents a massive missed opportunity. In my view, a significant portion of the current problems around SOEs – many of which are in poor financial and operational health – could have been avoided.

Chapter Four

The three-legged stool of BEE

The process of BEE is comprised of many components. As indicated elsewhere in this book, BEECom, for instance, identified ten pillars to BEE. The *Broad Based Black Empowerment Act* has always identified seven legs to BEE, up until recently when these were reduced to five. Therefore, there is certainly more to BEE than just the three legs which I personally concentrated on. And, indeed, all the legs are mutually complementary.

It has always been my view, since I started writing on the subject in the early 90s, that I will personally judge whether black economic advancement has occurred when I see decisively positive results in three areas: EE in the private and public sector, black business interests being significantly represented in major (mostly listed) private corporations of South Africa (the traditional view of BEE), and significant growth in the number of black-owned and black-run businesses, however large or small. For me, those have always been the key outputs and it is this approach that shapes the trilogy of books I have written on the state of black economic participation.

Of course, there is a whole raft of policies and initiatives around areas such as education, training, funding and regulations that must be on the input side of this equation. But, as any businessperson will tell you, the ultimate judgement is on the output side, not just the input. For example, South Africa has one of the largest budgets per capita on education in the world (input). At about seven per cent of GDP and 20 per cent of total state expenditure, this government spends more on education than on any other sector (see Southafrica.info), yet the product remains woeful. In fact, it has been proven that South Africa spends more on education than most of its peers, yet its results are consistently at the bottom of the pile (see Businesstech.co.za). Many of the business leaders interviewed in this book are dismayed at the state of education in this country. However, if one were to use an input-based approach (expenditure), one could argue that South Africa has one of the best education systems in the world! Of course that is not the case – the output remains woeful.

My approach has always been that the three major outputs that will convince me that BEE is well and truly on track, would be the aforementioned three legs. That is why in 1993 I wrote a book on one leg, AA, which I followed up in 1997 with a book on the second leg, black representivity in big business. The current book is essentially on the third leg, the state of black-owned and black-run enterprises in South Africa, 21 years into our democracy.

Leg One: Black corporate upward mobility and a brief history of AA in South Africa

My first book, *Affirmative action in corporate South Africa* (1993), was aimed exclusively at the corporate upward mobility leg of BEE. In the publication I actually argue that AA must be seen as a necessary economic intervention, rather than a grand political gesture on the part of the new ANC government, as was unfortunately widely believed at that time. It is incumbent on us to investigate the origins of AA in this country.

There is a popularly held misconception that AA was only introduced to South Africa when the ANC's assumption of power was imminent and inevitable, but AA as a concept and programme actually predates the establishment of the new South Africa. While AA has been used for black corporate advancement, as a concept it is much more far-reaching than that. It is therefore important to define the scope of this concept from the outset. AA, as it has evolved over the years and around the world (whether in India, the United States [US] or indeed South Africa), can be defined as any policy in which an individual's colour, race, sex, religion or national origin are taken into account by a business entity or the government in order to increase the opportunities provided to an underrepresented part of society (my definition).

AA as a programme was first introduced in South Africa via the *Wage Act* of 1925, a law which established a hierarchy of salaries, ostensibly in favour of white miners. This was followed by the *Mines and Works Act*, 1926, which, amongst others, reserved certain jobs for whites only. Of course it is worth noting that as early as the 1890s there were already various forms of job reservation around South Africa, although these had not been promulgated into law. It was in effect the 1922 bloody miners' strike in South Africa which triggered the first AA legislation in favour of white employees, mainly very poor Afrikaner miners from rural communities who were vulnerable to competition from black miners, who were attractive to mine owners because of their willingness to accept even lower wages than whites.

In so far as AA relates to black corporate upward mobility, it can be traced back to the mid to late 1970s. In 1976, there was an outbreak of student revolts that started in Soweto and quickly spread to other parts of South Africa. This triggered an international crisis for the then NP government in the form of multinational companies coming under tremendous pressure from their stakeholders to disinvest in South Africa. Some companies did indeed leave the country after these riots, while others opted to remain, for various reasons. One of the companies that chose to remain was the US automaker, General Motors. Companies that chose to remain realised that in order to justify the ethics of operating within a pariah state, they had to take ameliorative action. Under the leadership of its African-American Director, Rev. Leon Sullivan, General Motors implemented an AA programme in favour of its black employees in this country. The programme was subsequently codified and widely referred to as the 'Sullivan Code' (see https://en.wikipedia.org/wiki/Sullivan_principles).

Compelled by US legislation, various other American organisations operating in this country began to adopt the Sullivan Code, with varying degrees of commitment and success throughout the 70s and 80s. The irony in this hesitant implementation of the Code by both international and later even local companies, was that the programmes sought to ensure the empowerment of black employees who were, in legal terms, not full citizens of South Africa, because at that time blacks were consigned to various homelands scattered on the periphery of the country. "A situation where a black manager could be arrested for not having his passbook with him, spend a couple of days in prison (or be deported to a homeland!), and miss important meetings was not inconceivable" (Madi, 1993, p. 5).

AA as a programme picked up steam at the dawn of democracy in South Africa and became a cornerstone of the economic empowerment programme of the new government. It has to be acknowledged that some strides have been made in this arena, although there is still a lot of work to be done to achieve demographic representivity. An analysis and discussion of the state of AA in South Africa today falls outside the scope of this book. However, it should be noted that this leg of BEE has received its fair share of attention, for better or for worse, and indeed my first publication on matters of black economic advancement focused on this topic.

However, it would be remiss of me not to point out the dismay with which I read a report that was published literally as I was final editing this book, by the executive search firm, Jack Hammer. They essentially produced data that proved incontrovertibly that the number of black CEOs in the Top 40 companies in South Africa has declined from 15 per cent previously, to ten per cent in 2015. The report also indicates that of a total of 334 people constituting the executive teams in South Africa's Top 40 companies, only 21 per cent are black South Africans. More disturbingly, they conclude: "The implication of all of this is that, at least for the next five to ten years, we will continue to have peripheral transformation. Companies have certainly been attempting to deliver on their transformation agendas, but the big picture is showing that much of this is taking place in non-core functions" (see news24.com). It does feel like even on this leg of BEE we are taking three steps forward and five steps backward. But that is a subject for another day.

Leg Two: BEE through shareholding in established companies

This leg of BEE virtually became the standard-bearer of this process, practically to the exclusion of the other two legs. It is, however, understandable, given two factors: 1) due to the (at times) staggering monetary value of deals made in this arena, it has generally been seen as glamorous by the media and the public, and 2) it has indeed seen to the creation (often overnight) of a class of black millionaires and indeed billionaires, almost at a fairy-tale level. Almost through magical alchemy and a few signatures being added to documents, individuals have been transformed from economic anonymity to headline-grabbing, swashbuckling multimillionaires. And nothing fascinates the public, the world over, more than stories of dramatically secured pots of gold at the end of mystical rainbows.

My second book in the trilogy on black economic advancement concentrated on this leg in particular. Entitled *Black economic empowerment in the new South Africa – the rights and the wrongs* (1997), it looked at the good, the bad and, indeed, even the ugly side of the then fledgling BEE phenomenon, which was totally unregulated at the time. Written during the 'anything goes' era of BEE, the book concluded by advocating for a clarification of the rules of the game. It triggered the formation of the Black Economic Empowerment Commission (BEECom) the following year (of which I was founding member and commissioner). The commission began a process that was to lead to the drafting of legislation around, and regulation of, this process in the coming years.

This leg of BEE has, over the past 21 years, become the standard-bearer of BEE programmes, almost to the exclusion of the two other legs. In fact, in South Africa today when someone speaks of BEE, the assumption is that they are referring to the process of blacks buying shares in established, publicly listed companies, or at least a previously exclusively white-owned business. Of course the more recent (and unsavoury) connotation around BEE in South African parlance is related to tenderpreneurship, or indeed even downright corruption, as discussed elsewhere in this book.

Leg Three: Black enterprise development (the black sheep of the family)

The irony of this leg is that until the advent of democracy, this was principally what was generally meant by BEE. Indeed, a book by Paul Browning, entitled *Black economic empowerment* (1989), essentially concentrated on black enterprise and espoused the need use the black taxi industry as a vehicle for its development and enhancement. Until the late 80s, when it became clear that democracy was almost inevitable in South Africa, the only activity with regard to BEE was in the form of black enterprise, with black businessmen and women going through the trying work of setting up and running their businesses, with varying degrees of success, in townships and rural areas. In the early 90s, debates began to emerge around the other legs of BEE, namely black corporate advancement and black ownership of established businesses. Ironically, the ushering in of democracy almost relegated this leg of BEE to the shadows. After all, who would decline the promise of overnight BEE riches, and go to the effort of setting up and dealing with the day-to-day trials and tribulations of running your own enterprise? This leg became the black sheep of the family, with disastrous consequences for the country's economy and the creation of an entrepreneurial culture, as this book will argue.

In fact, the argument made here is that it is now time to place this leg of BEE at the core of the process, going forward.

The history of black economic disempowerment and the decline of black enterprise

Black economic disempowerment in general was neither an accident, nor did it begin with the NP government assuming power in 1948. This process was begun in earnest through the *Land Act*, 1913. The discovery of gold on the Witwatersrand happened almost at the same time as black peasants were beginning to be economically independent of white enterprise. The fledgling mining industry was in dire need of cheap labour, yet such labour was not available because of thriving black enterprise. This new law was therefore enacted to prohibit black people from owning land practically anywhere in 'mainland' South Africa. They could not own land even in the black reserves demarcated for them, because that was held communally by tribal chiefs. Therefore, with the passage of the *Land Act*, the black peasantry was destroyed and all black people, regardless of where they lived, were turned into a mass migrant labour force – a black proletariat which became totally dependent on the white-owned economy (Sparks, 2010).

As indicated earlier in this book, for those black South Africans who aspired to be economically independent and not simply providers of labour to the white community, the only avenue was to establish their own enterprise. The other two legs of the stool were not available as options (i.e., upward mobility within an almost always white-owned organisation or becoming a shareholder in such an organisation). Going the route of establishing an own enterprise tended to happen under the most daunting of circumstances. The broad political context at the time was that black South Africans were legally and constitutionally not regarded as citizens of the country; they were only deemed citizens of the Bantustans situated on the periphery of the country. Of course many blacks who lived in the homelands started their own businesses, with varying degrees of success. The main difficulty facing those entrepreneurs was that, because by and large the borders of these homelands were artificial, they tended not to be economically viable. It was very difficult to run a sustainable business in the backwater of South Africa. That some of those entrepreneurs managed to succeed and become titans is truly a tribute to the indomitable human spirit. Those who started up businesses within 'white' South Africa, in addition to being confronted with unsupportive government bureaucracy and denied access to established capital from financial institutions such as banks, faced a slew of laws and regulations that did not make for a conducive business environment. Hereunder is a brief list of laws that created an essentially hostile environment for everyday life, let alone encouraging black entrepreneurs (see Suzman, 2009):

- ### The *Group Areas Act*, 41 of 1950

  Forced physical separation between the races, achieved by creating separate residential areas for different races, led to the removal, by apartheid forces, of those people living in the 'wrong' areas, for example, coloureds living in District Six in Cape Town, or cosmopolitans living in Sophiatown, were relocated forcibly.

Amongst the laws which denied black people the option of appealing to the courts against forced removals were the *Natives Resettlement Act*, 19 of 1954; the *Group Areas Development Act*, 69 of 1955 and the *Natives (Prohibition of Interdicts) Act*, 64 of 1956.

- ## The *Suppression of Communism Act*, 44 of 1950

The apartheid government developed its own version of communism, hitherto unknown in the world. Essentially, communism was so broadly defined by the South African authorities, that an individual no longer needed to be a Marxist-Leninist to be regarded as a communist. The government had carte blanche to declare anything or anyone a communist, if it so wished, and its definition included any call for political change in this country. Indeed, calling for blacks to be allowed to trade freely in any part of the country could, in effect, be labelled as advancing communism! The consequences for a newly declared communist could be dire: such individuals were frequently banned from becoming members of a political organisation and were restricted to living in a particular area. Later on, especially after the riots of 1976, many so-called communists ended up being detained or tortured, and many simply 'disappeared'.

- ## The *Prohibition of Mixed Marriages Act*, 55 of 1949

This Act prohibited marriages between whites and people of other races. Between 1946 and the enactment of this law, only 75 mixed marriages were recorded, compared with some 28 000 white marriages.

- ## The *Immorality Amendment Act*, 21 of 1950; amended in 1957 (Act 23)

This Act prohibited adultery, attempted adultery or related immoral acts (such as extramarital sex) between white and black people. The social implication was that the Act had direct business-related consequences. For instance, potential business partners of different races, who were found in an establishment trying to transact legitimate business, could actually be arrested if they were of the opposite sex. The security forces of the time had carte blanche to break into private residences and snoop on people in an attempt to 'catch them in the act'.

- ## The *Population Registration Act*, 30 of 1950

This Act led to the creation of a national register in which every person's race was recorded. A Race Classification Board took the final decision on an individual's race, in disputed cases. The so–called scientific methods employed in determining someone's race were positively laughable, like the so-called 'hair comb test' (if a comb got stuck whilst being run through your hair, you were classified as non-European). This piece of legislation essentially formed the baseline of apartheid, as every human being in South Africa was defined and categorised on the basis of this law. Every human being in South Africa had to fall into some category set out in this law, no one was exempted.

- ### The *Bantu Building Workers Act*, 27 of 1951

  In terms of this Act, black people could be trained as artisans in the building trade – something previously reserved for whites only. However, they had to work within an area designated for blacks. The most sinister aspect of this innocent-looking law was that it made it a criminal offence for a black person to perform any skilled work in urban areas, except in those sections designated for black occupation. Therefore, a highly skilled black artisan could be arrested for trying to do business in a 'white' area, and could end up serving time in jail for his entrepreneurial spirit.

- ### The *Prevention of Illegal Squatting Act*, 52 of 1951

  This Act gave the Minister of Native Affairs the power to remove blacks from public or privately owned land, and to establish resettlement camps to house such displaced people.

- ### The *Bantu Authorities Act*, 68 of 1951

  The terms of this Act provided for the establishment of black homelands and regional authorities, with the aim of creating greater 'self-government in the homelands'.

- ### The *Natives Laws Amendment Act*, 1952

  Designed primarily to assist white businesses which were perpetually in need of cheap black labour, the Act narrowed the definition of the category of blacks who had the right of permanent residence in towns and other urban areas. Section 10 limited this to those who had been born in a town and had lived there continuously for no fewer than 15 years, or who had been employed there continuously for at least 15 years, or who had worked continuously for the same employer for at least ten years.

- **The *Natives (Abolition of Passes and Co-ordination of Documents) Act*, 67 of 1952**

Commonly known as the Pass Law, this cynically named Act forced black people to carry identification with them *at all times*. A pass included a photograph, details of the individual's place of origin, employment records, tax payments, and encounters with the police. It was a criminal offence to be unable to produce a pass when required to do so by the authorities. No black person could leave a rural area for an urban one without a permit from the local authorities. On arrival in an urban area, a permit to seek work had to be obtained within 72 hours.

This piece of legislation turned out to be the most odious and most reviled law of all the apartheid legislation. It caused untold misery and suffering within black communities, and had a devastating effect on family structures.

According to the Pass Law, government officials possessed the power to expel a black person from a particular area by adverse endorsement in the passbook or permit. This technique was known as 'endorsing out' and could be carried out at any time and for any reason. Officials were not required to provide an explanation for their actions. Family members of a worker who was 'endorsed out' also forfeited their right to remain in the area and faced eviction and exile to a bantustan. Forgetting to carry the permits or passbooks (disparagingly referred to as dompas), misplacing it, or having it stolen rendered one liable to arrest and imprisonment. Each year, over 250 000 blacks were arrested for technical offenses under the Pass Laws. As a result, the dompas became the most despised symbol of apartheid (http://wjhs7a.pbworks.com/f/Apartheid+in+South+Africa.doc).

- **The *Native Labour (Settlement of Disputes) Act*, 1953**

Another bizarre piece of apartheid legislation, it prohibited strike action by blacks.

- **The *Bantu Education Act*, 47 of 1953**

This piece of legislation is 'credited' with creating an under-educated, unlimited black labour force that was designed to effectively make black people permanent 'slaves' to white employers. Some have grudgingly given its architect, the then Minister Native Affairs, Dr Hendrik Verwoerd, credit for his unbelievable mastery of the art of subjugation.

This Act saw the establishment of a Black Education Department within the Department of Native Affairs, which would compile a curriculum that suited the "nature and requirements of the black people" (South African History Online, n.d.). Verwoerd, as author of the legislation, stated that its aim was to prevent Africans from receiving an education that would cause them to aspire to positions they would never be allowed to hold in society. Instead, Africans were to receive an education designed to provide them with the skills needed to serve their own people in the homelands, or to work in labouring jobs under white supervision.

The devastating consequences of this law are still evident today, 21 years after the collapse of apartheid. As the then Reserve Bank Governor, Tito Mboweni (EWN, 2011), once said, the biggest challenge around massive unemployment in South Africa is not that no new jobs are being created, but rather that there is an oversupply of unskilled labour in an environment where the new jobs being created require skilled labour.

- ## The *Reservation of Separate Amenities Act*, 49 of 1953

  This law enforced segregation in all public amenities, public buildings and public transport, with the aim of eliminating contact between whites and other races. 'Europeans Only' and 'Non-Europeans Only' signs were put up in virtually every nook and cranny of South Africa. The Act also specifically stated that facilities provided for different races need not be equal in terms of quality or number.

- ## The *Bantu Investment Corporation Act*, 34 of 1959

  This Act provided for the creation of financial, commercial and industrial schemes in areas designated for black people. In a rather cynical way, this piece of legislation was designed to force entrepreneurial blacks to effectively relocate to the homelands, where it would then be theoretically possible to raise funding for their ventures.

- ## The *Extension of University Education Act*, 45 of 1959

  One of the most pernicious abilities of the architects of apartheid was how they were able to design laws and give them labels whose effect was the direct opposite of what they purported to be doing. One example of such cynical naming is this piece of legislation, which effectively put an end to black students attending white universities (mainly the universities of Cape Town and Johannesburg – Wits and RAU). It went on to create separate and grossly under-resourced tertiary institutions for coloureds (University of the Western Cape), blacks (i.e. University of Zululand, University of the North, Turfloop) and Asians (Durban-Westville University). The newly created institutions intended to serve the black community ended up being labelled 'bush colleges'. That somehow these institutions, despite such daunting challenges, were able to produce the towering leaders we have today, is a tribute to the indomitable spirit of humankind.

- **The *Promotion of Bantu Self-Government Act*, 46 of 1959**

Another cynically named piece of legislation, this Act classified black people into eight ethnic groups. Eight commissioners-general were tasked with developing a homeland for each group, which was allowed to govern itself independently, without white intervention. Another unstated intention of this law was to entrench deep-seated ethnic divisions within black communities, in an obvious attempt to divide and rule.

- **The *Terrorism Act*, 1967**

This Act allowed for the indefinite detention without trial of black people, and led to the establishment of BOSS (the Bureau of State Security), which was responsible for the country's 'internal security'. This piece of legislation was the 'muscle', flexed to enforce the *Suppression of Communism Act*: once an individual was declared a communist, the authorities handed him/her over to the security forces, who, in accordance with this legislation, could do whatever they wished to that person. Again, terrorism was given a rather unique definition by the apartheid government: any individual who opposed government policies, be they social, economic or political, could be branded a terrorist and made to suffer the consequences.

- **The *Bantu Homelands Citizens Act*, 1970**

This Act compelled all black people to become a citizen of the homeland designated for their ethnic group, regardless of whether or not they had ever lived there, and stripped them of their South African citizenship. Amongst many of its effects was the fact that this law effectively made black South Africans aliens in their own country. The idea of not being permanent citizens was devastating from a black business point of view, and consequently trading under such circumstances was a Herculean task.

Of course there were many other laws and regulations – too numerous to mention here – that were designed to tighten the screws on black lives (including business licensing regulations, etc.). However, even without the additional regulations, the abovementioned laws stacked the dice heavily against blacks in general, and black entrepreneurs in particular. Collectively, all these laws can be regarded as having the direct effect of guaranteeing black economic disempowerment.

Generally speaking, those black people who ventured into business were extremely enterprising and bold, they were supercharged, visionary individuals with an irrepressible spirit. And, indeed, many of them did manage to make a success of it. Recounting my own family history seems apt at this point.

SECTION 2

BEE TRENDS IN A DEMOCRATIC SOUTH AFRICA

Chapter Five

The rise of strange breeds of black entrepreneurs

O
ne of the terrible ironies of present-day BEE is that it appears to have led to the decline of black enterprise, particularly in townships and rural areas. One of the legends of black enterprise, the former long-serving president of Nafcoc, Joe Hlongwane, has gone so far as to say: "BEE has done nothing for township businesses ... if township businesses fail, then South Africa fails" (*Business Day*, October 13, 2013). And Hlongwane should know: Nafcoc is the chamber of commerce to which many black businesses have belonged over the years (including my own parents, during their lifetime. I have vivid recollections of my father dragging me, as a young boy, to meetings of the local chapter!). If one uses membership of Nafcoc as a barometer, there definitely has been a significant decline in black business activity in townships. In 1998, Nafcoc had 155 000 members in good standing. In 2013, that number had declined to a meagre 50 000 – a staggering 68 per cent drop! Current serving President of Nafcoc, Lawrence Mavundla, expands quite eloquently on this point later on in this book.

The decline of black enterprise is further amplified in the following table, which originates from Statistics South Africa. It indicates that the number of individuals who have been trading for their own account has consistently declined over the years, since 2008:

Table 1: Employment status, 2008–2014 (numbers are in thousands)

Employment status	Q4 2008	Q4 2009	Q4 2010	Q4 2011	Q4 2012	Q4 2013	Q2 2014
Employee	12,456	11,836	11,693	12,187	12,313	13,036	12,996
Employer	850	728	791	741	745	780	796
Own–account worker	1,344	1,287	1,310	1,302	1,381	1,256	1,235
Unpaid household member	119	122	104	107	86	104	67
Total	14,769	13,973	13,898	14,336	14,524	15,177	15,094

Source: Human Capital Labour Reports: South Africa, 2015.

Tenderpreneurs

The rise of this strange breed of entrepreneur has given South Africa a rather dubious honour: the term 'tenderpreneur' now appears in Wikipedia, which defines this concept as follows:

> A tenderpreneur is a South African term for a person in government who abuses their political power and influence to secure government tenders and contracts. The word *tenderpreneur* is a portmanteau of 'tendering' and 'entrepreneur'. Some commentators believe that this practice might give rise to a kleptocracy as a deviant mutation of a democracy if left unchecked. In this regard a kleptocracy is defined as the condition arising when a political elite manipulate the three arms of government (legislature, executive and judiciary) with the intention of capturing resources that will enrich that elite, a general phenomenon known as elite capture. (https://en.wikipedia.org/wiki/Tenderpreneur)

The South African daily newspaper, *The Star* (February 21, 2010) defines a tenderpreneur as "someone politically well-connected who has gotten rich through the government tendering system".

It has been common practice amongst many of these tenderpreneurs to try to legitimise the nefarious means by which they acquire their wealth, by covering it under the honourable cloak of BEE. Needless to say, this has provided ammunition to detractors of BEE. Indeed, those who have never supported BEE have latched onto this phenomenon, conveniently equating BEE with tenderpreneurship.

> These tender mongers are often given projects like fixing roads, building public clinics, schools and RDP houses that they either don't finish or are constructed poorly. They use poor quality raw material for building with cracks on the walls emerging because the concrete mix is poor. The piping and reticulation systems are bought cheaply from dubious sources resulting in the whole neighbourhood dripping with water and stinking due to burst pipes.

> No inspection is done on the work because those at the top know that the contractor is a friend who has never handled a spirit level or tape measure in his or her life ... This is what tenderpreneurs do for development. They scupper it. (Naki, 2012)

Even the current general secretaries of the ANC, the South African Communist Party and the Congress of South African Trade Unions (Cosatu), in a joint report to the alliance summit, recently lamented this fact: "This tendency has resulted in incompetent companies doing business with government, causing a serious failure in service delivery" (*The Sowetan*, June 29, 2015).

Former Governor of the Reserve Bank, and now private entrepreneur, Tito Mboweni, referring to his newly established company, said: "We are not a BEE company. If you want a BEE [partner], don't come to us; we don't do BEE" (*Financial Mail*, August 7, 2014). Clearly, his utterances were influenced, amongst other things, by the bad reputation that BEE is beginning to acquire amongst honourable men and women. It has almost become a swearword. Tendencies like tenderpreneurship have done immense damage to the standing of BEE, not to mention its aims and reputation in the eyes of ordinary South Africans.

Politpreneurs

This is a term that I have coined myself. Politpreneurship manifests itself in two situations:

1. It denotes an individual who is a partially active politician, but also quite active in business. In debates I have had with colleagues, some have argued that these individuals could well be categorised as lobbyists, just as one would find lobbyists in Washington, DC. However, there are certain subtle differences between these individuals and lobbyists as they are traditionally known. Lobbyists a) offer a legitimate consultancy service which is performed in the open and is, in many instances, regulated; b) aim to influence only the policy and legislation that results from such policies; c) derive their income from this consultancy service and are not necessarily actual or potential shareholders/partners of the organisations for whom they do lobbying.

> Another term that may closely resemble these characters is 'political rent-seekers'. In his recent article titled 'Rent seeking is gobbling up our economy" (http://mg.co.za/article/2015-09-10-rent-seeking-is-gobbling-up-our-economy), political analyst and academic William Gumede defines various manifestations of politpreneurship, including:
>
> > A new phenomenon increasingly reported is that of politically connected BEE businesspeople, in cahoots with corrupt government tender officials, stealing the business plans submitted

by entrepreneurs who are not politically connected, reworking them slightly and then resubmitting them to the same corrupt officials with successful outcomes.

Well-connected political deployees to government who lack the necessary competence push out talented potential incumbents. We often see the same people being appointed to senior positions, such as director general, in different departments, or as executives and board members at state-owned enterprises, even when they fail. They hop from one post to another, even if there are many talented black professionals out there.

Incompetent public sector deployees often cause waste, mismanagement and inefficiencies. Service delivery gets stunted and a negative cycle of corruption, nepotism and mismanagement ensues. They demoralise those working under them, decrease their productivity and undermine the whole system.

2. The term can refer to those individuals who join a political party (naturally a governing one, in a particular constituency) with the sole purpose of accessing public resources to use for their own individual benefit not necessarily to serve the public. To them, political service is a means to an end, that end being to secure their own commercial interests. Some may go through the motions (and use the rhetoric) of your average politician, but beneath the surface they are furiously engaged in business dealings in one form or another, to feather their own nests. In his keynote address to the ANC National General Council in Port Elizabeth, on July 12, 2000, the then President of the ANC (and serving head of state) Thabo Mbeki commented on the insidious tendency of politpreneurship within his own party and certain wings of government:

> The result I am talking about is that we have attracted into and continue to retain opportunists and careerists within our ranks. These are the people who join the movement not because they respect or support any of the strategic objectives I have mentioned. They join with the great ease that our procedures as a mass movement permit, with the sole aim of furthering their personal careers and using the access to state power we have as a ruling party, to enrich themselves. (Mbeki, 2000)

Essentially, politpreneurs are people to whom serving the populace is a distant afterthought. Their primary focus is to access state resources and plunder them.

Unfortunately, once again they make haste to wrap their machinations in the respectable cloak of BEE.

It would be justified to state that BEE at times looks like a soiled and discredited endeavour because of these two species of black entrepreneurs: tenderpreneurs and politpreneurs. These strange breeds have done immeasurable harm to the once hallowed and noble BEE. It has given BEE the whiff of corruption and venality, that is why, on the one hand, when I am in my neighbourhood in Soweto and I mention BEE, the response usually from these humble (and mainly poor) folks is: 'Don't mention that corruption to me! It's just a den of thieves gorging themselves silly on our blood and sweat.' Similarly, during lighter moments with captains of industry at various official functions, I commonly hear mutterings along the lines of the following: 'BEE has mostly been dignified bribery we've all been compelled to do, otherwise government won't do business with us.'

That is throwing the baby out with the bathwater! The baby, BEE, remains noble and it needs to be protected and nurtured. Let us throw out the venal aspects of BEE and see to the health of the baby, and watch it grow to its full potential. Later on in the book I introduce a new approach and fundamental paradigm shift on how we can restore the nobility of this endeavour. We all need to remember, as Mark Barnes (2013) puts it: "You cannot sleep well in Sandton until they can eat in Soweto."

Chapter Six

SOEs as BEE laboratories

There is no doubt that, ever since the debate arose about whether they should be subjects of massive privatisation (as indicated in an earlier section), SOEs have been contested terrain. On the one hand, official policy – as recently reaffirmed by the National Planning Commission – has consistently maintained that SOEs are crucial to the economic development of South Africa, as well as the delivery of vital services to the populace. On the other hand, critics of this approach argue that local politicians approach SOEs as a kind of laboratory for all sorts of BEE and AA experiments, and as vehicles of patronage for friends and associates. Currently, virtually all prominent and vital SOEs appear to be in a state of deep crisis.

South Africa is home to more than 400 SOEs, and it would be grossly unfair to argue that all such enterprises are operating in crisis mode. However, the difficulty is that those SOEs that dominate their sectors – some to the extent of being monopolies – are the ones that appear to be in a permanent state of upheaval. As at the time of writing, the following major SOEs were in dire straits and virtually hogging newspaper headlines on a daily basis.

Prasa – the Passenger Rail Agency of South Africa

This organisation is being ailed by the following maladies (Fin24, 2015):

- It is running one year behind on a rail and locomotive modernisation programme that is estimated to cost R5 billion;

- Its Chief Executive Officer, Lucky Montana, was dismissed by the board after what appears to be a serious fall-out with the Chairman, Popo Molefe (who served two terms as Premier of the North-West Province and is widely regarded as a stalwart of the governing party). Montana himself has a long track record as an ANC activist, especially within its youth ranks. The Chairman, Molefe, has argued that there is a plot by certain interested parties to assassinate him, and he recently opened a case with the police. It would appear that the main contention is around contracts and tenders awarded by PRASA, with some parties crying foul;

- Its senior engineer, "Dr" Daniel Mthimkulu, has turned out not to have the qualifications that he professed to have. A case of fraud has been opened against him, and he has since tendered his resignation. This individual is said to have been at the helm of a recent acquisition of trains by the organisation – a project costing billions.

These dramatic events are unfolding at a time when there are heated debates in the media about whether the locomotives that have recently been acquired by PRASA were purchased at an inflated cost. There are rumours that the locomotives pose a safety risk to passengers because they are not compatible with the South African railway network already in place (Fin24, 2015).

PetroSA – The Petroleum, Oil and Gas Corporation of South Africa

The state-owned oil company currently faces its own serious problems:

- It is expected to suffer a loss of R14.9bn this year – the biggest financial loss by any state-owned company;
- Last month the company suspended its chief financial officer as well as its chief executive officer, which resulted in serious divisions within the board;
- While there is speculation about what led to this massive exodus, the widely held view is that it can be attributed to poor decisions regarding its Project Ikhwezi, PetroSA's plan to prolong the life of the Mossgas gas-to-liquids plant near Mossel Bay, by exploring further resources southeast of the current drilling fields.

Sapo – the South African Post Office

Another flagship organisation that is in trouble is the South African Post Office, which appears to be experiencing fairly serious cash-flow issues.

- It owes almost R245m to more than 2 000 suppliers;
- It is in arrears on various payments by up to six months;
- 879 creditors have not been paid for a period of more than 60 days;
- Employees' salaries also fall into arrears from time to time;
- A number of branches have been closed by landlords due to the non-payment of rent;

- In an attempt to deal with its cash-flow crunch, in May this year the government facilitated a short-term overdraft of R270m, with further borrowings guaranteed.

SAA – South African Airways

The state-owned airline, SAA, is also experiencing turbulence:

- Close on R14bn in various forms of government bailouts have been spent on SAA over the past 15 years;

- Over the past five years, SAA has introduced one turnaround plan after another;

- It is currently operating with an interim board of four people, after the director walked out last year;

- It does not have a proper board of directors or a permanent CEO after the acting CEO, who had been plucked out of a subsidiary company, was himself recently replaced by a human resources director;

- There is widespread media speculation that its current chair is very close to the president of the country, and has been deployed to the airlines not thanks to her competence, but essentially because of this relationship.

Eskom – the Electricity Supply Commission

There is no SOE whose maladies have had a more direct and painful impact on the lives of average South Africans than this one. On many an occasion this organisation has literally plunged South Africa into darkness. A lack of infrastructure maintenance and failure to plan for a growing consumer base are two of the reasons given. Naturally, at an economic level the impact has been nothing short of devastating.

> If we'd had enough electricity since 2007 and it was not a limiting factor, the economy could have been about 10% bigger than it actually was by the end of 2014. That is more than 300 billion rand ($25.3 billion), or more than a million job opportunities. (Vollgraaff, 2015)

> South African mining magnate, Patrice Motsepe, recently bemoaned the current state of affairs, saying that Eskom had led South Africa down very badly: "If electricity was available at a competitive price ... a huge number of jobs could have been created, not only by ARM

but various other mining companies as well" (*Business Day*, March 17, 2015).

To list all the maladies that have plagued the commission would be to detract from the main purpose of this book. No doubt a plethora of books will be written on what went wrong at this subsidiary. However in summary, the following can be stated:

- Eskom has been plagued by management instability, which recently saw almost its entire executive suspended and eventually being let to go by the government. It currently has an acting CEO and an acting chairman;

- It has received a cash injection of around R23bn, but still needs billions more to be able to fulfil its mandate;

- It is trying to convince the electricity regulator to increase its prices by more than 25 per cent over the next two years, arguing that these hefty price hikes are needed for it to have sufficient funds to complete major construction works on new power stations;

- It anticipates more power cuts over the next three years at least, due to insufficient capacity to meet the country's power requirements. Therefore the pain is expected to continue.

From a BEE point of view, Eskom deserves special attention because it has been at the heart of the most recent (and at times fairly irrational and highly animated) debates and discussions. It is somehow regarded as the poster boy for an AA or even BEE programme gone mad, with disastrous consequences for the nation's economy. This is indeed understandable when one takes into account the direct impact its failure to deliver has had on the lives of everyday South Africans, not just the business community.

In particular, it becomes instructive if one studies a March 2015 document compiled by the Southern African Institute of Race Relations (SAIRR), entitled 'The rise and fall of Eskom and how to fix it'. While it is generally a well-researched document, some of its conclusions can only be categorised as emotional and political in nature, as exemplified by the following assertions:

- After 1994, highly skilled and experienced white engineers, managers and technicians were given generous packages "to get out and make way for persons of the correct skin colour and political affiliation" (SAIRR, 2015, p. 5);

- The state seemed intent on taking away Eskom's obligation to supply. In 1998 it forbade Eskom from building new power stations;

- ANC ministers seemed to regard Eskom as a sort of magic machine that would automatically generate as much electricity as was needed, but could also be diverted – seemingly at will – for other purposes;

- "Eskom became blighted with a damaging combination of ANC ideology and business school fashion" (SAIRR, 2015);

- The 2008, blackouts were caused by a decision to start buying coal from a variety of small black-owned mines, which provided poor-quality coal;

- In starting up a coal furnace, the procedure is to first put in a flame before feeding in coal powder. Instead, the enterprise fed flame into a furnace filled with coal powder, and it exploded;

- The government seemed to be bowing to a trend for private electricity supply, but without any commitment or coherency in terms of strategy;

- Eskom should remain under state ownership, but only if the state refrains from interfering in Eskom politically;

- In a rational world, the choice of energy sources for generating electricity would be based on scientific and economic facts. Instead, in this country it is fraught with ideology and superstition;

- Eskom must be depoliticised and resume its old function, which is to provide sufficient, reliable electricity. In the process it should cover its costs.

Given the difficulties outlined above, many detractors of black advancement argue that the state of these flagship enterprises indicates that BEE is a catch-all term for cronyism and nepotism, dressed in honourable robes. I would, however, argue that the problems currently besetting these enterprises have nothing to do with BEE at all. I would rather agree with the treasury ministry that the problems are mostly a result of governance failures and inadequate policy frameworks (*Business Day*, February 26, 2015).

The National Planning Commission (NPC) alluded to these problems by stating in its report that "accountability in state-owned enterprises has been blurred through a complex and unclear appointment process and at times, undue political interference" (NPC, 2011). It therefore follows that if these two key weaknesses are addressed across all SOEs, the problems that have continuously beset these institutions will be a thing of the past. It is absolutely vital that government earnestly and decisively ensures 1) that there is impeccable corporate governance at these institutions, and 2) that there is clarity about the policy and mandate of each.

It is vital that we avoid arriving at a position that is reductionist and perhaps even racist in its character, by assuming that where black management and leadership are in charge (as has indeed been the case in many of these SOEs), widespread failure and bad governance naturally follow.

Chapter Seven

The JSE mirage

One of the most vexing aspects of BEE has been the aspiration by black South Africans to obtain a meaningful stake in Johannesburg Stock Exchange (JSE) listed companies. Indeed, one of the stated objectives within the BEE commission's report was that the JSE must be 25 per cent black owned. Following the original frenetic activity of deals post South Africa's democratic elections, black businesses were reported to have acquired about ten per cent of shares on the JSE in the first four years (Jacobs, 2002). But by the beginning of 2015, all these gains were widely regarded as having been reversed, with President Jacob Zuma maintaining during his State of the Nation Address that blacks own only three per cent of the total shares listed on the exchange. However, it must be pointed out that the statistics are contested by the JSE's CEO, Nicky Newton-King (2013), who contends that black share ownership of the Top 100 companies now stands at 23 per cent.

Despite this, it can still be argued that attempts to increase black shareholding to the originally envisaged 25 per cent have, 21 years on, actually declined to below the levels obtaining in 2002. This begs the question whether we are not perhaps obsessing over an ephemeral target. I do not hereby contend that chasing the 25 per cent target is a waste of time. However, the model that has been utilised so far in trying to meet this target has really been that of heavily leveraging acquisitions. In other words, purchases that are dependent largely on loan financing and are serviced by expected dividends will hopefully be paid off through capital appreciation for acquired shares. However the vagaries of the market will generally frustrate this development, given the fact that whenever there is a stock market correction, or indeed a crash, whatever capital gains the shares may have acquired are eroded, thereby leading to an inability to service loans that were utilised to acquire such shares in the first place, thus these shares frequently revert back to 'white capital'. This then leads to a reversal of all the gains realised up to that stage. This explains why there has been this almost continuous cycle of gains by black shareholders on the JSE during boom times, which erode back to square one once there is a market correction.

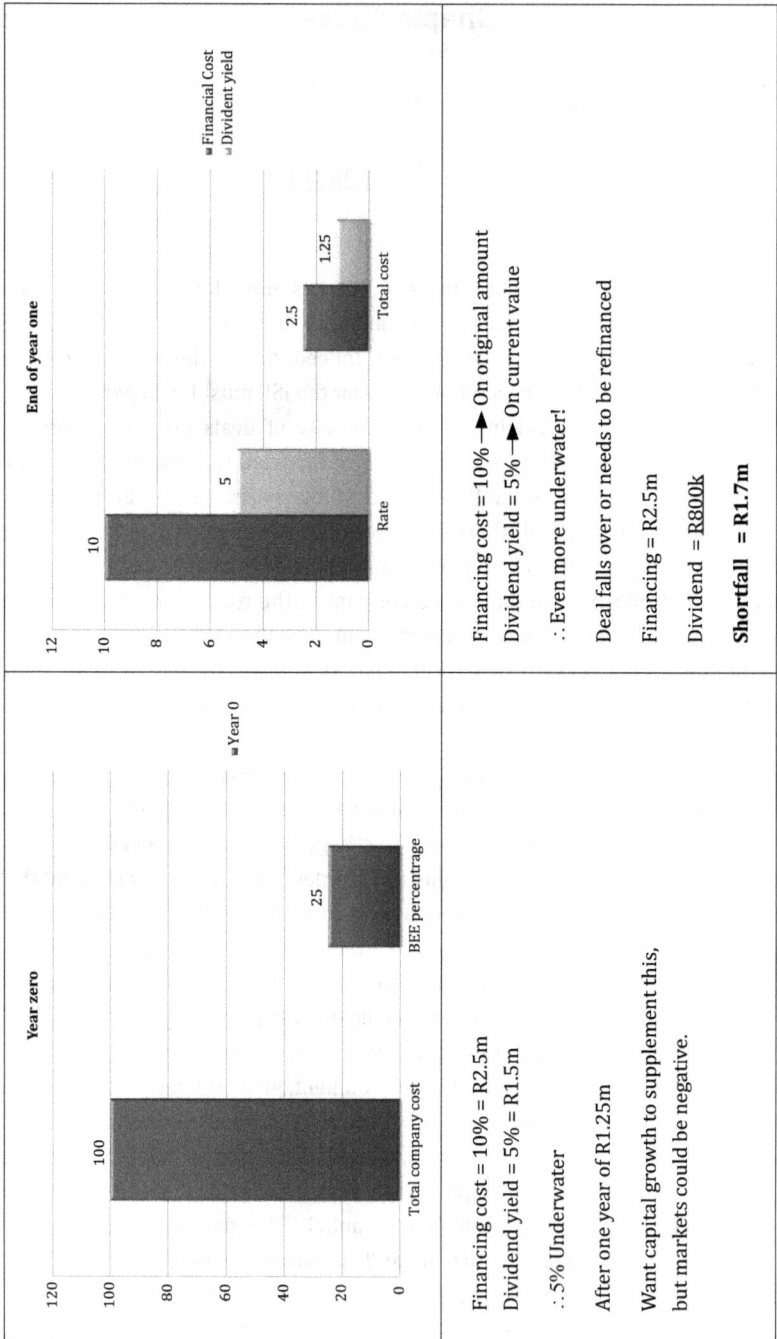

Year zero

120
100
80
60
40
20
0

100

25

Total company cost BEE percentrage

■ Year 0

Financing cost = 10% = R2.5m
Dividend yield = 5% = R1.5m

∴5% Underwater

After one year of R1.25m

Want capital growth to supplement this,
but markets could be negative.

End of year one

12
10
8
6
4
2
0

10

5

2.5

1.25

Rate Total cost

■ Financial Cost
■ Divident yield

Financing cost = 10% ⟶ On original amount
Dividend yield = 5% ⟶ On current value

∴Even more underwater!

Deal falls over or needs to be refinanced

Financing = R2.5m

Dividend = R800k

Shortfall = R1.7m

Figure 1: BEE deal structure scenario

Source: Stuart Milroy CFP®, Wealth Manager at Sanlam Private Wealth

This conundrum is well articulated by Mark Barnes in his article 'Time to re-design black economic empowerment' (*Business Day*, October 7, 2013): "I can't remember any time in South Africa's history when dividend yields exceeded the prime overdraft rate."

The average dividend yield over the past 20 years has been about 3.8 to four per cent, and the prime overdraft rate has been above 15 per cent for most of that time. You cannot service a 15 per cent interest rate with a four per cent income. You do not need a PhD in astrophysics to figure that out. It's not politics, its arithmetic.

When BEE funding structures were put in place, everyone knew that they would not be self-funding – there is a 'negative carry' between the dividend cash in and the interest cash out (less exaggerated in low-interest rate cycles, but still there). Compounding this flaw is the fact that interest on capital borrowed to purchase shares which yield after-tax dividends (if any) is not tax deductible.

How was it ever expected that this gap would be filled? Most likely either through capital appreciation or vendor support. The hope has always been that the capital appreciation in the shares over the life of the structure would outstrip the negative carry embedded in it. Even if this is so, it cannot solve the whole problem. If interest rates are at ten per cent and dividend yields are at five per cent there is a negative carry of five per cent. If the share price appreciates at ten per cent a year (double the negative carry), then there will still only be about a net 28 per cent appreciation in the capital value after five years. Once the scheme is wound up after five years and the loan is repaid, the BEE beneficiaries will only end up with about six per cent free equity, if they bought 25 per cent in the first place.

Start again, hope again – the cycle continues. It is nothing short of silly to put one's trust in this process.

A former ANC treasurer summed it up well recently when he said: "I wonder if those with empowerment shares in struggling commodities feel empowered today, or do they feel overwhelmingly indebted" (http://businesstech.co.za/news/business/98793/bee-isnt-doing-what-its-supposed-to-former-anc-treasurer/).

The question that therefore needs to be asked, is whether the emphasis should not actually be on helping blacks to first become successful entrepreneurs, who will then grow sufficient capital via being involved in starting, developing and growing their businesses to a point where, at a later stage, they will be in a position to acquire shares on the JSE using mainly their own capital. In such instances loans will only serve as a supplementary mechanism, rather than as the base. In my opinion, unless and until there is a new mechanism for providing soft loans to those black entrepreneurs trying to acquire shares in established companies on the JSE, this predictable vicious cycle will continue. The emphasis should be on growing black enterprise. It is imperative that government enable black entrepreneurs to acquire sufficient wealth to eventually acquire shares by predominantly using their own resources.

In any case, the question can be asked, legitimately, beyond the symbolism of it all, what intrinsic value it ultimately adds to the economy, if blacks are able to own a substantial portion of the JSE. Surely the challenge should be to create a vibrant black entrepreneurial class as a priority?

Chapter Eight

The threat of a Mzansi Spring – How real is it?

The implementation of BEE in the new South Africa was not without controversy. This may well have been fuelled by the fact that the first BEE deals tended to include people with strong political connections and backgrounds. Indeed, some have theorised that BEE was not necessarily designed to empower the many, but rather to pacify the political elite so that they would abandon their original radical and transformative policies. Moeletsi Mbeki, the socio-political commentator, has consistently argued that

> [b]ig business had anticipated all the questions and came up with its own solution. It offered to transfer a small part of its assets to individual leaders of the black resistance movement in return for them leaving the business environment as they found it. The leaders found this offer of instant wealth hard to resist. The co-option of the black nationalist elite by big business came to be known as Black Economic Empowerment or BEE. (Mbeki, 2009)

I would argue that this definition is somewhat reductionist (throwing the baby out with the bathwater!). Mbeki almost intimates that the black intelligentsia never applied their collective minds to issues of black economic advancement. Obviously this is a fallacious argument, as other parts of this book indicate that blacks were engaged in economic endeavours long before even the anti-apartheid struggle began. The Black Management Forum (BMF), which has been a vocal proponent of black economic advancement, was formed in 1976. The legendary (and all-powerful) black chamber of commerce, the National African Federated Chamber of Commerce (Nafcoc), was founded in Orlando, Soweto, in 1964! Therefore, by the time South Africa became a democracy black intellectuals and businesspeople had long been applying their minds to the question of how they could accelerate the involvement of black people in the mainstream economy. Black leaders did not simply sit back and wait for white established capital to determine the agenda. True, there is no doubt that certain key white business leaders may well have, in a Machiavellian fashion, determined that the only way to prevent a radical attack on their assets (and comforts!) was to effectively attempt to 'bribe' certain leaders. And certain of those leaders may well have succumbed.

Sadly, that a large segment of the South African population has not benefited from BEE cannot be denied. Gwede Mantashe, Secretary-General of the ANC, recently noted: "If you understand BEE for what it is, I think if we philosophise we are being less than honest. BEE creates black capitalists. Simply, that's what it does, so it will produce capitalists" (Mantashe, 2015).

Even former treasurer of the ANC, Mathews Phosa, recently stated:

> The present black economic empowerment policy... is with respect, not a cure-all to real broad-based black economic empowerment. Millions of black people feel left out and are very sceptical since they cannot enter the formal economy. They only see a few that largely benefited from tenderpreneurship and not from hard work. (http://businesstech.co.za/news/business/98793/bee-isnt-doing-what-its-supposed-to-former-anc-treasurer/)

Indeed, it is now widely acknowledged that South Africa currently has a more unequal distribution of wealth and resources than at any other point in its history. Some have warned that this situation poses a serious threat to social stability going into the (not-so-distant) future. Some statistics – especially as they relate to youth unemployment – are extremely unsettling.

Given the prevailing unequal distribution of income and wealth, as well as high unemployment rates, the question can be asked: Is South Africa heading for its own version of the Arab Spring?

The Arab Spring refers to a wave of protests – both violent and non-violent – that began on December 18, 2010, in Tunisia and quickly spread across several countries in North Africa and the Middle East. These protests, while largely led by the youth, were so dramatic and effective that by the end of February 2012, regimes had been toppled or dragged into civil war.

> In Tunisia, Egypt, Libya and Yemen; whilst civil uprisings had erupted in Bahrain and Syria; major protests had broken out in Algeria, Iraq, Jordan, Kuwait, Morocco, and Sudan; and minor protests had occurred in Mauritania, Oman, Saudi Arabia, Djibouti, Western Sahara, and Palestine. Weapons and Tuareg fighters returning from the Libyan Civil War stoked a simmering conflict in Mali which has been described as 'fallout' from the Arab Spring in North Africa. (Wikipedia, https://en.wikipedia.org/wiki/Arab_Spring#cite_note-Mali_coup:_Arab_Spring_spreads_to_Africa-18)

Stunned and at times bewildered by these uprisings, many authorities responded with an iron fist. These dramatic developments have led many in South Africa to wonder aloud whether we will be going down the same path. One person who has focused on this is political trend analyst, J.P. Landman, who contends that for any country to see an eruption of an Arab Spring-like revolution, *all five* the following conditions must be present:

1. The countries where the movement gained a foothold were all middle-income nations with high rates of inequality and poverty;

2. The demographics also showed a 'youth bulge' with 30–32 per cent of the population aged between 15 and 29;

3. High levels of poverty;

4. High levels of inequality;

5. Very restricted political and civil rights (Stokes, 2012).

Landman contends that only four of the five requirements are present in South Africa, where there is a high degree of political and civil activism, but also of civil liberties. He therefore concludes that the chances of an Arab Spring occurring in this country are slim. However, some counter that not all five elements need necessarily be present in order for a revolution to occur, and that perhaps having 'most' of these prerequisites manifest themselves in a particular society is sufficient to trigger such an event. Mark Barnes, the economic thinker and financier, mused: "Unemployment figures can only grow so much before we end up with an economic disparity that will result in a fight" (*Rand Daily Mail,* July 7, 2015).

Clem Sunter, South Africa's foremost strategist and scenario 'seer' has argued that, despite this country only meeting four of the five requirements, we are tipping towards mayhem (Sunter, 2012). He cites the very tragic Marikana killings where, on August 16, 2012, miners were so desperate for better pay that they were willing to literally fling themselves at a hail of police bullets during a wage strike in which 43 men were killed. Sunter cites this as an ominous sign, combined with the almost daily occurrence of service delivery protests in the country.

> All in all, we could be at a pivotal moment in our history where we could tip into the no-holds-barred anarchy of a Failed State; or we could accept that the game has to change in order to create an economic democracy that goes with our political democracy – in other words, begin the process of transforming our economy into an inclusive one

offering genuine economic freedom and the chance for ordinary people to better their lives and circumstances. (Sunter, 2012)

> Indeed, even within the upper echelons of South Africa's dominating political party, the ANC, one can observe a growing trend of public ruminations by senior officials about a serious possibility of social upheaval. Recently the Chairman of the ANC in Gauteng, Paul Mashatile, issued this ominous warning to corporate South Africa: "Share the wealth or South Africa will suffer" (*Times Live*, 2015).

Some analysts have come up with their own worst-case scenario prognostications. R.W. Johnson, in his recently published book, *How long will South Africa survive?* (2015), predicts that, punch-drunk from misgovernance and malfeasance, South Africa is destined to implode in two years!

Of course there have been some prominent South Africans on the other side of the fence, the most notable being the co-founder of FirstRand, Paul Harris, who has strenuously rejected any possibility of the country going up in flames. His private letter to a friend and South African expatriate in Australia went viral, inspiring a great number of his compatriots (*Business Day*, October 28, 2012). The most quoted sentence in that letter sums up his view: "However, for as long as I can remember there have always been people who think SA has five years left before we go over the cliff. No change from when I was at school in the sixties. The five years went down to a few months at times in the eighties!"

While I would not go so far as to predict a cataclysmic collapse, like Johnson does, and am not as starry-eyed as Harris, there is reason enough to be concerned. In its document, the National Planning Commission (2011) points out that, based on current official statistics, chances are minimal of an individual who is above 24 years of age and who has no prior working experience securing a job. This becomes spine-chilling information, given that South Africa, which constitutes only .08 per cent of the total world population, accounts for almost two per cent of total youth unemployment on planet Earth (*Business Day*, January 26, 2015). South Africa's youth unemployment currently hovers at around 53 per cent. And as the graphic hereunder shows, it has been stubbornly low for the past two decades, even at times when there were relatively good economic growth rates.

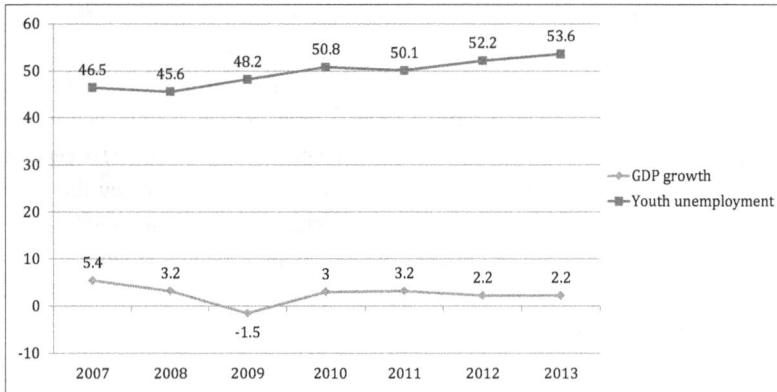

Figure 2: South Africa's GDP growth and youth unemployment
Source: Human Capital Labour Reports: South Africa, 2015.

Even if one were to set aside the issue of whether or not the country is ripe for an Arab Spring, history has shown that if there are hordes of unemployed youths roaming the land, it generally tends to lead to a rise in racism, xenophobia and other sociopathic tendencies.

South Africa has been dubbed the protest capital of the world. Since 2002, more South Africans (on a proportional basis) have protested than any other country's citizens. Since 2008, more than two million people have taken to the streets in protest every year (Plaut, 2012). Njabulo Ndebele (2012) argues that "[w]idespread 'service delivery protests' may soon take on an organisational character that will start off as discrete formations and then coalesce into a full-blown movement".

Following this trend, some have argued that we as a country are indeed experiencing a 'low-scale' Mzansi Spring, which may (or may not) go full scale, depending on whether or not people's despair is assuaged. That there are ominous signs, cannot be denied. My contention is that given these signs, we should not wait for our own version of an Arab Spring to occur (a Mzansi Spring?). We must act now to prevent such an occurrence, and the only way of forestalling this is to facilitate large-scale entrepreneurial activity across the length and breadth of this country, thus ensuring that our youth is gainfully employed. It does not have to be on a grand scale; as long as we ensure that people (especially the youth) are engaged – whether they are selling newspapers on a street corner or running a kiosk somewhere, or indeed whether they eventually develop into full-blown industrialists – that is the only way we can safeguard against a Mzansi Spring ever coming to our shores.

That South Africa is, by just about every measurement, possibly the most unequal society on Earth is a given, as illustrated by the data above. My alluding to this point earlier, and the discussion on it, was premised on its implications for social instability. But an even bigger economic argument has been raised by the recently published international bestseller, *Capital in the 21st century* (2013), by the French economics academic, Thomas Piketty. To say the book caused a stir in both academic and business circles, let alone generated hitherto unknown social chatter on economics, would be an understatement. Why did it generate such hype? It made some extremely uncomfortable, yet relentlessly logical, arguments along the following lines:

1. Capitalism is, by its very nature, likely to create an unequal society. Therefore, in a capitalist system (for which, by and large, the developed world has now settled) inequality should be expected to exist;

2. Once inequality becomes extreme it begins to have negative effects, not just in terms of social cohesion, but also in terms of economic efficiencies. This point, in summarising Piketty's views, is well captured by, of all people, the world's richest man, Bill Gates, in his treatise *Why inequality matters* (2014):

I very much agree with Piketty that:

*   High levels of inequality are a problem – messing up economic incentives, tilting democracies in favor of powerful interests, and undercutting the ideal that all people are created equal.

*   Capitalism does not self-correct toward greater equality – that is, excess wealth concentration can have a snowball effect if left unchecked.

*   Governments can play a constructive role in offsetting the snowballing tendencies if and when they choose to do so.

Piketty, an avowed non-Marxist and pro-capitalism, argues that inequality in any society may actually be good because it triggers an aspirational factor amongst the less privileged, who are inspired to work harder in order to reach the same level as the privileged, thereby triggering innovation and economic growth. He goes on to warn that such inequality can become extreme (defined in the formula r>g, meaning that the wealthy are continuously 'making money' even if there is poor economic growth, i.e., they are living off accumulated wealth without necessarily adding anything new to the economy). Piketty (2014) alluded that a skewed Gini coefficient can be a major indicator of extreme inequality.

Essentially, once inequality becomes extreme (which is the case in South Africa), it begins to drag the economy down, since those with capital continue to live better even when an economy is underperforming, while the vulnerable, who are without capital, slide ever deeper into poverty. That is the 'hard facts' part of the argument. But there is also a soft part to the argument, Piketty argues. That is when the underprivileged, being gradually squeezed off capital markets and the economy, begin to lose hope and become resigned to the fact that there is no escaping from the cycle of poverty. And once people lose hope, whatever innovation they could have brought into the economy, is lost. As a once famous poem, written by Kaizer Ngwenya during the 1970s student anti-apartheid protests, put it: "dreams wither slowly" (in Motluoase, 1981).

Therefore, my conclusion is that, even if extreme inequality does not eventually trigger a Mzansi Spring, it is inflicting debilitating damage on the South African economy. It will continue to stifle innovation and entrepreneurship for many years to come.

To deal with extreme inequality, Piketty suggests a punitive annual wealth tax. I personally am not convinced that this is the best way to deal with the matter since, as we all know, the wealthy always have an army of the brightest lawyers and tax experts at their disposal. History has taught us that the wealthy are almost always a step ahead of the authorities. With regard to South Africa, instead of proposing a wealth tax that may swell the coffers of the state (and such revenue may well end up being squandered in all sorts of nefarious ways, as we have recently observed), I propose a migration from BEE programmes to BEN programmes, as explained in the 'Way forward' section of this book. I believe only BEN can help us address extreme inequality in South Africa, not BEE.

Looking forward – the baby must survive!

SECTION 3

SO WHERETO
FROM HERE?

Chapter Nine

Revisiting the groundbreaking work of BEECom

I t is rather unfortunate that the sterling work done by BEECom (established in 1998), appears to have been largely forgotten within present discourse around BEE. Ironically, a revisit of the commission's report does indicate what the original aim and intention of BEE were, before it was unfortunately corrupted and hijacked, mainly for personal gain.

As stated earlier in this book, in 1997 I published *Black economic empowerment in South Africa – the rights and the wrongs*. Essentially, this book decried the absence of uniformity in the implementation of what was being promoted as BEE initiatives country-wide. It was literally a free-for-all environment where something of a Wild West culture was beginning to predominate. All sorts of initiatives, many of which acquired a slightly nefarious character, were being promoted under the banner of BEE. In addition to pointing out this rather unfortunate development, the book sought to advocate for the codification of good BEE practices and policies, so as to ensure uniformity as well as legitimacy. The book, along with many other utterances by leading figures in South Africa, began to espouse the view that the time had come to codify all local BEE practices. A year after its publication, in May 1998, the BMF took the decision to form a commission to ensure uniformity in BEE implementation (BEECom), under the chairmanship of Cyril Ramaphosa. I became a member of this commission.

It is not uncommon these days to hear the original members of this commission, when reflecting on the state of BEE today, saying that this is not what they had in mind when they formed and eventually produced a report from BEECom. (See the later section featuring Peter Vundla who, like the author, also served on the commission.)

The direction that BEE has taken in the past few years, as characterised by such practices as tenderpreneurship, was definitely not what was originally envisaged, as attested to by many of the contributors featured in this book.

Indeed, there is consensus even amongst present-day commentators, that BEE has taken a previously unintended route. Thabo Masombuka, Executive Director of Transformation Services at Siyakha Consulting, a former Director of BEE Charters and Partnerships at the Department of Trade and Industry (DTI), said blacks needed to change the way they amassed wealth, instead of focusing on buying BEE stakes from white companies:

> We approach BEE from a minimalist point of view. The top 20 rich black South Africans have stakes in white companies and they have rarely created wealth by starting companies from scratch.
>
> If blacks want to create meaningful wealth, they must start their own companies instead of buying small stakes from white companies. (*City Press*, April 29, 2012)

Perhaps the question should be asked as to what exactly the original commission had in mind when it defined BEE. The definition from the commission's report is indeed telling:

> There is often a tendency in South Africa to define BEE narrowly and to equate it with the development of a black capitalist class. The narrow definition focuses on the entry and transaction activities of black people in business, especially what is commonly referred to as BEE investment companies. (BEECom, 2001, p. 1)

The commission proceeded to define how BEE must be approached in South Africa:

- An Investment for Growth Accord between business, labour and government aimed at reaching agreement on a concrete strategy to lift the country's levels of fixed investment and economic growth;

- The design and implementation of an Integrated Human Resources Development (HRD) strategy;

- The implementation of the Integrated Sustainable Rural Development Strategy and the creation of an agency to streamline and co-ordinate funding and other initiatives in rural areas, including land reform;

- A National Procurement Agency located within the Department of Trade and Industry aimed at transforming the public and private sector procurement environment;

- A *National Black Economic Empowerment Act* enabling legislation aimed at creating uniformity in policy and establishing the necessary institutional support and instruments with which to drive the BEE strategy. The Act should define BEE and set uniform guidelines that will facilitate the deracialisation of economic activities in the public and private sectors;

- An Empowerment Framework for Public Sector Restructuring that outlines empowerment principles to be followed;

- An enabling framework aimed at improving access to finance for households and businesses through disclosure and reporting requirements in the banking sector and targets to encourage service delivery and the enhancement of existing state capacity in the Post Bank;

- Recommendations on the streamlining and co-ordination of public sector funding initiatives through a National Empowerment Funding Agency (Nefa);

- Recommendations on building the capacity of business structures, especially black business structures;

- The strategy incorporates national targets to be met by the stakeholders. These are discussed in the following chapters. (BEECom, 2001, p. 2)

While it cannot be said that BEECom was a perfect body that produced a perfect document, a cursory glance at the points listed above does indicate that had these recommendations been implemented aggressively and concretely, today there would have been a vibrant black entrepreneurial class. The absence of a coordinated and comprehensive implementation of BEE nationally has led to a situation where, essentially, all that has thus far happened within BEE has been the closing of equity transactions and half-hearted sporadic attempts at enterprise development.

It is also important to note that several support mechanisms and institutions were identified in the commission's report which was, unfortunately, subsequently ignored by policy and law-makers:

1. *An Investment for Growth Accord between business, labour and government aimed at reaching agreement on a concrete strategy to lift the country's levels of fixed investment and economic growth.* Recently there have been calls by business luminaries in the country, Clem Sunter in particular, to this effect:

What better way of kicking off 'Walk Together' – the scenario which offers a populist but peaceful path into the future – than an Economic Codesa? The design of such a Codesa should be open to popular debate and not be centrally imposed by any of the key actors. Of course, the government through the National Planning Commission will play an essential role in getting the initiative off the ground. Only one non-negotiable condition has to apply: any economic sector covered by this Codesa – whether it be mining, banking, agriculture, manufacturing, small business – should involve a give-and-take negotiation process between all the parties involved. Nobody would be omitted. (Sunter, *Unfinished business*)

2. *A National Procurement Agency located within the Department of Trade and Industry aimed at transforming the public and private sector procurement environment.* It can be argued that many unseemly practices that have recently characterised BEE, such as tenderpreneurship (see elsewhere in this book) could have been largely averted, as most misdemeanours tend to happen at local level, and go almost undetected. Credit must be given to the Treasury, which recently established a central database of all suppliers to government, in an attempt to root out corrupt service providers. Better late than never, although a lot of damage has already been done (*Mail & Guardian*, March 6, 2015).

3. *Recommendations on building the capacity of business structures, especially black business structures.* The lack of action in this regard has been nothing short of tragic, as explained elsewhere in this book. The recent establishment of the Ministry of Small Business is a promising step indeed. Again, better late than never!

4. *An enabling framework aimed at improving access to finance for households and businesses through disclosure and reporting requirements in the banking sector and targets to encourage service delivery and the enhancement of existing state capacity in the Post Bank.* The lack of a national risk fund for black entrepreneurs in particular, as bemoaned elsewhere in this book by entrepreneurs such as Richard Maponya, and as eloquently explained by young dynamic entrepreneur, Vusi Thembekwayo, has been a major omission. Until such a fund – which would have a higher risk tolerance and broader time horizons than conventional banks – is established, the development of black enterprise will remain crippled.

Chapter Ten

One hundred black industrialists

Towards the end of 2014, the South African government announced its policy geared towards the development of 100 black industrialists over a period of three years. This policy was designed to address concerns arising since the start of the BEE process, namely that most BEE initiatives had really been passive investments by a select (the same!) group of black investors in well-established white companies, without any operational involvement, new value add or new jobs being created in the process. Therefore, the concern is that most BEE programmes and initiatives have not created black entrepreneurs who were operationally involved from the outset, or had the requisite business know-how:

> Over the next five years, a host of working opportunities will become available to South Africans. For example, a new generation of Black industrialists will be driving the re-industrialisation of our economy. Local procurement and increased domestic production will be at the heart of efforts to transform our economy, and will be buoyed by a government undertaking to buy 75% of goods and services from South African producers. (Masina, 2014)

> BEE has been a bit slow and to a certain extent, has been manipulated. When the concept of BBBEE [broad-based Black Economic Empowerment] came in, it meant that rural villagers had shares, but they were not very significant [...] It had spawned a new class of rich black people – such as Tokyo Sexwale, Cyril Ramaphosa, Mzi Khumalo and Saki Macozoma – *but now we don't see rich black people altering the structure of the economy.* (Masina in *City Press*, October 19, 2014)

These pronouncements have undoubtedly generated much debate, ranging from supportive through skeptical to (at times) downright dismissive. But that this is a major development in BEE policy thinking cannot be denied. There is at least, at policy level, an acknowledgement of some of the pitfalls in the traditional approach. But these commentators' pronouncements, as stated earlier, have not been without their critics. In an editorial entitled 'Like black sheep to the slaughter', *Financial Mail* (April 9, 2015), the editor could not hide his dismissal of this government ambition. The paper took the somewhat unusual view that government had been motivated by the economic empowerment of Afrikaners in drawing up this policy, and set about highlighting the flaws in this 'Afrikaner-inspired policy' by stating the following key impediments:

1   Afrikaners built or created monopolies that didn't have to compete with established businesses(*Rand Daily Mail*, 2015);

2   They were operating using a vast pool of cheap black labour;

3   Trade unions were outlawed when the Afrikaners performed this miracle of which the ANC is in such awe;

4   South Africa was a siege economy, increasingly isolated. Much of its industry has turned to import substitution, whereas we now live in an era of much more open trade;

5   The South African rand in the early 1960s was worth more than US$1,50. Its value was gradually eroded by poor government, as remains the case today;

6   The dollar price of our labour renders the export of all but the most unique manufactured products unviable;

7   If the product of black industrialists is to sell domestically, the state will have to find ways to stimulate local demand, the exact opposite of what the DTI is trying to achieve;

8   Palming the project off onto the shoulders of the deputy minister at the DTI is a sure sign that it is not a priority.

Probably the most rational critique, in my view, came from commentator and entrepreneur K.K. Diaz, in his article 'The Myth of 100 Black Industrialists' (LinkedIn Pulse, November 18, 2014), who issues the following caveats:

1.   The nation needs to know who the people responsible for this initiative are. Who can we hold accountable for failure, and who can we celebrate, should there be success? There will never be any success if no one is accountable;

2.   Why the policy obsession? There is no need for additional policies to be drafted, or for legislation to be amended, to support government's aim. In fact, I believe most of the three years will surely be eaten up by this process. Politicians should facilitate and assist businesses, not seek to control how business operates.

3. The use of the word 'create' in all the communication surrounding this idea implies that government believes it can simply wave its policy wand and we'll have our 100 black industrialists. Real business means hard work, commitment and truly transparent leadership. We will have to start right at the beginning and come close to killing ourselves to slowly grow the commercial experience needed to create 100 new black industrialists. There is no easy way out of this paradigm. We should stop looking for one.

4. What about female entrepreneurs? In 2014, the Entrepreneur category for the Businesswoman of the Year Awards was removed from the Business Women's Association programme because not enough females met the qualifying criteria. Can we truly produce 100 black industrialists, across the nationally agreed gender balance requirements, in three years? It doesn't look likely.

5. What about education? Achieving strong, sustainable economic growth is a bottom up process. We need to grow our future generations of moguls from a foundation of literate and numerate matriculants. Our education system, in its current form, is unable to provide this foundation.

While I could contest the other concerns that Diaz raises, where I fully agree with him is at point 3, where he cautions against the narrative that it is the government that has to create these 100 black industrialists. We need to be very careful about the language we use, because creating the impression that the government will somehow miraculously conjure up – literally out of thin air – 100 black industrialists, is fundamentally flawed. The government can only 'facilitate' the emergence of black industrialists, not create them. I expand later on this by contending that government language in the past ('we will create x million jobs, we will build x million houses, we will... we will...') has been largely disempowering to the citizenry on the one hand, while creating unrealistic expectations on the other.

Needless to say, in so far as genuine black involvement in the economy is concerned, this is a step in the right direction. Principally, it addresses the fears that have been voiced since the beginning, namely that most participants in BEE transactions were not adding value to the economy, or gaining operational experience. This type of approach is, therefore, designed to breed hardcore businesspeople who know how to run corporations and manage operations, how to add value to the economy, grow it and, in the process, create jobs. Clearly this is a step in the right direction. However, the question that arises, given certain events of the past, is whether this process will not somehow end up being hijacked by parties that are not necessarily well-intentioned. In other words, will this process become just another mechanism for crony capitalism or patronage? How does one ensure that the truly deserving become the beneficiaries of this process? At this stage it behoves us to interrogate global best practice on government-directed industrialisation within a non-communist policy framework, and any lessons that could be learned.

South Korea and the *chaebol* system

One country whose development from an essentially agrarian society in the 60s to a global industrial powerhouse in the 21st century has been nothing less than spectacular, is South Korea. The country's dramatic economic development has come on the back of phenomenal government-sponsored and government-directed industrialisation. To illustrate how phenomenal this change has been, it is hard to believe that in the 60s the South Korean economy was exactly at the same level of output as the Zimbabwean economy. The starting point of South Korea's heavy industrialisation project, spearheaded by its government, was that those individuals who were targeted for special assistance were already involved in some kind of industrial effort, however lowly or impressive it may have been. They had already displayed initiative and had been 'around the block', in a manner of speaking. They were not pseudo-entrepreneurs following an opportunistic approach, nor were they merely undeserving beneficiaries of crony capitalism. And there is a lesson to be learned there, that in order for such industrialists to eventually become successful and government efforts not to end up squandering funds, the focus needs to be on people who have already shown an entrepreneurial, hard-core industrial-productive bent. After all, it is impossible to turn a previously disinterested or unengaged individual into an industrialist overnight (Mu-hyun, 2015).

Of course it is worth noting that any system that requires active involvement and direction on the part of government is unlikely to find favour with free-market purists. True purists would view such government intervention as being at an almost unacceptably high level. But that it worked wonders in the case of South Korea (and many other examples subsequent to that) cannot be disputed. To quote China's post-Mao Zedong leader, Deng Xiaoping, who steered the country from hard-core communism to the capitalist global industrial giant it is today: It doesn't matter to me whether the cat is white or black, as long as it catches the mice (Xiaoping, 1962).

The South Korean system eventually gained wide renown as the *chaebol* system, consisting of a business conglomerate of typical global multinationals owning numerous international enterprises, controlled by a chairman who has power over all the operations. While the government provided the blueprint for industrial expansion, the *chaebol* realised the plans. The *chaebol* was able to grow thanks to two factors: foreign loans and special favours. Access to foreign technology was equally critical to the expansion of this system throughout the 1980s. Under the slogan of 'guided capitalism', the government selected companies to undertake projects and channelled funds from foreign loans. The government guaranteed repayment, should a company be unable to repay its foreign creditors. Additional loans were made available by domestic banks. In the late 1980s, the *chaebol* dominated the industrial sector and were especially prevalent in manufacturing, trade and heavy industries. This is how companies like Samsung, LG and Hyundai, to name a few, eventually became global brands, manufacturing everything from toothbrushes to large container ships, television sets to cars.

It is my view that, in pursuit of efforts to create black industrialists, much can be learnt (both positives and in some instances negatives) from the South Korean model. The main positive points to take from the *chaebol* system is that government, having identified legitimate fledgling industrialists, helped them to secure funding from mainly foreign institutions with a different risk appetite and longer time horizons for payback. Currently, in South Africa, this is a major drawback for budding entrepreneurs: our funding institutions simply do not have the appropriate mindset or indeed systems in place to implement a similar system. Banks are governed by a stifling form of conservatism. It is, of course, not uncommon to hear all and sundry arguing that we have the safest and most stable banking structure in the world, but I contend that this is because banks basically sit on the money – they never lend it to deserving but obviously risky enterprises. It is a widely known fact in business circles in this country that it is easier to raise R1bn to buy five per cent of a JSE-listed blue-chip entity, than it is to raise R1m to finance a small shoe factory! In fact, some argue that South African funding institutions take pride in how miserly they can be (although I would not go that far).

One major drawback to the *chaebol* system, which I would urge policy-makers to avoid at all costs, is the creation of diversified conglomerates in pursuit of accelerated industrialisation. The minute any organisation becomes a conglomerate that manufactures both toothbrushes and television sets, all sorts of economic inefficiencies arise. Therefore, to my mind, a Mzansi *chaebol* would have the following distinct features:

1. It is owned and run by a full-time hands-on entrepreneur, not an investment holding company;

2. It is run and owned by an entrepreneur who has been in that business, even if at a low or even subsistence level, for not less than three years;

3. It has a demonstrable capacity to grow and survive without relying exclusively on business from a government department or state-owned agency.

An oft-repeated saying is that Africa consumes that which it does not produce and produces that which it does not consume. There is no doubt in my mind that this conundrum can be solved by the heavy industrialisation of South Africa. In fact, it can be argued that local de-industrialisation has disadvantaged economic development across the continent. In the event that South Africa is industrialised via this strategy of facilitating black industrialists, the rest of the continent can only benefit. But, more importantly, it would solve the problem of Africa being the only economic bloc in the world that does very little trade amongst its own. If South Africa establishes a huge industrial base, then it will have a ready consumer market in the rest of the continent. South Africa can become an export powerhouse, trading up into Africa. With Africa's population growing at a phenomenal rate, thereby creating a vibrant consumer pool, it has had to rely on imports from the rest of the world to satisfy its needs. A rapidly industrialising South Africa can efficiently serve this fast-growing market. This country would be a convenient exporter to Africa's growing economies.

Another highly innovative idea that can be adopted to fast-track the development of black industrialists, comes from an article by Peter Bruce (*Business Day*, 2015).

I have opted to let the eloquent Mr Bruce speak for himself, without my trying to interpret what he meant to say:

> I have three thoughts on how that might happen.
>
> First, big listed and non-listed companies should be required by the JSE or the law to mentor small to medium-sized black businesses. Not microenterprises, but companies turning over between, say, R20m and R100m a year.
>
> The mentoring would place at least one senior director (not, please, human resources) on the mentee company board, and that board would contain one member from the dominant union in the business and its main banker. The mentor would include a report on its mentee in its JSE filings and annual report (or its tax returns), would pay for an

annual external audit from a reputable black-controlled firm, and take a degree of responsibility for its mentee's performance. The better the performance, the better the scorecard. Mentees could be suppliers or not. The aim would be to ensure good governance and sustainable jobs.

Second, the JSE itself should come to the party. I'm sure it does *tons* for empowerment, but an old idea (there is some dispute as to whether it was Stephen Mulholland's or Jacko Maree's) is still powerful. It would require, under JSE supervision and possibly its enforcement, all listed companies to raise their share capital by 1%, and to pool it. At the current market capitalisation of the JSE that would raise about R120bn.

The idea would be for control of the pool to totally exclude the state and any political interest. It would be the responsibility of a board of trustees drawn from the great and the good of the private sector (think retirees such as RMB's Paul Harris, Tsogo Sun's Jabu Mabuza, and SAB's Norman Adami). Their job would be to distribute the money as quickly as possible to big and small (even micro in this case) black businesses that can make a case for it. Some will stick, some not. It doesn't matter...

A third thought is that the state should ensure that when the president or a minister conducts a trade visit abroad it should be to get actual business, and not merely to introduce potential black partners to possible foreign investors. UK prime ministers have been doing this to great effect since Margaret Thatcher began visiting foreign countries to sell British goods.

Leaders of big, established local manufacturers should always be a part of the delegations politicians take with them. And if the state helps them win a foreign order, the business needs to be shared with a local black-owned company.

These are the only ways established (call it white) and emerging (call it black) companies are ever going to meet each other on terms not dictated by political interests. And none is beyond our reach. (*Business Day*, 2015)

Well said, Mr Bruce.

The major point to be taken here for policy-makers is that, to ensure success in creating a pool of black industrialists, it cannot be 'business as usual'. Employing new and innovative ways, like the ones suggested here, should be the key approach. That would require government to 'loosen up' and develop such programmes *jointly* with the private sector and hard-core entrepreneurs, not solely with the input of bureaucrats and policy apparatchiks.

SECTION 4

PROMINENT VOICES
ON BEE BY
SOUTH AFRICAN
BUSINESS LEADERS

Khanyisile Kweyama
Chief Executive Officer, Business Unity South Africa
(Busa)

Ms. Khanyisile Kweyama has been the Chief Executive Officer, Business Unity South Africa (Busa), since December 2014. Prior to that she served as Executive Director at Anglo American. She has held several executive positions in some of South Africa's major corporations and continues to serve on several boards as a non-executive director.

For me, BEE is like corrective surgery. It is designed to fix that which is broken, namely the reality that black people, being a clear majority in this country, do not have any meaningful stake in this economy whatsoever, due to a history of deliberate exclusion. That, to me, is like an abnormality in the body which requires surgery. And, like any surgery, it is painful. That is the part I think many people tend to overlook. This *is* a painful process, which can at times be very messy. Some of us somehow expected the process to be sanitised, clean and orderly, but it cannot be. It is these unrealistic expectations that sometimes cause people to be unnecessarily critical of the process. There is no surgical procedure that is completely non-invasive, orderly and painless. And, given the discomfort accompanying the pain, if we decide to yield to the temptation not to perform corrective surgery, the deformity will continue and will eventually compromise the health of our young democracy. I would rather that we deal with the pain now, than being squeamish and ending up paying the ultimate price much later. Yes, at times we will disagree, both as individuals and organisations, on how to best perform that surgery. But that's fine – as long as we do not abandon it.

The organisation of which I am the CEO, Busa, was born out of a sincere attempt to unite all business formations in South Africa which had been divided due to our past as a nation. In 2003 we had an amalgamation of the (predominantly black) Black Business Council with the predominantly white Business South Africa. Of course, as everybody knows, in 2011 the Black Business Council decided to leave the formation for reasons they stated publicly. However, Busa remains an agglomeration of business organisations from all sorts of backgrounds. We all bring our perspectives to the table. As a result we have vigorous debates amongst ourselves, including on matters related to BEE. But our commitment is always to move towards common ground. And, as business leaders, we realise that we have to be torch-bearers for change. Many of our members are captains of their own respective ships. We are therefore very aware that, however different our points of departure may be, we need to be very clear and articulate in our support for mechanisms designed to correct the economic injustices of the past, regardless of how uncomfortable and painful such processes may be.

Of course it does not mean that we do not have our own critics as an organisation. As mentioned earlier, the Black Business Council decided to leave us in 2011 because, essentially, they were concerned about the speed of our movement towards transformation. We respect their view and have continued to have very constructive interactions and collaborations on many matters of common interest. I think it would be fair to say we all look forward to the day when we will be united once again. I am particularly pleased at the level of cooperation we have shown, especially at business/government forums where we speak with one voice on numerous issues. Even where we differ, I am satisfied with the mature way in which we have handled those differences.

Coming to business generally embracing corrective measures like BEE and EE, I think it would be disingenuous to argue, as some of us do, that there has been little or no change at all over the past 20 years. There is always room for improvement, of course, but to ignore the fact that some black business executives have climbed the corporate ladder with aplomb, would be both untrue and unfair. For instance, as of now, two of the four big banks in South Africa have black CEOs. You cannot ignore that, given our past as a nation. Looking at the boards of some of the major companies in South Africa, you will see a lot of high-calibre black professionals amongst their members. These are high-level people who are not just there for decorative purposes: they constitute serious intellectual capital and their contributions to these boards is immense. I myself, being a black African female, am CEO of the biggest business federation in South Africa. Surely that should count for something. We therefore cannot allow ourselves, especially as black professionals, to be sucked into effectively throwing the baby out with the bathwater just because we are perhaps not happy with the pace of change. We have to give credit where it is due, and acknowledge progress where it has occurred. Sometimes the tendency to be dismissive can be very frustrating to the business leaders of major corporations. On numerous occasions I have had white business leaders, who are active in Busa, privately expressing their frustration to me, almost throwing their hands in the air with despair that, whatever they do, they feel they are constantly on the receiving end of criticism for not being committed to transformation. We need to be careful, as black professionals, that we do not end up alienating even our supporters from big business in South Africa, by being continuously dismissive of their earnest efforts.

Indeed, some of us black professionals tend to carry our own individual experiences into public platforms and generalise. I'm sure that many of us, including Madi as the author of this book, have had nasty experiences which we would prefer to forget, as regards our dealings with white people in general, and with white colleagues, associates, or even bosses for that matter. We have all been on the receiving end of scorn, rudeness and outright racism in our lives – after all, we grew up at the height of apartheid. But we cannot allow our past experiences, bitterness and anger to colour our assessment of everything that is happening in business at this moment. Some of us have to really reign in our anger. We cannot be prisoners of the past. Even our founding father, Nelson Mandela, had to overcome horrific memories of the past, for the sake of building this nation. We need to take a leaf from his book.

Some of us have allowed our past bruising experiences with BEE commercial deals to colour our view of the process. We may have been partners in BEE deals that went sour, we may even have suffered heavy financial losses, but we cannot allow such experiences to colour our view of the process globally. After all, BEE transactions are mainly private commercial deals between consenting adults. They may go well, they may falter, they may make someone rich, but equally they may potentially leave someone a lot poorer. Relations in these transactions may prosper, or they may fracture. Egos may be built, or they may be severely bruised. That's life. It's no good carrying these bad memories into public platforms and articulating them as general trends.

Some of us, in our haste to be seen as serious BEE players, rush into transactions that are economically unsound. Because of our desperation to make the headlines and build public profiles, some of us plunge into deals that would just never have worked. We allow our egos to drive our thinking, instead of making sound, sober assessments. I have personally witnessed situations where black consortiums competing over a BEE deal outbid one another to foolish levels in their desperation to be the ones who bag the elephant. Of course, this can only serve the interests of a white business organisation that is being courted, since, after all, the executives there have a duty to act in the best interests of their shareholders. So if you have two or three black consortiums going overboard and being willing to pay stratospheric premiums to do a deal, the incumbent shareholders can only be happy. Any shareholder, black or white, would be. Then somehow we expect someone to bail us out if things go wrong. And when our expectations are not met, we cry foul. When a business deal flounders, we look for scapegoats, we blame government's lack of support or a white partner's sinister motives, and so forth. We must just accept that, in the end, BEE is essentially comprised of ordinary business transactions. Yes, the transaction may have been done within the context of a national programme, but the laws of economics are not suspended simply because someone has done a BEE transaction. Sometimes the best BEE deals are the ones you walk away from. We need the intellectual rigor and discipline to assess every opportunity for a BEE transaction as essentially a normal commercial transaction. If the numbers don't add up, walk away.

We need to be careful about our public articulations, too, or we may well end up delegitimising the very process we all support. We also need to be mindful that the younger generation is coming through the ranks, and is beginning to carefully assess what is happening in the BEE space. We do not want to be sending conflicting or even negative signals to them. We don't want the next generation to end up concluding that BEE is essentially a scam before dismissing it accordingly, to the detriment of the long-term economic emancipation of black people.

We must also be realistic about the fact that we are dealing with the consequences of deliberate economic exclusion which was entrenched over centuries. So, much as we would like to, we are probably unlikely to see this legacy being reversed fully in our lifetime. Our job as the current generation is to ensure that we put in place systems and mechanisms that, over the coming decades, will begin to have a telling effect on this legacy, by steadily and resolutely reversing it. But there will be no overnight results.

Of course my cautionary comments must not be misread to mean I am happy with the status quo – far from it! We need to ramp up the integration of black people into the mainstream. That is my unequivocal position. But as we do that, we must also be rational.

With regard to the way forward, access to funding remains a major impediment to black business generally, not just BEE transactions. We have raised this issue numerous times with government during our regular meetings. Until we find a mechanism to address this, the integration of black people into the mainstream of the economy will be near impossible. The stringent criteria adhered to by private commercial banks are simply excluding many budding black entrepreneurs. Public funding institutions will therefore have to ramp up their involvement.

Our education system is also creating a great deal of frustration amongst business entities. We are simply not producing the quality needed by industry, and this is an area of serious concern. Personally, I am baffled about how, even during apartheid, learners were regarded as having passed a grade if they obtained a mark of 50 plus per cent. But in a democratic government, with huge resources having been poured into education, we have lowered the bar to 30 per cent. This is just mind-boggling. And from industry's point of view, it is delivering people who are pretty much under-educated and often hopelessly ill-equipped. This adds to our stubbornly high unemployment rate, especially amongst the youth and is a threat to our social stability.

I would also like to appeal to my colleagues in the labour movement to come to the party and put national interests ahead of the interests of their membership. It's no use putting exorbitant demands on the bargaining table. Being aggressive and unyielding may in the end win you huge settlements, only to result in massive retrenchments a few months down the line, because a company was arm-wrestled into making unsustainable concessions. This has contributed immensely to the job losses inflicted on our economy. It also intimidates potential new investors, as they perceive our labour unions to be essentially hostile to business.

We as Busa would like to see government aggressively helping to remove red tape, and continue to raise these issues at various forums. Truth is, there are just too many cumbersome regulations that make starting up a business, or getting a licence, or travelling, or recruiting talent from abroad so cumbersome. The Department of Mineral Resources recently set up a one-stop-shop to issue licences and get mining operations off the ground. This has worked exceptionally well. We would like to see these one-stop-shops being replicated in every sector of the economy, as it would make a huge difference. However, my observation is that all this red tape is not solely confined to South Africa. Other BRICS countries (Brazil, Russia, India, China, South Africa), for instance, are also bogged down in bureaucracy. We recently had our own delegation to China being fragmented as some had the requisite papers issued timeously, whilst others simply did not receive theirs at all! So, as the entire BRICS block, we need to work towards eliminating unnecessary barriers to sound economic cooperation.

Broadly, as Busa, we are happy with our joint interactions and liaisons with government. Yes, there are many challenges that we have to contend with, but we are heartened by the cooperative spirit that is at the heart of our interactions.

Andile Mazwai
black stockbroking pioneer

Andile Mazwai is widely regarded as a pioneer, having been amongst the very first black professionals to qualify as a stockbroker in the new democratic South Africa. He started Mazwai Securities which rapidly grew and eventually merged with one of South Africa's premier broking firms, Barnard Jacobs Mellet (BJM). Andile became the CEO of the merged broking company. After a few years at the helm of BJM, he took a break from the hectic stock-broking world. In 2013 he decided to return to the financial services industry, but on the *stokvel* side this time around. He is the current CEO of the National Stokvels Association of South Africa (Nasasa)

When the discourse on BEE and AA kicked off at the dawn of our democracy, my sense is that it was primarily driven by corporate South Africa. And it was a very defensive discourse from corporate South Africa's perspective: 'No, we don't mind AA, provided it does not lower OUR standards. No, we don't have a problem with BEE, provided it is understood that these are OUR assets, we are not just going to give them away. This is OUR economy, we will decide how much of it we are willing to share.' There was so much of 'OUR', 'OUR'. The point of departure for many established businesses and serious economic players was: 'We have this asset that we have built up. It is now under threat. The only way to protect it, is to let the new powers-that-be have a piece of the action. But we will decide the parameters.' It was clear that black people were regarded as intruders in the world of serious business. And if you look at economic value, from a corporate's point of view, whatever value they were going to 'give away', it would be peanuts. As for me, I found this very patronising. I therefore truly did not like the tone of the original discourse on BEE and AA. It was clear to me that we were perceived as outsiders. Our legitimacy as participants in the world of serious business was in question. I think these processes started off on the wrong footing. There was no sense of us being equal partners in this world. We were almost like tenants, and corporate South Africa was the landlord.

Effectively, we were going to have to settle for whatever was thrown our way. The narrative was practically: 'You may make up 87 per cent of the population, but this is our economy, so be glad if we let you nibble at a crust. Be happy with a 10 or 15 or 20 per cent stake in this company.' I therefore think that, from the get-go, as BEE and AA were rolled out in this country, black people were already on the back foot. This imposed limitations on our entry points as black entrepreneurs, thereby creating a virtual scramble amongst ourselves from the beginning.

Personally, I think if you were to ask the original BEE dealmakers, quietly and privately, they will concede that many of the deals done during those early days were poorly structured, and many were even uneconomic. The funding structures were exorbitantly expensive, paying massive fees to banks and advisors. For the deals to be viable, all economic forces had to remain positively aligned. The share price had to keep going up, interest rates had to remain favourable, our currency had to remain strong, dividends had to be continuously and punctually declared or banks would levy hefty penalties, amongst others. If any one of these factors was out of kilter, it would scupper the deal. So, for five years during the tenure of the deal, you had to pray to the gods that all the stars would remain aligned in your favour. For many black participants in BEE deals, immediate real value lay in the directors' fees. Those fees paid the bills, kept the kids in school, paid the rent, etc. But the 'billion rand' deal, the one being spoken about in the newspapers, *that* proved to be illusory. It was like having your nose pressed against the window, you could look at this 'fortune', but were unable to touch it, or feel it or enjoy it. Of course, while enjoying those director's fees, you had to protect the organisation so that one day the big payday would finally arrive. The director's fees kept you trapped, well-behaved and on your knees in prayer.

The original participants did these deals because of the lure of overnight riches and the desperation to reap the first-comers benefits. Furthermore, many of the deals tossed their way were really on a take-it-or-leave-it basis. Corporate South Africa knew that many of us were desperate to do these deals, to get into the game and become players. Indeed, we were so desperate that on many occasions it was a stampede as we formed competing consortiums and tried to outbid one another. The approach would be that if Consortium A gave us a hard time by questioning the economics of the deal, Consortium B would take it without question. We would be played off against each other, and be taken advantage of in the process.

These deals were designed to effectively kill two birds with one stone for corporate South Africa, by protecting as much as possible of their asset base and ensuring political leverage. They were not really designed to ensure genuine economic empowerment for the beneficiaries. If economic empowerment happened, well great. If you study some of the original BEE deals, you will note that the people who made the real money were (almost exclusively) *white* financial institutions and corporate advisors. That bunch made a ton of money. I know of many white corporate advisors who made so much money from the initial wave of BEE transactions that, at its conclusion, they retired with handsome profits and have pretty much lived happily ever after. Of course, some black participants – many with strong political backgrounds – also made fortunes in the process. Many of these deals were designed to ensure that, if somehow the economic winds blew against them, political allies especially would not suffer losses, since that would obviously have eroded the political leverage these organisations were aiming for.

I would argue that the biggest BEE winner, by far, has been corporate South Africa, rather than the average black person in this country. Corporate South Africa was able to 'give away' a tiny bit of its capital, but in return received advantages that far exceeded whatever was given away. Corporates were able to secure political immunity, so their asset base was not in any way attacked by the new powers-that-be. Thereafter they could consolidate aggressively, and grow their businesses and their balance sheets. Those in retail were able to move into black areas and trade freely, in the process decimating much of black enterprise there. They aggressively moved up into Africa now that they had political legitimacy and were no longer suffering the effects of sanctions. Many moved their headquarters and treasuries to territories outside South Africa. Established banks made vast sums of money from BEE transactions. Given all these examples, in my view BEE has been fantastic for established business over the past 20 years. While a few of our folks made money, many were left stranded, really.

Of course the protests by those who did not make money from the initial wave of BEE deals will not resonate with ordinary black folk. You won't get much sympathy from others if you say: 'Damn, I should have made a billion, but I only ended up with a hundred million.' So I concede this is an elitist cry. Now that we are all reflecting on the situation 20 years down the line, many lessons have been learnt. I personally remain a firm supporter of BEE. I think we are all wiser now. I also like the approach of moving towards creating black industrialists, instead of black entrepreneurs merely being passive shareholders. But we also need to be careful that these sorts of interventions don't end up being self-perpetuating, especially not without any fundamental economics underlying them. To give an example: in our desperate need to create black industrialists, we must not create a situation where even the lazy and unproductive amongst us take advantage. We must not be left with a situation where a black enterprise is propped up when there is no economic rationale for its existence. Opportunists will take advantage of that, knowing that it does not matter whether they perform or not, we are so desperate to create 'success stories' that we will prop them up anyway with our taxes. So there is a risk that we will be taken for a ride, unless we build in strong checks and balances, and do not allow our desperation for success stories to cloud our judgement.

We also need to be certain that our definition of success, within the BEE context, does not become trapped in the lure of shiny accoutrements and bling. There is now truly a danger that unless you show off your flashy possessions, you are not regarded as a success. This is the case, irrespective of how your business is performing. Theoretically, you could therefore have a 'successful' black industrialist because he lives in a mansion and drives a massive, fancy car. If that becomes the accepted norm, then it encourages our new crop of entrepreneurs to rush to acquire flashy items, to the detriment of the business. You might end up with a situation where a dedicated entrepreneur will drive a beat-up VW Beetle so as to ensure that the funds go into growing his business, but sadly, because of the prevailing culture many a black entrepreneur ends up directing funds towards acquiring flash items simply to confirm to everybody that he has arrived. He knows that if he does not display the trappings of wealth, he will be regarded as a failure. And he may also know that, even if the venture suffers, just because we are desperate for success stories, we will probably continue to prop him up.

Let us concede that it is natural for any human being to wish to be acknowledged by society as a success. But in our society, the only way to be acknowledged as such, is to accumulate fancy possessions – there appears to be no other way, really. Many people, in my view (entrepreneurs in particular) have made a marked contribution towards developing and maturing black progress by going where angels fear to tread. Many have not made a fortune in the process, but they were trailblazers who chipped away at established stereotypes. Indeed, many of them feel like failures today because they have no vast possessions to show off. To me, that is a tragedy. They should be walking with their heads held high, knowing that society honours them for their pioneering efforts. Sometimes I wish South Africa had something similar to the British honours system where, if you have done well for the nation, despite not having fancy possessions, you are awarded an honour that stays with you for the rest of your life, like Sir So-and-So, or Joe Soap, OBE. I know we have national honours which are conferred on people, like The Order of Ikamanga, but I am talking about letters behind your name, which are uttered every time your name is mentioned. Of course the academic world has such honours, honorary professorships and honorary doctorates. But by their very nature, in order to preserve their currency, these are quite rare and are justifiably jealously guarded by academic institutions. There is no annual event where a slew of honorary doctorates or honorary professorships are announced, as you have with the British system. And by their very nature, these honours are reserved for academic effort. If we were to have these titles, almost akin to the British system, I think it would help to change our focus from defining success as being linked purely to riches.

I also think as black people we have retained certain contradictions in our psyche about our definition of success. Everybody knows we are generally communal in our orientation, rather than individualistic. While that has advantages in terms of the tendency to help one another, as expressed in the philosophy of *ubuntu*, it can be limiting at times. You want to be successful, but not so successful that you leave your folk far behind. An odd situation may arise where you own two cars, for instance: a humble one for attending family functions in order to downplay your success, and a fancy one when interacting with peers! That puts unnecessary pressure on you and may actually hold you back from unleashing your full potential. It can become debilitating. You want to inspire others by showing off the fruits of your hard labour, but you also need to be mindful that you are not perceived as showy and elitist. It is a bit of a schizophrenic situation that we really need to resolve as a people.

We as a nation are also quite punishing of failure. We crucify failures, irrespective of whether vital lessons were learnt in the process. In this culture, those who tried something in business and did not manage to make a runaway success of it, are brutally judged. I am sure this accounts for our low levels of entrepreneurship. People are so terrified of 'not making it', they would rather not try at all.

Coming back to BEE itself, I can only sum up the last 20 years as *painful lessons learned*. But we cannot live in the past. Our responsibility, as black entrepreneurs and leaders, is to ensure that the next 20 years are decidedly better than the last. After taking a brief respite from the world of stockbroking, I had some time to reflect on these issues. I came to the conclusion that I have to get back into the BEE scrum, but to do so differently by ensuring that, going forward, there is real economic empowerment for black people, rather than just enrichment of the elite.

For a long time I had been troubled by the fact that ordinary, hard-working black people, who have effectively been shunned by financial institutions, have come together over the past few decades to form mutual saving societies or so-called *stokvels*. There is an estimated R50bn that is collected by our people through these groupings. Naturally they hand over the collected funds to traditional banks, but when they need the very same banks' help, they are given the run-around. In my view this is a gross injustice. People who don't even have that much money, who have struggled all their lives, pool their resources together to save for a rainy day and hand their monies over to our banks. But when the rainy day comes, their funds end up financing major developments in privileged areas, funding the consumption of the elite, or the enterprises of the privileged. I received a calling to get stuck into the world of *stokvels*, to see how we can try to reverse the huge and grave injustice of our people not being able to benefit from the fruits of their own hard labour.

Just under two years ago I joined the National Stokvels Association of South Africa (Nasasa) as its CEO. Nasasa was founded in 1988 by black entrepreneurs who wanted to mobilise the disparate *stokvels* scattered across South Africa's black communities, to use their collective leverage. Nasasa is a self-regulatory organisation authorised by the South African Reserve Bank. Our mission is to improve people's lives by delivering enabling products and services that will create wealth or reduce the cost of living. Our strategy is to harness the cooperative power of *stokvel* groups to structurally change risk pricing and bargaining power to favour *stokvels*.

For me, this has been a life-changing and rewarding experience. Certainly, it is different from the hallowed and pristine worlds of high finance and the trading floors of stock exchanges or dealing rooms that I had been accustomed to for many years. But it is the arena of real empowerment. This is not the world of computer screens spewing out numbers and graphs, or traders shouting 'buy' and 'sell' orders. This is trudging it on the dusty streets, addressing people in community halls, at township taverns and at month-end functions. It is a world where you cannot assume that the person you are talking to understands such high-flown economic and financial concepts as leveraged buyouts, or complex financial instruments. It is a world where, at times, you have to spend an hour explaining the power of compounding. It is a world where people sometimes literally circulate a hat around the room, dropping off their monthly contributions! But it is the world of my people. I have found fulfilment here. All my intense and sophisticated financial training is now being deployed for the direct benefit of our folk. I am happier in this world.

In interacting with established banks, it was a bit of a rude awakening for me. I remember when I had my first meeting with a certain banking official to try to negotiate for concessions for our members. I started our conversation by saying: 'I am here on behalf of our members at Nasasa.' He quickly interrupted me, saying: 'No. You are here to talk about MY clients!' The meeting went downhill from there. It became clear to me that banks regarded *stokvel* members as they would any ordinary client, rather than seeing them as something special. The bank did not feel these members deserved any special attention, or unique services and products. And by indicating that they were nothing special, they effectively disempowered them. So, when our members went to banks for help, the usual forms and requirements were thrown at them: at people who live in backyard shacks, who work as taxi drivers, miners or street hawkers. The banks wanted proof of permanent address, pay-slips stretching over years, electricity bills, and so on. Naturally, the person concerned was unable to provide these, and it definitively killed off his/her application for a loan. We at Nasasa subsequently had to first instil a sense of power in our members; reminding them: 'This is YOUR money, you must use your leverage. We will help you assert yourselves. Do not be intimidated or allow yourselves to be dismissed so easily, especially when you are pumping so much of your funds into these institutions.' Admittedly, we have rather uneasy relations with established banks, but hopefully this will improve, going forward. We want our people to start flexing their collective muscle. We want them to benefit directly from the fruits of their labours. We don't want the banks to treat them with respect when they bring in bags full of cash, only to shut the door in their faces when they need help. We have also started strategic relations with other established organisations like cell phone and consumer goods providers to create special products and services for them, taking into account their realities while not throwing unrealistic qualifying criteria at them. The banks need to understand that many of our people are still trapped in townships which were effectively created as labour camps, not permanent areas of residence. They must respond to that reality and not be oblivious to it.

We want *stokvels* to become a true vehicle for the economic empowerment of our people. To that end, our struggle for real empowerment has now begun in earnest.

Gaby Magomola
black banking pioneer

Gaby Magomola is one of South Africa's most distinguished business and thought leaders. This he has proven thanks to a career spanning more than 35 years in both his native land and other parts of the world. He is Executive Chairman of VRG Enterprises and Thamaga Holdings. After overcoming the hardships of life as a political prisoner on Robben Island, where he first met President Nelson Mandela in the mid-60s, Magomola travelled to New York, where he became an acclaimed banker at the World Head Office of Citibank. He was later transferred to Wall Street where he rubbed shoulders with top investment bankers and stockbrokers. During his career in banking, he worked in NYC, London, as well as Athens.

It is your view as the author of this book, that a group of young executives whom I had assembled at African Bank in the 80s – of which you were a member – saw themselves almost as disciples of the gospel of black economic advancement which I was espousing at that time as your leader. That compels me to go back to explain how I had arrived at that point in terms of my philosophy on this critical matter, since it was a journey. I left South Africa in the late 70s to study banking and finance in the United States. I ended up staying there for a period of around eight years or so. Being outside South Africa for all that time was a life-changing experience for me, in many respects. I was to return to South Africa a completely different man, especially in terms of what I expected of black people's role in the economy. I was no longer willing to settle for less.

After obtaining an MBA in America, I had started climbing the corporate ladder and was settling in quite well. But I also observed that although African Americans at that time constituted around ten per cent of the total American population, there was nowhere near that number in terms of representivity across the various levels of the corporate sector. I encountered a group of highly capable black executives who seemed stuck at middle management level, despite their talent. It became clear to me that, comfortable as I was settling into the corporate world in America, I was likely to meet a similar fate at some stage in the future. Knowing that I was also destined to hit the glass ceiling, I took a decision to someday return to the land of my birth, rather than getting bogged down in the States.

I realised that I would need to equip myself well and become a fully developed executive by the time I went back home. It wasn't all doom and gloom, because at that time I also witnessed certain positive events unfolding in my career.

The bank I was working for seemed to be going the extra mile in training me, and exposing me to their various branches in the major capitals of the world. In addition, the then chairman of the bank was keeping a fairly close eye on my career progress and I had frequent meetings with him where we would exchange notes. It was much later that I was to become aware that the powers-that-be at Citibank had resolved to groom me for a leadership position in their South African operations. Like many American companies that had decided not to disinvest from South Africa, Citibank was under tremendous pressure to train and develop black South Africans, as espoused by the Sullivan Code. As a result there was some commonality of thinking there: not only had I resolved to go back home one day, but the bank also saw me returning to South Africa at some future date. Of course, their hope that I would end up leading their South African operations was a bit unrealistic, as it would have been against the laws of the day!

Nonetheless, they spared no effort in equipping me, as they knew that appointing me at a senior level in South Africa would subject them – and me – to intense scrutiny and skepticism. They wanted me to be super skilled to hold my own in what would possibly be a hostile environment. While all of this was happening, it had a tremendously positive effect on my self-esteem. I was already holding my own amongst the best and the brightest in the financial capital of the world, Wall Street. And I emphasise this part because if there is anything that apartheid did to the psyche of our people, it was to grind down our self-esteem and self-confidence. For me, in addition to being technically equipped as a world-class banker, I was being given back the best gift of all: my self-esteem.

By the time I returned to South Africa, I had far outgrown the psychological damage that apartheid had inflicted on us as black people. As a university student and later as an executive I had met and worked with brilliant Africans from across the entire continent. I had also frequently interacted with black American entrepreneurs. This proved to be quite pivotal in my thinking on matters around BEE. These black entrepreneurs were ardent proponents of BEE, and I imbibed their philosophies wholeheartedly. Their exhortations resonated with me as an Africanist, so much so that I just could not wait to begin espousing these philosophies when I returned home. Clearly, it was going to be impossible for me to be relegated to a tight little corner by the apartheid regime, to sit quietly and toe the line. So, you fellows who eventually worked with me at African Bank met a completely different person then, hence my evangelising on black economic self-reliance.

I remember shortly after my return to South Africa in the 80s, I was being interviewed by a white reporter from the SABC. In the course of our interview he called me 'cocky'. He said to me: 'Mr Magomola, you keep saying all these provocative things about black people lifting themselves up economically without looking at white people for salvation. You keep talking about the rand circulating several times within black communities before it goes out, isn't that a bit cocky?'

There he was referring to my advocating what Chika Onyeani, the author of *Capitalist nigger*, eventually came call the 'Spider-Web Doctrine'. The basis of Onyeani's argument is that blacks must mimic Asian people. I had been saying on television that blacks must in the main purchase black-manufactured goods, patronise black-owned stores, eat in black-owned establishments, etc. By adopting this approach, blacks would be able to attract wealth to their communities, and trap it there just as a spider traps flies. Now many white viewers found my views to be outrageous! If Twitter had existed then, it would have created a Twitter storm! Remember, I was saying these things at the height of apartheid. Whilst what I was saying was not breaking any laws as such, you could say I was sailing close to the wind. The Establishment perceived my pronouncements as too brash.

At that time I was mostly doing foreign-exchange financing, import–export letters of credit, etc., for Citibank in South Africa. Naturally I was dealing mostly with white captains of industry and many of them were rather intrigued that a black person could be comfortable in such high finance circles. They used to marvel at me, and the irony is that I also marvelled at the fact that they were marvelling at me! I remember one white fellow whom I was in a meeting with, calling his wife and saying: 'I wish you were here dear. I am sitting with one hell of a black guy here. You've never seen anything like this.' I am saying these things just to reflect how far we have come.

Clearly we were slowly chipping away at some of the established stereotypes of that time. Remember, this was the context in which black people were generally expected to be low-level clerks or ordinary labourers. It was a bit of a novelty to find black people moving comfortably in sophisticated business circles, especially in the world of high finance. We must also remember there were no private schools at that time; the only education that black people received was through Bantu Education. The expectation was that we could only think to a certain level, so, understandably, for many of our white compatriots to meet a black person who was comfortable in this milieu was just mind-boggling.

What I have also subsequently learned from some of the black people I interacted with at that time is that they also found me something of a novelty. I remember one black journalist saying to me, many years later after our initial encounter, that he was very keen to interview me because he thought some of the things that I had been saying at the time, for instance that black people need to own mines, were a bit outlandish. So he wanted to verify whether I was of sound mind!

My view as I returned to South Africa was that we needed to use whatever economic might we had as yet another tool in our struggle for liberation. As a member of Nafcoc, I was fully supportive of the Chamber of Commerce's ideas, as espoused at that time, that white business interests should not come into the townships, and that they should not ambush our guys close to the townships. That had already started happening on the periphery of townships, in places like Devland where big white wholesalers and some retailers were already setting up shop. That is why, over time, Nafcoc set up Afrimet, which was meant to become a distributor to smaller retailers in the townships. Nafcoc also went on to create the retail supermarket, BlackChain, in Soweto, and of course it had already created African Bank, where I was to eventually assume the position of Managing Director. For me in a way it was a huge advantage when my employer Citibank disinvested from South Africa, as it created an opportunity to finally join African Bank, after a short stint at Barclays Bank where I learnt retail banking. Naturally, as an active member of Nafcoc I had been having discussions with the founders to join African Bank at a future date. Again, under the auspices of Nafcoc, we worked with the likes of Richard Maponya, Nthato Motlana, Gibson Thula and Cyril Kobus and bought a bottling plant, which was probably the first milestone of what we now call BEE. I drove that process with Chris Ball at Barclays Bank because I saw it as an opportunity to create a first black entity of scale. That bottling plant, Kilimanjaro, was eventually listed on the JSE.

Subsequent to that we tried looking around for another opportunity. We identified Molope Bakeries in GaRankuwa, helped them with their plans for expansion, they made some additional acquisitions, we assisted them with finance, and helped them until they eventually listed on the JSE as the Molope Group. So there were now two black-owned businesses of scale that were listed on the JSE and playing with the big boys. That was our model at Nafcoc: build black-owned and black-run enterprises and equip them to graduate to the premier league. Building black enterprise brick by brick was our approach.

Then, of course, with the ushering in of our democracy in 1994, the BEE model underwent fundamental changes. That very same year a new era of BEE emerged via the Metropolitan transaction that created New Africa Investments Ltd (NAIL). Suddenly it looked possible that we could be financed to acquire an old established white enterprise and, at the stroke of a pen, we were in the premier league. It all looked so painless. With it came the possibility of overnight riches, of course, and all sorts of trappings. It was alluring. We were all captivated by this new easy way of doing business, but little did we know how ephemeral it was. And I am not being critical of the guys, I am simply relating the story as it unfolded. Yes, we were all captivated by it. A similar transaction happened elsewhere and it created Real Africa Holdings (RAIL). Both NAIL and RAIL are of course gone now, but that was the turning point.

Next we started looking at different ways of doing business as African people. We said: 'Oh, so we can knock at the door of other companies and ask for shares? This is easier than rolling up your sleeves.' In a way we were naive. Having not been involved in the guts of these businesses all along, we did not appreciate the complexities of running and growing them fully.

Now, looking back, I question whether this new model really was what we had meant by BEE when we started out. Yes, some did well through this new way, and that is fine. But it wasn't the original plan. We meant to create a pool of black businesses that would grow and graduate, in the process also creating a vibrant black middle class.

Going forward, I would say that this new talk about the black industrialist programme and radical economic change is encouraging. Of course, whether the results will come out of those announcements is a different matter, but the narrative from policy-makers and business leaders is different, and that is good. We must now channel our disappointments and frustrations in a way that will bring positive results. We must hope that there aren't long delays in policy implementation, because our people's patience has been tested. Policy-makers need to realise that people's patience is running out and they cannot sustain it forever.

What is it that will assist in accelerating the implementation of policy proposals and pronouncements? It is the institutions: strong, well-functioning institutions both inside and outside government. My contention is that we now need to prioritise the strengthening of institutions, otherwise all policy pronouncements and initiatives will simply fizzle out. We also need to ask ourselves: Where are the institutions outside of government to help those in government? Democracy, good governance and progress in civilised societies ought to be underpinned by institutional arrangements that are well governed, that would work collaboratively. If you do not have a properly constituted institutional framework, then policy pronouncement may not be implemented on time and chaos may follow. Where in civilised societies we have laws, and we have law enforcement and good governance, we also have successful societies. So, even with regard to institutions like Busa and Nafcoc, we need to ensure that they are properly resourced, that they are strong enough to continue to push policy-makers in the right direction. We also need to ensure that those leading these institutions put national interests ahead of personal ones. For instance, the question can be asked as to whether it is good policy to have institutions like these being led by active entrepreneurs. Isn't there an inherent conflict of interest somewhere in there? And this issue is about the principle, not necessarily about casting aspersions on any personalities.

Herman Mashaba
founder of Black Like Me and pioneering
black industrialist

Herman Mashaba is an entrepreneur and founder of the company Black Like Me. One of the few black industrialists South Africa has, and a business icon, Mashaba rose from poverty in the North West province and defied apartheid to open his own hair business which became the biggest hair brand in South Africa. He recently published his second book: *Capitalist crusader – fighting poverty through economic growth.*

~~~~~~~~~~

For me, this book on BEE could not have come at a more opportune time, as I am busy reflecting on these issues at public speaking engagements and lectures at universities and so forth. It highlights what I personally call the contradiction of South Africa's economic freedom. It becomes a contradiction to me when I reflect on my own life journey: I was born in 1959 at the time this country was under H.F. Verwoerd, the grand architect of apartheid. I was born into an environment where, with the passing in 1950 of the *Suppression of Communism Act*, I was automatically classified as a communist since that piece of legislation essentially classified anybody who opposed the policies of that government as such. The fact that I, as a black person, aspired to be the best I can be and to realise my full potential, basically put me at odds with the apartheid government which expected me to just be a good labourer, that's it. Although this law was eventually repealed in 1982, it was replaced by the more odious *Internal Security Act*, which the state security apparatus used to detain, torture and kill opponents of the apartheid regime.

The environment I was born into naturally made blacks resentful of anything associated with apartheid, including capitalism. We grew up believing that capitalism and apartheid were bedfellows. What entrenched this view was that just about all the major capitalist nations of the world – the United Kingdom, the United States, etc., were propping up the apartheid regime, while the only help available to anti-apartheid liberation movements came from Eastern bloc nations like Russia, and China. Of course to us ordinary black folk it wasn't self-evident that there was a cold war raging, which meant if the West opposed something, the East would automatically support it. To us it was very simple: the West equaled capitalism which equaled apartheid, while the East equaled communism/socialism which equaled non-racialism.

We therefore grew up equating apartheid with capitalism. The irony, of course, which I got to learn much later in life, is that the apartheid state was actually very communist in the way it went about doing things: massive government ownership of major corporations, no tolerance for individual freedoms, totalitarianism, and so forth. So, as a young man I decided to become a lawyer in order to fight this oppressive system. My university education unfortunately was constantly disrupted due to our then widespread campus activism and the anti-apartheid movement. Fired by this activism, at that point in my life I decided to go into exile and join the liberation fighters. My attempts in that regard were not successful due to difficulties in securing resources for my passage to leave the country. So, having been displaced from university, and having had difficulties in establishing contacts to skip the country, I had to take a decision about what to do with my life.

With nothing to lose, and my restless spirit at full throttle, I decided to go the business route. That was to eventually culminate in me and my associates starting what was to become a hugely successful black-owned cosmetics and hair-care brand, Black Like Me. Out of defiance and a heavy dose of self-reliance, despite the trials and tribulations of building a black industrial enterprise within a hostile apartheid environment, we built what was to be become this iconic black company.

Like many black South Africans, when our liberation movements were eventually unbanned and our leaders returned from prison and exile in the early 90s, I was extremely excited. Prospects for our nation looked very bright. Practically all of us voted for the ANC, exhilarated that the iconic Nelson Mandela was going to be our first democratically elected head of state. His vision for the future and his emphasis on forgetting the horrors of the past were truly inspiring.

He was to be followed in office by the immensely intellectual and talented Thabo Mbeki, whose dream of an African Renaissance had all of us captivated. But as the Mbeki vision soared in our minds, we saw our next-door neighbour, Zimbabwe, going in the opposite direction. There was more repression and violence there. Like many, I assumed that our president, Mbeki, the clear articulator of the African Renaissance, would unreservedly condemn the downward spiral in Zimbabwe. To my shock and disappointment, he did not. He seemed to be treating the situation with kid gloves. I started to question his African Renaissance gospel. In my mind there seemed to be a dichotomy between principle and practice. Zimbabwe virtually collapsed while we sat with our arms folded: there were reports of beatings, torture, killings, farm invasions. Zimbabweans were literally being driven out of their country and forced into exile the world over, with millions coming to settle here in South Africa. It was all happening under our noses. Our government, which had espoused freedom, the rule of law and human rights, just sat there and pretty much did nothing. This distressed me immensely.

My sense of foreboding was to grow deeper when suddenly there were fierce and ugly power struggles within the ruling ANC itself, culminating in President Mbeki being unseated from power a mere three or four months before his term of office expired. And this unseating of a serving head of state was done in flagrant disregard of the constitution of the country. My confidence in our former liberators began to waiver.

Suddenly the fears for my personal freedom and liberties that had existed during apartheid times began to come back to me. But I am businessman, so first among the many liberties I fight for, are the economic ones. I began seeing economic spaces closing up, largely because of the leftwing policies that were being implemented with zeal. It appeared as if the socialist and communist elements within the governing party's alliance partners were seizing control of the policy apparatus, to the detriment of our economy.

Coming back to BEE, when it was first introduced in this country, I was very excited because all my life I had believed there should be no impediments to anyone's economic empowerment. I understood BEE to mean that in the opening up of economic spaces, black people would receive priority given their deliberate exclusion in the past. Of course when BEE was introduced, as you know I was already a successful industrialist. Therefore I continued to prioritise my business, while observing from a distance how the BEE process was unfolding. Like many people, I assumed it was going to trigger a wide-scale opening up of opportunities for black people. But what I have witnessed over the past two decades is basically crony capitalism. To me it looks like the people who have benefited the most are politicians and their associates. It is really difficult for me to think of major entrepreneurs with zero political connections, who have emerged from BEE and done well by themselves. Almost all major beneficiaries have massive connections to the ANC. So it appears as if, perhaps with very few exceptions, politicians have been using BEE to take care of themselves and their circle. I believe the masses have little to nothing to show from BEE, 21 years after the advent of our democracy.

If we look at the economy, it is underperforming compared to practically every other economy on the continent. Our unemployment rate has remained the highest over the longest period for any country in the world. Almost 60 per cent of our youth are roaming the streets. Many are either trying to eke out a living from criminal activity, or are existing in a drug-induced stupor. Drugs like *nyaope* are running amok in our communities, with idle youngsters seeking refuge in them. With my family foundation we have managed to help some vulnerable youth in various parts of the country. The devastation that drugs is wreaking on our youngsters has reached epic proportions. I have seen it with my own eyes. Idle youths are having children they cannot care for. We are fast losing an entire generation. To me, there is no mystery about why we have these violent so-called service delivery protests. Most of them feature disaffected youths who just want to trash and burn. Our police force spend most of their time suppressing these protests, instead of protecting ordinary citizens from crime. It almost feels like a low-scale revolution by the underclass is underway. It is heartbreaking. Then you have almost 40 per cent of local households living on social grants paid by government, and government bandying about this statistic with pride. As if people find honour and dignity in joining the social welfare system. In a way, instead of unleashing the entrepreneurial spirit of the masses, I see a government that uses its energy in buying popularity by dishing out favours in terms of social grants to the masses, and BEE deals to friends. Even AA, on many occasions, has been used especially in SOEs, to recruit and advance political comrades and friends. We have recently had an embarrassing spate of exposures of people with fake qualifications holding top positions in the public sector and being in charge of budgets running into billions. Surely this is not the path that Mandela envisaged for us?

I am talking here as an unashamed capitalist and a crusader for economic freedoms. It looks to me like many of government's policies have been hijacked by communists, and it is doing immeasurable harm to the economy. It is time for us to face the realities before it is too late. And I emphasise the fact that I am a capitalist, because there are political opportunists in our country who continue to peddle the lie that capitalism equates apartheid. They condemn capitalism publicly, yet enjoy lives of conspicuous consumption.

And if you look at our current education system, you will notice that it produces kids who are barely ready for employment, let alone for tertiary education. Without educating our people there is just no way we will get anywhere as a country. A few weeks ago, the *Mail & Guardian* newspaper reported that 80 per cent of our public schools are dysfunctional. It is almost as if we are consigning a generation to a life of misery and unemployability. Frankly, I just don't know what has gone wrong with our former liberators. It is mind-boggling. But as patriots and citizens we cannot just sit back and watch. It is time to stand up and be counted.

Democratic systems all over the world succeeded not by chance, but because citizens took an interest in their lives. That's the challenge I would like to pose to my fellow citizens.

As you know, with the support of the Free Market Foundation board, we are challenging a piece of labour legislation at the Constitutional Court. We believe this legislation is unconstitutional, in addition to destroying small businesses. It essentially states that, once big companies and major trade unions have come together and agreed on payment packages for particular sectors, the minister is required to impose this arrangement on all entities operating in that particular sector, both big and small. So, at the stroke of a pen, without having agreed to a particular payment and staff benefit regime, a small business person may find himself having to pay exactly the same benefits as a large corporation. This is insane. These laws are destroying jobs, and we as citizens must stand up and fight against them. In this matter the government is cosying up to its trade union allies, but its actions are leading to multitudes of our people living a life of hopelessness and poverty, as small businesses close down countrywide. It is unacceptable. My stance on this matter has so incensed the government's trade union allies, that Cosatu recently called for a boycott of my company's products. Instead of deferring to the courts of our land to determine the outcome, economic warfare is now being unleashed on my business! And the government has not come out to condemn this threat from its alliance partner. Our government, which now has a policy of developing black industrialists, is allowing one of the very few black industrialists to be bullied by its partner! Hopefully the Constitutional Court will find in our favour. Unfortunately, our opponents in this case have used every trick in the book to delay this matter for the past two years, hoping that we will lose heart and walk away. We are not going to walk away.

We have all sorts of laws and regulations that seem to be hostile towards the creation of a vibrant small business sector in this country. And yet the rest of the world has accepted that a thriving small business sector is the ultimate job creator. This explains why we have persistently high unemployment rates, there is no mystery in all this. In order to please its alliance partners in the trade union movement, the government passes laws that by their very nature drive small business into the ground. Laws are passed that prescribe minimum wages. So, even if an unemployed person is willing to work for less for his own dignity and sustenance, the government says: 'No, rather stay at home and wait for your social grant.' Some people have even theorised that our government would prefer multitudes living off social grants, since that guarantees votes at every election. This creates an environment where an individual needs government's generosity to survive on a day-to-day basis. The individual becomes so dependent that he can no longer imagine himself surviving on his own, and is thereby perpetually indebted to the government. I must say that while I initially dismissed this theory as being too cynical, I am beginning to believe there is some truth to it. I just cannot find any other explanation for why our government seems to be entirely comfortable with – and in fact even proud of – the fact that 16 million out of its 55 million citizens live off social welfare. Other than the fact that it is unsustainable and will eventually bankrupt our economy, it is a statistic any nation should be ashamed of. If a great nation such as Greece can go bankrupt because of non-productive government policies, what will stop us? The unthinkable can happen here. I believe that all patriotic South Africans must stand up now and challenge this gradual decline in our nation.

There are a number of things I'd like to see happening with regard to the economic advancement of our people. Firstly, I believe we must scrap race-based laws and give freedom to everyone to achieve their dreams. I believe that race-based laws like AA legislation and BEE as it exists today have pulled our people backwards instead of carrying them forward. These race-based laws have discouraged and intimidated potential investors because they are cumbersome, punitive and divisive. You therefore have a situation where the economy is virtually grinding to a halt. It is a tragic irony that, at the height of apartheid, while I was growing up in Hammanskraal, practically everybody was working. They may not have been earning great salaries, but they had pride and dignity. In fact, those who did not work were despised, as it was a widely accepted fact that if you wanted work, you would get it. Today, when I visit my old neighbourhood, virtually nobody is employed. And, in a painful reversal, it is now an accepted fact that only the very lucky few are able to find work. People stare at you with blank faces, all hope gone. Youngsters stare at you, if sober, with anger and resentment, almost as if they are about to unleash their fury on you. I fear that the generations that come after us will have nothing but contempt for us, unless we stand up and arrest this decline. In a way, just as we developed contempt for our parents' capitulation to apartheid in the 70s, our kids are going to develop contempt for our capitulation to these self-destructive policies.

Some of my business colleagues have called for an economic summit, almost akin to an economic Codesa. I don't support this. What needs to be done is so patently obvious. We don't need conferences. If our government were to scrap the legislation which is aimed at destroying business (like the ones I mentioned earlier), it would unleash such entrepreneurial activity that our economy will easily grow by five per cent or more. Imagine the tax revenue that will then be available to government to fund infrastructure, etc. Right now, our tax base is shrinking year on year, because of all these restrictive policies and a declining economy, while virtually all our neighbouring countries are leaving us in the dust.

We as blacks also need to study some of the unintended consequences of initiatives like AA, especially from our fellow blacks in the United States, who have had decades of experience in this regard. There is now a growing body of literature, written by black intellectuals, denouncing AA. I would urge every South African, especially my fellow black compatriots, to read *Please stop helping us – How liberals make it harder for blacks to succeed*, by Jason L. Riley. That book demonstrates some of the soul-destroying aspects of race-based legislation.

It is time for us as blacks to outgrow the notion that we need government's help in order to succeed. I would contend that, looking at the record of BEE and AA so far, these programmes have done more harm than good.

Iqbal Surve
prominent black entrepreneur
and community leader

Dr Iqbal Surve is the Executive Chairman of the Independent Media Group and founder of the Sekunjalo Group, a pioneering black empowerment conglomerate established at the dawn of democracy in South Africa. Starting out as a medical doctor to liberation icons like Nelson Mandela, this anti-apartheid activist has, over the years, become a recognised global business leader and philanthropist.

Our point of departure here in the Western Cape, when we became engaged in the anti-apartheid struggle, was our deep concern about issues of poverty, social justice and development. It is that original point of departure that also informed our thinking on BEE from the get-go. We came from a point of view that black people had every right to fully participate in the country's economy as a means to address poverty, social justice and their own development. The fact that our negotiations for a democratic South Africa led to a political settlement did not automatically mean the transfer of economic power as well. Some other vehicle had to be found, and BEE was that vehicle. We were realistic enough to understand that BEE would not necessarily lead to an egalitarian society, which could only be achieved through a more complex socio-political process. We've learned lessons in this regard from what happened in China during the Cultural Revolution, and how that process brought to its knees what had been the world's largest economy, 400 years earlier. (Of course Deng Xiaoping was to subsequently rebuild the Chinese economy into the world's second largest one as we have it today, after painful lessons had been learned.) We also observed similar trends in our most immediate neighbour, Zimbabwe. So the idea was to open up the economy for black participation, without unleashing wanton destruction.

Of course the reality of our economic system is that if you do not have capital, you are already on the back foot. It is this reality that confronted us as newly liberated black people who also sought to complete our liberation through economic empowerment. The fact that white capital rules the roost is a stark and formidable reality, now as it was then. Capital, by its very nature, tends to coalesce and self-perpetuate where it resides, rather than naturally flowing outward. It is institutionalised within a particular community, or indeed a family like the Ruperts, and is passed on from one generation to another. It does not easily and naturally flow to new settings. It does not like strangers. By nature, rich people like to keep to themselves, and to hang onto their assets and fortunes. They use every trick in the book to keep outsiders out. They do not like to share (which is actually ironic, considering how poor people tend to have a propensity to share). Redirecting capital in the direction of black business activity was therefore going to be a major challenge, because it effectively meant trying to dislodge it from where it had coalesced and congealed. And BEE as a process was meant to trigger the rerouting of capital to where it was now most needed: within black communities. It was a big challenge then, and it continues to be to this day. That is why black enterprise continues to struggle. Capital remains largely congealed where it has been all along. Of course I am the first to admit that having capital by itself does not guarantee success. Knowledge of running a complex enterprise is absolutely necessary. But a lack of capital almost guarantees a false start, irrespective of how talented an individual is. Unfortunately, some detractors of BEE tend to conveniently overlook this formidable challenge, and use the patchy success of black business as evidence of blacks' so-called natural lack of business acumen. They also conveniently overlook the fact that some black entrepreneurs, like Richard Maponya, succeeded in our townships at the height of apartheid, when every obstacle was being thrown their way, including a legislated denial of capital.

In the first decade of our democracy, most BEE transactions were really structured in a way that decisively favoured established capital. Many white captains of industry, their bankers and their legions of advisors made a fortune for themselves, while many black entrepreneurs were left with little to show for their troubles. These deals would be done at the peak of the market, when they were more favourable to white entrepreneurs than new black partners. Our naivety and newness in the world of big business was taken advantage of. It is only in the second decade that the structuring of BEE deals began to improve, because many of us were now battle-scarred veterans and had gained enough experience to begin to assert ourselves during these transactions.

Naturally, our foray into serious business as black entrepreneurs has been marked by both successes and failures. And that is natural. For me, it is an important point to make that failure is natural to business, it is not just confined to black enterprise. Apartheid has skewed our thinking, especially amongst BEE detractors. There is a tendency to regard black failures in business as confirming a natural ineptitude. As black leaders we need to attack this posture since it may lead to the demobilisation of the black entrepreneurial spirit, intimidating our budding entrepreneurs into timidity and causing them to withdraw from the hustle and bustle of business. And this will certainly ensure that there is no transformation within the South African economy, which is precisely what BEE detractors want. To maintain the status quo, the detractors overplay black business failures and downplay success, building a narrative of a natural lack of business acumen amongst blacks – as if all white business ventures end up being successful!

The challenge to change the narrative of black effort is significant, too, because negative expectations in this regard are unfortunately still the norm in this country. That is why I make it a point that my children, from a very young age, are exposed to black intellectuals, scientists, business leaders and academics, so that they don't grow up having bought into the idea that blacks are inherently incapable of high achievement. And I believe it is the responsibility of every black leader from all walks of life to do so, lest our children begin to buy into the narrative that is perpetuated in the media today, that blacks are venal underachievers. I don't want my children to have the same experience as I did, when I first reported for class as a young, black medical student at the then whites-only University of Cape Town Medical School. I had professors there saying that my being there (instead of being at a university specifically set up for black students) would inevitably lead to standards being lowered! Today, this mentality is evident in South African business circles. There is very little that is welcoming in South Africa's established business, if you are black.

Because of constant exposure to black achievers, my kids now are at an intellectual stage where they challenge stereotypes of black underachievement. Not very long ago they even went so far as to demand that I begin to challenge these negative stories through our publications. For instance, where we don't just report the failings in our country and on the continent of Africa, but highlight, as loudly as possible, many of the successes that are being realised every day. For me, harping on children is key, because the best legacy we can leave our children is the sense that they are as good and as capable as anybody else. If we become immensely wealthy, but we do not leave our kids with a legacy of self-confidence, our work will have been in vain. Whatever riches we leave them, will soon dissipate.

Another reality we are confronting as black business is the almost perpetual resistance from established business, the never-ending push-back. This exerts extra pressure on us to be continuously vigilant, because the minute we think we have built momentum and start to take our foot off the pedal, established business uses its critical mass and financial heft to move in, even into territories where we thought we had successfully carved a niche for ourselves. And, naturally, once they move back in, very soon their entire economic ecosystem does the same. Before you know it, we are outsiders again.

Another challenge we face as black entrepreneurs is to try to live according to the expectations of what traditional business defines as hallmarks of a successful business entrepreneur, namely snobbishness and conspicuous consumption. This riles me greatly, to see many successful black businesspeople, in an attempt to be seen as such, mimicking some of the most opulent and decadent habits that are prevalent in the white community. They acquire massive and opulent residences, and take pride in being admitted to previously exclusively white, upper-class establishments, etc. This they do in the midst of grinding poverty amongst our people, almost as if they are rubbing it in. Many do this because they are desperate to be seen as 'one of us' by the white Establishment. We, as black entrepreneurs, need to retain the discipline and frugality we exercised during the liberation struggle. Unfortunately, amongst many of us, that has now gone. Opulence is becoming the order of the day. Rich black entrepreneurs have migrated completely, both physically and mentally, away from their own people. This is why, despite my success in business, I decided to remain in my old house and basically have the same lifestyle as I had prior to my success. This has inspired many of my kinsmen. Some would say it has cost me greatly in terms of not being seen as part of the 'new elite' and not joining the 'old boys' networks in this country. But I believe it has helped me to retain my original spirit of continuously fighting for the liberation of our people from poverty, disease and poor education. I believe that once you migrate to that world of snobbery and conspicuous consumption, as a black executive, you completely lose your identity. You end up essentially being a rich, white snob in a black skin. Not only do you adopt the habits of our former oppressors, you begin to think like them, and before you know it you become their agent, protecting their interests. We as black entrepreneurs need to be very careful of this co-option and assimilation. Unfortunately, many of us have fallen into this trap, and that is why many of our people are starting to view BEE as a honey trap for black achievers, instead of it being a tool which liberates common black folk from poverty and want. For me, the spirit of humility and dedication to your people is aptly captured in a picture that was doing the rounds on social media the other day, of a policeman sharing bread with a homeless woman. I said: 'This is it, this is what we were fighting for. This policeman, wearing a uniform that not long ago was a symbol of terror amongst our people, instead of being "captured" by this uniform as a symbol of power, is now using it as an instrument of service.' That is how those who have benefited from BEE must behave towards our people. BEE must push them to put themselves at the disposal of our people, rather than it being a new wall separating them from our folk. As a proud product of BEE myself, I firmly believe in this principle. The alternative is that, very soon, our people will hate us with the same passion with which they hated their former oppressors.

Some in this country have begun to argue that it's time to scrap BEE. I disagree completely. Those of us who have benefited from BEE constitute such a tiny minority that we have barely moved the needle in terms of black representivity in the South African economy. There is still a lot of work to be done. We need a critical mass of successful black entrepreneurs, and we are nowhere close to that. To abandon BEE now would see to a quick reversal of the gains made thus far. Those are the hard facts. But there are also 'soft' issues involved here. BEE gives hope to our people. They know that their democratically elected government, still mindful of their economic plight, wants them to be fully integrated into the mainstream of South Africa's economy. Our people are realistic. They know that not every black entrepreneur is going to be a millionaire because of BEE, nor that every black person will be in business, for that matter. They know that the chances of cracking the concrete walls and glass ceilings installed by apartheid are still there, but once BEE is scrapped as a national policy, we will be killing our people's hopes. They will feel that they have been abandoned by their government and its elite. And who knows what our people will resort to, once the flames of hope have been extinguished? After all, many of us joined the anti-apartheid struggle when we lost hope of ever being able to realise our potential under the previous regime. We need to keep our people's hope alive.

We also need to be careful not to allow a narrative to settle – one that equates BEE with corruption. Such a perception is designed to delegitimise the process, thereby allowing old patterns of economic power to re-emerge in our country. I personally am not afraid to say that I am a product of BEE, but I did not steal or rob (unlike the way in which our former oppressors obtained their wealth in the first place). Unlike BEE detractors who have inherited vast ill-begotten fortunes from their predecessors, as a new breed of black entrepreneurs we started from virtually nothing. In fact, as is a common experience amongst many black professionals, when my father died, instead of inheriting a fortune, I actually had to work extra hard, as a medical student, to settle the debts he left behind. And this is a common experience amongst many black folk. So, those who seek to judge and condemn us must first condemn their ancestors, who were part of a process of dispossessing indigenous peoples on a massive scale. They have no moral ground to stand on. They are essentially the beneficiaries of a process of grand corruption which we call apartheid and colonialism. I have worked extremely hard to get to where I am. Therefore we, as entrepreneurs who have benefited from BEE, should not be forced to hang our heads in shame, especially not by the very same people who used colonial and apartheid corruption and dispossession to build their vast fortunes. I am aware that some of our black entrepreneurs have been cowed into silence on these issues. I have had some people quietly saying to me that my being vocal on these issues may have cost me a lot in terms of accumulating more wealth. I would rather have less wealth than know that, in the pursuit of wealth, I sold my soul. I would argue that we need a more aggressive form of BEE now, instead of retreating on it. The cumulative lessons that we have learned from BEE processes in the past two decades can now be used to strengthen it even further.

I personally believe one of the reasons BEE so frequently comes under attack from established business is that, if black business grows to the extent where it is able to make its presence felt, even in the political and policy-making institutions of this country, the voice of black business will become so powerful as to be the normative voice. And that is what established business fears most – losing voice and influence in the corridors of power. This is what I always say to my comrades in public office, that it is important that they help us grow as black business, so that we can provide them with an alternative view of the world and help them to shape policies differently. Right now, because black business is relatively weak compared to established white business, it is the voice and worldview of white business that tends to own this contested space. And they would prefer to keep it that way.

It is therefore the duty of our government to aggressively seek out fledgling black businesses and support them. Government should, for instance, advertise aggressively in black-owned media. Us growing from strength to strength will also see our government growing from strength to strength, otherwise government will always be at the beck and call of established business. This is something our democratic government needs to remember: for as long as black business remains weak, government risks being at the beck and call of established business. We as black business still remain largely in touch with the hopes and fears of our people, thus we are likely to provide counsel and insight to our government that is close to the ground, unlike established business. We also are more grounded to the soil. The truth is that many of my white compatriots still have a transitory loyalty to this land. I can say without fear of equivocation that, while talk of migrating to Australia, the UK, Canada or the US is commonplace in the white community, it barely exists in the black communities of this country. Many white business leaders have family members scattered around the world, and talk fairly regularly of eventually joining them. Therefore, there is a strong tendency to 'accumulate-as-much-as-possible-and-as-quickly-as-possible-because-you-will-probably-be-leaving-this-country-at-some-stage-in-the-future', within the white communities. This kind of mentality is virtually absent amongst black entrepreneurs. Our government needs to develop clarity of mind on this issue: Do we prefer to be guided and counselled by people who do not see their roots here, or do we prefer to give our ear to the people who are here for keeps? Surely someone who sees himself leaving at some stage in the foreseeable future is not likely to care that much about the effect his actions will have on this country in 50 years' time, when he does not see himself living here at that time.

One of the major disappointments for me, 21 years into our democracy, is the resistance to change that one still sees from many of our white compatriots in certain sectors of our society. After many years of being an active member of the University of Cape Town council, for instance, I eventually resigned because at times it felt like I was swimming against the tide. Many of my white colleagues, who were furious at my publishing my resignation letter, are blind to what I call subliminal racism. This is racism which manifests itself in engaging in activities, or taking positions that, while not necessarily aimed at disadvantaging blacks on campus, have the exact same effect. This happens on a wide scale: from not being concerned about the paucity of black professors, to being oblivious to the offense statutes of colonial characters like Cecil John Rhodes give people of colour, to awarding all service contracts to white-owned enterprises, etc. I think many of my colleagues there, as is the case in South African society generally, have over the years become so socialised to an apartheid way of life that they have become blinded to certain anomalies which, to us black folk, are so patently obvious. The abnormal has become the normal to them. I challenge my white compatriots to do some serious introspection on subliminal racism.

In terms of the future outlook, I think we need to tighten up legislation on BEE, so that we close all the existing loopholes and incorporate the lessons learned over the past 20 years. But certainly there must be no retreat, whatever the onslaught on BEE may be.

I really like the talk of creating black industrialists, but we must not confine ourselves to only a hundred. Even a thousand, if at all possible. Let's aim high. But we should not just focus on the high-end of black business activity, to the exclusion of small and micro enterprises. A lot of jobs will be created at small business level, as international experience has shown. We therefore need to lay solid foundations by doing good groundwork. We need to learn from what Ratan Tata has done in India, or Muhammad Yunus did with Grameen Bank in creating unique micro-lending mechanisms to help small and micro entrepreneurs get off the ground. One way to do this would be through the securitisation of poor folks' assets – even informal settlements, for that matter, to grant them some asset that can be used as collateral for raising start-up capital. I recently saw something similar in Beijing. We always think of China as this massive manufacturing base, but I was recently exposed to a part of Beijing where, instead of seeing gleaming high-rise buildings or mega industrial parks, you see vast areas with rows upon rows of micro-entrepreneurs, selling all sorts of items: from vegetables to meat. Clearly, beneath the massive whale of huge factories in China there is a shoal of sardines in the form of small and micro enterprises.

One more thing I learned from that observation in Beijing, is that in our quest for major successes in BEE we must not forget that, at times, building a family's asset base can begin at a very humble level, like a micro enterprise. The main thing is to get started. Yes, the results will not be stories of overnight riches or vast fortunes. But it will create an asset base which will grow and be passed on from generation to generation, to ensure a sustained (albeit gradual) improvement in people's lives. We must also understand that the process of black economic emancipation will not entail vast empires being built overnight; it mostly will be a multi-generational process of gradual improvement.

Koko Khumalo
Chartered Accountant and Deputy President,
Black Management Forum

Koko Khumalo is a qualified and practising chartered accountant. She is currently a partner at Ernst & Young (EY), and is the Africa Leader for Risk Management. She serves on the Executive Committee of both the South Africa and Africa Region. She is responsible for legal, compliance, independence, risk management and regulatory services in EY–Sub-Saharan Africa. Ms Khumalo is also Deputy President of the Black Management Forum (BMF).

~~~~~~

My approach to BEE is going to be from a black professional's perspective, and of course more as a chartered accountant. Let me start by proudly stating that I am a product of AA. I am proud to proclaim that, because elements in our society mischievously try to delegitimise this vital transformational initiative. Had it not been for AA, I would not have been able to break into this profession which, until recently, was completely closed off to black people, let alone women. After obtaining my junior degree, I joined one of the big four banks and was included in their accelerated development programme, which helped immensely in terms of rapidly exposing me to areas it would have taken me years to access. While I remain thankful to that bank for the opportunities afforded to me, I had a pretty tough time there, as I suddenly found myself in a predominantly Afrikaans-speaking male-dominated environment. The fact that my command of the language was pretty weak, having been educated in a Roman Catholic school, made it very difficult for me to be perceived as a member of the team. This difficulty in integrating into the team eventually led me to leave and join a beverages company. This troubling experience at that bank was also instrumental in moving me to join the Black Management Forum when it launched in my hometown, Polokwane, in 1995. I identified fully with its vision of helping black executives to break through glass ceilings in corporate South Africa.

However, even in my new company it was clear to me that the fact that I had obtained my junior degree from a formerly apartheid-established university, Turfloop, made my colleagues think I was not properly qualified. One even went so far as to state that he did not recognise my degree as being worth much. That truly made me angry. However, I decided to convert my anger into a positive experience. A year later I left that beverages company and started my articles at Price Waterhouse Coopers (PWC), where I eventually qualified as a chartered accountant and was made a partner. The fact that I was to become the first woman in the history of PWC to be made an executive committee member was a high for me, considering how rough my initial entry into the corporate world had been.

As regards BEE, my main observation over the past 21 years has been that, while some of us have done well financially out of the process, gaining deep knowledge of the organisations or industries where we have been BEE partners has not necessarily been part of the process. So, even where there was good money to be made, often there was scant mastery of the entity concerned. The initial phase of BEE was characterised by our people simply being passive shareholders who, after a deal had been done and was announced with pomp and fanfare, slid away into their little corners, waiting to be called in when dividends were declared. Many joined boards as non-executive directors, thereafter relying on management to tell them how the company was doing. Some new BEE shareholders were useful to the organisation by running political errands for the company, or lobbying government for this or that favour. But being involved in the day-to-day operation of the business was a no-no. They were not, in any way, expected to acquire in-depth knowledge of the business. For me, tragically, on many occasions it was evident that they themselves never really insisted on being involved whatsoever. It was merely a question of collecting fees as directors or consultants during that time, hoping for dividends at the end of financial year, and, of course, keeping their fingers crossed that when the BEE scheme matured in a few years' time, the share price would be kind enough for them to pay off their main debt and be left with a hefty profit. A few made a lot of money in this way, but many others did not. Regardless, once a particular share transaction matured they repeated the cycle all over again, either within that particular organisation or with a new one. This approach has continued virtually with predictable regularity ever since BEE was first implemented.

This was not my initial understanding of how BEE would be done. My initial expectation was that BEE deals would be accompanied by black professionals being hands-on within their organisations, getting involved in daily operations, and in the process acquiring expertise. But, in general terms, that unfortunately has not materialised. Some of us have made a great deal of money from the BEE process, but have we acquired the requisite know-how? In many instances, certainly not. My approach to BEE has always been that making a ton of money is not enough, in itself. In fact, I would argue that making money without gaining the technical and operational knowledge is the opposite of being empowered. Yes, if this were the exception rather than the rule, I would understand that. Even in other economies of the world, some merely view themselves as investors, not necessarily as operators – people like Warren Buffett, Carl Icahn, etc. But generally those are developed economies where technical skill and operational knowledge are abundant commodities within the population. These investors are simply niche players, they are not the norm. Here in South Africa, where operational knowledge and technical skill are so scarce, especially amongst black people, I would have expected BEE to become our bridge to acquiring these skills. Sadly, the exception has become the norm. On very rare occasions have BEE partners joined an organisation and got involved in running the business. On paper, a huge number of BEE deals have been done, but have they been accompanied by wide-scale skills growth for our people? I would argue that they have not. As a rule, it's all been about doing the deal, about waiting for the dividend and for the big pay day. Surely that can't be right. After all, money is ephemeral, while knowledge is permanent. In essence, I would say our empowerment appears to have been artificial and illusory. I have to indicate that I am aware of a number of situations where BEE black partners' attempts to be operationally involved have been thwarted by their white partners as they would be loath to have 'outsiders interfering in their business'. This is unfortunate, but has been quite commonplace.

Still on this trend of passive BEE relations, I would truly have expected our political leadership to be vocal in condemning this scenario because it has, in my view, created an illusion of empowerment simply because big sums of money are bandied about without the acquisition of industry-related skills. I would have expected our leadership to come out clear and send a message that skills acquisition is far more beneficial to the nation than overnight riches for the few. Some have argued that our leaders perhaps prefer to look the other way because they are active players in this process. Nonetheless, I believe South Africa has squandered a massive opportunity for black professionals, through BEE deals, to become the drivers of the economy. Now, 20 years on, although we are supposed to be playing in the big league thanks to BEE deals, we are not knowledgeable enough to run these operations. As a consequence, the prevailing situation sees the best and the brightest black professionals not truly being part of the guts of the business world, running organisations or sweating it out in the engine room of the economic ship. It begs the question: Empowerment? What empowerment?

This brings me to my second point, the currently woeful statistics regarding black executive representation in corporate South Africa. They remain decisively skewed in favour of white males. There is no mystery to this, in my view. Being excited about BEE deals, we took our eye off the ball when it came to EE. While BEE deals were announced amidst much hype and headline-grabbing reports, in a way organisations were deflecting our attention away from AA, which demands true knowledge and skills acquisition. Now we are stuck with a situation where black advancement in corporate South Africa has virtually ground to a halt. I view this as a big tragedy, since this is where the development of a significant pool of black talent with skills, technical know-how and, more importantly, experience, should have emerged by now. In fact, I would personally have been happier if the situation had been reversed over the past 20 years: there should have been fewer BEE deals, but significantly more training, development and advancement of black talent in corporate South Africa. Unfortunately, 20 years later, the opposite is true. Black people are still largely absent from the top echelons of corporate South Africa, therefore they are not able to move things in the direction of fundamental transformation there. We are conspicuous by our absence from decision-making bodies. Even those black professionals who have broken through into the executive ranks – possibly because they are such a tiny minority in those echelons – find themselves isolated and incapable of making their presence felt. They are unable to drive their organisations towards transformation. Of course, one also has to acknowledge that some executives who have broken through take the perks of high office and do not want to rock the boat. For me, sadly, the past 20 years have largely constituted an opportunity lost in terms of true, lasting empowerment. I also need to point out that many white executives have continued over this period to see themselves as gatekeepers of the executive power corridors, thwarting almost every attempt to have them integrated and representative of South Africa's diversity. A very unfortunate situation indeed.

Coming back to BEE, this poses a big question: Is the cry for BEE a national cry, or is it a cry for individual achievement? If it is the latter, perhaps there is cause to sit back and let those who have 'arrived' enjoy the fruits of their achievements. However, if it is a national cry there isn't much to celebrate, really, as at a broader level our achievements have truly been patchy. I have also observed a trend towards the individualisation of black economic achievements. I deem this trend dangerous because it has a demobilising effect: it makes people happy that they have excellent jobs with great perks, and they then forget that there is a bigger national question at stake. After all, from an individualistic point of view, if you have a nice job and are well paid, then what is there to worry about? You are fine in your corner. Life is good to you, so why worry about everybody else?

The great Zimbabwean leader, Joshua Nkomo, once said that a nation can never be free if its peoples, en masse, are not free. From this I take the lesson that we cannot, as black professionals, separate our own individual economic freedom from the freedom of the nation at large. If large numbers of our people are mired in poverty and despair, it makes whatever successes some of us have achieved, rather hollow.

The individualisation of economic advancement also trivialises the liberation struggle. Essentially, it reduces the struggle to a quest for good jobs for some,

BEE deals for others, and elections once every five years for everybody. It reduces BEE to a cry to be let into the old, established networks and their grand tables, so that you too can enjoy the delicacies on offer. That cannot be right. There was more to our struggle than merely allowing some to sneak through and have a great life, while the vast majority are left to fend for themselves.

Frankly, even youngsters don't know anymore what we mean by BEE. Do we mean being awarded government tenders? Do we mean a few elites are invited to the lush table of big business? Do we mean quick hit-and-run business relationships where the focus is on grabbing the money and running? Do we mean bling and fancy possessions?

I believe the large-scale failure to hone our skills as black professionals while we were focused on overnight riches via BEE has also deprived our government of a significant pool of black talent that would have matured over the past 20 years and been available as a resource by now. I am certain this new talent, coming from our background, would have provided a development focus to our economic policy, as well as a new perspective. Right now, our government mostly relies on the advice of what I would call traditionalists and consultants with a conventional First-World bias. At times this becomes evident when new policies and regulations are presented which have absolutely no development focus. In fact, some have a direct opposite outcome. To give an example, I come from a rural area in Limpopo. My folk there have needs that are completely different from the needs of people in Soweto. But sometimes you see infrastructure being developed there which does not meet the needs of ruralites in Limpopo, although it would have been perfect for Soweto. This makes you wonder who exactly advises our government. We, as black professionals, given our background (coming mainly from deprived communities), may be engineers, physicists, economists or accountants, but we are likely to be influenced by our background when providing counsel to policy-makers. We will not just recite the rules according to the International Monetary Fund (IMF) or Harvard University. This uniqueness is what is required to bolster the development of South Africa, and it would have been widely available by now, had we concentrated on honing our technical skills post-apartheid. As an auditor, given my background, in addition to seeing to it that our codes of good practice are by and large implemented, I need to ask: Is this rule helping to meet South Africa's needs, or not? I won't just recite International Financial Reporting Standards (IFRS) rules in a robotic manner. And that is the unique perspective I would provide to policy-makers. I know that, at times, as black professionals we get scared off from providing a unique perspective, fearing the cry: 'Please don't lower our global standards!' But are some of these so-called high standards useful in a developing economy like ours, or they are hindering development and service delivery? Sometimes we get hoodwinked into thinking and operating as if we are in Zurich, when we are in fact dealing with a municipality in Alexandra township.

As black professionals we need to be careful that our approach to BEE and EE does not see us wanting to be assimilated and becoming mere clones who maintain the status quo. We need to develop our own view of processes and events, and must be willing to challenge them if they are not in line with our vision. For instance, the accounting profession, my profession, is known for being very stringent about rules and processes. But, as black accountants who understand the challenges that our country faces in trying to improve the lives of our people, we should be willing to ask whether a particular set of rules is helping or hindering such a move. If it isn't, we must be ready to challenge it, and not just parrot that it is 'in line with international standards'. By way of an example, if an official who has a budget to build 400 low-income houses for the local community, because of his energy and initiative ends up building 650, our rules currently would condemn that official. Instead of noting that development and actually encouraging the individual, s/he may well end up being dismissed. Why? Because in terms of global 'world-class' accounting standards, which we all at times blindly recite, this official is in the wrong, despite the fact that he actually did well in terms of improving people's lives.

I am making a clarion call to all black professionals to defer the rush for perks, to rather dedicate the next 20 years to aggressively honing their skills and technical know-how in all sectors of society.

Going forward, I would contend that for any transaction to be regarded as a genuine BEE deal and be awarded a high score in terms of our BEE Codes of Good Practice, it must, amongst other things, include a high component of skills development and EE. My proposal is that if it does not exceed those requirements, it must not be regarded as a BEE transaction at all. It must merely be branded an ordinary commercial transaction where the buyers just happen to be black, rather than a BEE transaction.

In 1956, the leaders of our various progressive movements came together and asked: 'What kind of South Africa do we want? We know the South Africa we DO NOT want, but let's dream for a moment. What kind of a nation are we struggling to create?' That was a pivotal moment in our quest for liberation, because from that point on they knew precisely what they were fighting for. It was no longer just platitudes and slogans, the vision was clear. The vision was not expressed in highly technical language, but it reflected our aspirations and resonated with people from all walks of life. It was to guide the liberation movement for decades to come. I personally think the time has come for us to develop an economic freedom charter. We need to answer the basic question: What should a truly economically liberated South Africa look like?

Right now, the answer is not obvious. A great deal of improvisation is happening; there are pockets of what looks like excellence, amidst patches of despair. We need to get to a point where we can answer simple questions like the following: If a black individual has made a ton of money, but has acquired zero knowledge of that particular business, has there been true empowerment as understood within the BEE context in that scenario? And conversely, if a black entrepreneur has not made a fortune out of a particular endeavour, or indeed has even experienced failure but has in the process acquired immense knowledge and skills, has there been genuine empowerment? Have our people acquired sufficient knowledge to be able to design our own programmes and policies, or do we rely on others to do that for us?

As black professionals, entrepreneurs and economic thinkers we need to come together to design our own economic freedom charter. When all is said and done, and we all set off in different directions, we must know precisely what we hope to achieve. Such a charter must reflect our common vision.

Lawrence Mavundla
President of NAFCOC, the legendary black business chamber of commerce

Lawrence Mavundla is the Founder and President of African Co-operative for Hawkers and Informal Businesses (ACHIB), one of the key constituencies of the National African Federated Chamber of Commerce and Industry (Nafcoc) which he also leads as the National President. Nafcoc, formed in 1964, is the oldest black business formation and arguably one of this country's oldest and largest business chambers. Mavundla has a long track record in small business activism and he has been a voice of conscience in matters affecting small business for over three decades.

As you know, Nafcoc is the oldest black business organisation in the country, having been first discussed in the 1940s by traders in and around Sophiatown and other suburbs of Johannesburg, only eventually to be formally constituted in Orlando, Soweto, in 1964.

It is a humbling honour for me to serve as its president. I came into Nafcoc having first organised street traders who were continuously being harassed by apartheid police in the streets of Johannesburg in the mid-80s. We formed an organisation called ACHIB (African Cooperative for Hawkers and Informal Businesses), growing rapidly from nothing to 45 000 members – at one point we had 110 000 members across the country. I was young and, quite frankly, angry! I wasn't a politician, I just wanted people to be allowed to earn a living. To me, it was abominable that the apartheid police seemed hell bent on seeing people starving. However, at some point I was privileged because I was accepted into the stately and much calmer Nafcoc, where I served under founding fathers such as Dr. Sam Motsuenyane, Dr. Archie Nkonyeni, Rev. Joe Hlongwane, Steve Skhosana, and, later on, Patrice Motsepe. I learned at their feet and they were kind enough to mold me from an angry young man into a seasoned, calm campaigner for BEE. I remain forever thankful to them.

At the time I became aware of Nafcoc, moves were afoot by the leaders to form a national black-owned retail organisation. Their vision was to graduate us from our little corner shops into competing with the big boys like Checkers, PicknPay and Spar, amongst others. This was to culminate in the formation of the first (and, ironically, only) entirely black-owned retail chain called BlackChain, which opened its doors in Soweto in 1976, literally rising like a phoenix from the ashes of that township, right at the height of apartheid. This shows the calibre of our founding fathers.

Their dreams were not just confined to retail – in fact, a year before Soweto erupted, Nafcoc had formed the first (and, again sadly, the only) entirely black-owned bank, African Bank. Our leaders began moving on to other sectors: Sentry Assurance was formed as a black foray into the insurance sector; Nafcoc Via was our foray into a travel agency business; Soshanguve Shopping Centre became our own black-owned shopping mall; African Development and Construction Holdings (ADCH, a construction company created to compete with the big boys like Group Five, Murray & Roberts, etc.); Black Business Publications and a Management and Leadership Development Centre to train managers for the future. The author of this book, Phinda Madi, is himself a beneficiary through the Joint Management Development Programme (JMDP), a joint venture between Nafcoc and the French Chamber of Commerce, established in the 80s. Nafcoc also instituted the Masekela-Mavimbela Scholarship Fund. As is evident, Nafcoc's vision from way back when has always been to have black business represented in all sectors of the economy, not just retail. And it is worth noting that all these major endeavours which I have mentioned were set up at the height of apartheid, virtually in total defiance of the regime. It is as if apartheid extracted the best from us.

When I grew up, it was a common sight in the townships to see big Unilever trucks delivering goods to black establishments. These big suppliers were comfortable in supplying (and growing) black-owned enterprises. But at some stage – perhaps for security reasons following anti-apartheid revolts in black areas – they gradually disappeared. Some wholesalers, like Metro Cash and Carry, began setting up on the periphery of townships to supply traders. As a result, our traders now had the additional expense of travelling to these wholesalers, which added to their cost structure and further eroded their margins, rendering many enterprises less viable. The point I'm making here is that those were the beginnings of our undoing as vibrant black entrepreneurs in townships and rural areas. The seeds of our annihilation were gradually being planted.

The woes of black retail and black enterprise in general since the apartheid era are well known, so I won't recount them here blow by blow. Save to say that when our leaders came back from exile and prison, like all South Africans we were excited. We thought they would make it their priority to reverse our decline and help us rebuild as black business. We thought they would help us mobilise funding, infrastructure and other necessary resources. We believed they would help us tie up with stronger white business partners whose hearts and minds were in the right place. I have recollections that out of sheer excitement, many businesspeople in the townships had pooled their resources so that we could smuggle funds to the liberation movements, to facilitate their return and resettlement in the country! We envisaged the dawn of a new golden age for black business.

But then came BEE. Initially we were excited because this was going to be the vehicle for black and white business to begin to work together for the good of all. To us, BEE was going to be the fuel that black business had been desperate for all those years. Instead, a different animal emerged. It quickly became nothing but a get-rich-quick scheme.

Our people saw others with virtually no business history or any track record to speak of, becoming millionaires overnight after signing a couple of papers with white business partners. Instead of grinding it out on the dusty streets of the township, and sweating it the good old-fashioned way, suddenly BEE seemed the easy way out. There was a scramble to get in on the act. Of course not all entrepreneurs in black areas could access BEE – only a lucky or connected few did. Many of our entrepreneurs were left scrambling for crumbs and trying to eke out a living. While small township entrepreneurs were reeling under this blow, suddenly there came the invasion of behemoth white-owned shopping malls, taking advantage of the situation. As our people scrambled for cover, we looked to our political leaders for help but none was forthcoming. We expected our leaders to say to established white business: 'It isn't BEE if it isn't helping fledgling businesses in black areas.' That didn't happen. White retail giants were setting up in our areas with a free hand, pushing our traders to the edge of extinction. If all these giants were entering via joint ventures with local traders who had been slaving there for ages, we would have been very happy about it. If our political leaders had insisted on that, we would have been in a much healthier position today. Instead, these new behemoths completely ignored us and brushed aside township entrepreneurs. When we approached these large white retailers to explore the potential for working together, they would refer to the fact that they were compliant with BEE codes, because they had done BEE deals through their JSE-listed holding companies with people who were barely members of the community. In a way they felt they had bought a licence to operate with abandon in black areas. They felt they were entitled to trade in our areas because of BEE.

This created untold anguish and devastation in townships. There was also a lot of anger, with some taking out their anger on foreign small traders, triggering cries of 'xenophobia'. It's not simply xenophobia, it's deep-seated but misdirected anger at being wiped out in our own back yards. Nafcoc reeled under the blows just as our core membership did, yet we had to step up to the plate. Sadly, we have had to accept that, much like during apartheid, unless we gird our loins and do something almost despite our government's promises, black business will die a slow and painful death in the townships and rural areas. And again, sadly, we have had to accept that BEE provides no solutions for us. In fact, it has actually has cost us a lot. We took our eye off the ball because of BEE. So as Nafcoc, we have now decided to go back to our roots, to do business the good old-fashioned way by getting stuck in and getting our fingernails dirty through a number of initiatives.

We have subsequently pooled our resources and bought prime properties (like the prestigious conference centre, Gallagher Estates), to generate rental income. We are in the process of rebuilding our retail infrastructure through a new brand of wholesale, warehouse and retail chains. We are going to start supplying our traders in the townships, and they will be part-owners of this network. Instead of being angry at the big boys who are eating our lunch, or small-time foreign traders, we have decided to fight back by pulling ourselves up by our own bootstraps. We have started almost by stealth, but it will only be a matter of time before we surface fully with new brands. Our traders and other entrepreneurs in the townships are now extremely excited and full of hope once more. Already we are unable to cope with the demand for our new services. We are channelling entrepreneurs' and traders' anger in the right direction.

We want to transform the retail industry. We want our people to begin to buy through our members in our structures. We plan to go further than retail – we have already signed up black farmers to supply produce to us. We want consumers to buy products that are produced by our own people. We want them to buy mealie meal produced by our own farmers and black milling operations. Our people understand that we are under siege, that if we survive, they survive too. It is pleasing to see our people beaming again. We recently hosted a delegation from Zimbabwe who like what we are doing, and we are beginning to establish genuinely empowering partnership with some white businesspeople who see our success as their success. I am confident we are rising from the ashes, developing a new model. Our position is that while government busies itself with slogans, we will be developing our own model and moving forward. There's no time to waste.

What makes me especially sad is the fact that only three industries in this country are black-owned and operated: the taxi industry, hospitality/taverns in the townships, and the street hawkers who appear to have been singled out for victimisation by our very own government:

- The taxi industry receives no help from the government, unlike other public transport that is subsidised. Instead, people are left to scramble at the bottom of an industry where profits are menial and in-fighting for survival is commonplace. We are always under the jackboot of aggression from authorities.

- Similarly, street hawkers are being swept off the streets like vermin. They receive no support or alternative trading facilities and infrastructure. They are merely seen as an eyesore, not as entrepreneurs who are employing people and feeding families.

- The new liquor regulations state that it is illegal to sell liquor within a certain radius of residential areas. These new proposed regulations by themselves are about to wipe out township taverns and the hospitality sector, which are anchor industries for township economies. It is mind-boggling and most disheartening!

We have almost come to a point where we expect no help from the authorities. Unless we improvise, we will die. Our backs are against the wall, so this is a fight for survival.

This is the gospel we are also beginning to preach to our people now; that unless we stand up on our own and help ourselves, it's all over. Sometimes I see guys in the streets 'toyi-toying' and shouting 'Government must build me a house'. I mean, come on, let's empower ourselves so that we can afford to build our own homes, otherwise we will be toyi-toying forever. We must develop self-reliance now.

At times I must say that I feel for the president of our country. We black businesspeople bombard him with so many contradictory messages at times that it can be bewildering. Some of us conveniently punt the message that BEE is all about owning a piece of white business, while others lobby for their own, individual projects. Some use their access to him as a selling proposition to white business. What we need to be saying to the president is: 'Give us the tools to help ourselves.' Unfortunately, not all of us want to do it the hard way. Why don't we go back to doing business the way our forebears did it: by getting down and dirty, not through scheming, all sorts of machinations, and get-rich-quick scams. Those are illusory. At Nafcoc, just as our forebears did in the 60s, we want to preach the gospel of black self-reliance and getting rich the good old-fashioned way – through hard work.

One final and important point I want to make, is this. There is this misconception that black businesspeople in the townships need loans. No, we don't need loans. Our entrepreneurs there don't have massive overheads. All we need is credit – trading credit. If we had funding mechanisms to enable us to access credit, we would give all our competitors here a run for their money.

Dr Len Konar
prominent independent
director of companies and accounting academic

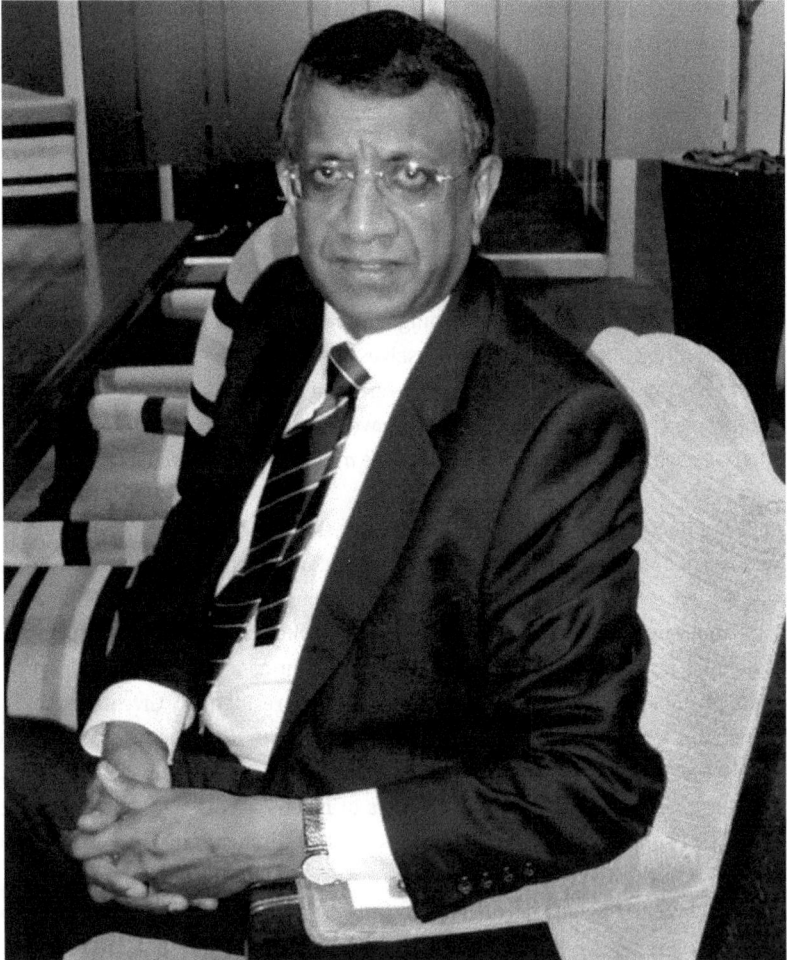

Dr Len Konar, DCom (CA, SA) was a member of the King Commission on Corporate Governance, past Chair of the Ministerial Panel for the Review of Accountants and Auditors in SA (2002–2004), co-Chair of the Independent Oversight Panel of the World Bank (2009–2010) and past Chairman and member of the External Audit Committee of the International Monetary Fund (IMF) in Washington. A past member of the Ad Hoc Ethics Panel of the United Nations, he serves on and chairs a number of major public companies in South Africa. He also lectures and presents seminars and workshops at universities and to both private and public companies, corporations and NGOs in South Africa and elsewhere.

My thinking on BEE over the past 20 years is that we haven't really implemented it in terms of the constitution, certainly the initial wave of these transactions, which singled out 'poster' boys and 'poster' girls, and empowered them. High-profile politicians or highly politically connected individuals were identified and then essentially gifted these BEE transactions, and as a consequence they became seriously rich. The thinking then was that this would give those 'empowering' organisations particular political leverage as the new South Africa took shape. My disappointment with this initial wave is that the transactions were very narrowly focused – there was nothing broad-based about them. I would therefore argue that they were not in line with our constitutional imperatives, since BEE was supposed to be broad-based from the get-go.

However, I would not be so reductionist as to say, as some critics have done, that this was a wide-scale 'capturing' of our political leaders by corporate South Africa. My sense is that 60 to 70 per cent of organisations in the private sector want to do the right thing. Some may have made hasty mistakes as the dust began settling at the birth of our democracy following the chaos of the anti-apartheid conflict. Furthermore, this trend of politicians receiving overnight benefits was not confined to private sector BEE deals. A number of very senior politicians have had (and some continue to have) their spouses or family members occupying very senior positions in public institutions – some deservedly so, others not. So many political figures were certainly involved in a scramble for enrichment, both in the private sector thanks to this initial wave of BEE deals, and some by attaining top positions in public institutions like the SABC, amongst others. Some of the recently exposed lapses in SOEs, for instance, occurred exactly as the result of this scramble. Take South African Airways, for example – an organisation with a turnover north of R30bn, it has a board of only four people, with only one member having the requisite skills.

My preferred approach to BEE is totally contrary to the initial approach of merely singling out a few individuals, and then empowering them lavishly. My preferred model, which I espouse very assertively in the companies on whose boards I serve – especially where I am the chairman – is to initially look at employees of that particular company as the first line of beneficiaries. This moves from the premise that charity begins at home. Employees must be given a stake in the company. If I take Steinhoff as an example, 11 000 of our employees are shareholders. If we have to help them raise funding, so be it, but they HAVE to be shareholders in the company. When we did our empowerment deal, the share price was between R12 and R22. Today, the share price is above R80. That means there has been serious value growth for all our shareholders, including our employees. Another example is the scheme we used at Kumba Iron Ore. When it matured in five years' time, each employee shareholder ended up pocketing an average of R345 000. We did a similar scheme at Exarro Resources, where each employee shareholder ended up pocketing an average of R135 000. In this way, significant wealth was created amongst a wide section of mostly ordinary folk.

Remaining employee focused, the second leg of my preferred model is still confined to staff (especially black staff) and involves their training and development. That way, we grow our own timber. At Exarro, for instance, we are sponsoring three chairs around some of the top universities in the country, at significant cost to the company, to ensure that those universities help us identify and train black mining engineers who will come and join us once they graduate.

The key motivator here is to align the interests of the employee with those of the company. At every one of these organisations and their operations all over, employees know exactly what the budget is; how much production needs to occur to meet targets, etc. With this kind of approach, you have everybody pulling in the same direction.

The third leg is to improve the lot of the communities surrounding the businesses where we operate. We need to investigate what amenities local communities lack, especially around education: Do the local schools have libraries, laboratories, WIFI and so forth? We also focus on healthcare issues: Are local clinics properly resourced? Is primary healthcare functional? Is childcare available? The intention is simple: I want to see an improvement in the quality of people's lives, particularly in the communities in which we operate. We have to go even further and source all the required skills (be they fitters, artisans, etc.) from the local community. We will then go aggressively and recruit and train only from such local communities.

The fourth element would be to use our premises creatively, for the benefit of local communities. Over the weekends, for instance, can we make our facilities available for local students to study, or to pursue recreational activities.

Going forward, I believe all major corporations in South Africa need to encourage their executives to make themselves available for mentorship programmes. That way, you would have your top executives spending approximately ten per cent of their time, one or two days a month, getting involved in social upliftment activities. Our executives need to be very active in mentoring not just aspiring executives, but also budding entrepreneurs, because that is exactly where employment creation will happen in the future.

I also believe that we, as big organisations, need to scan our entire procurements profile and identify all services that we can outsource, before pro-actively going out to seek (and where need be, even help) start-up black-owned enterprises to provide messenger services, carpet cleaning, catering, landscaping and other services. As companies, we should even be willing to stand as guarantors to these fledgling enterprises to help them access funding from banks. As you can see, the focus should not just be on headline-grabbing grand BEE schemes. These kinds of services can make a huge difference in people's lives, while creating a vibrant entrepreneurial class amongst peoples from disadvantaged backgrounds.

If I had the power, I would decree that one to two per cent of the profits of major South African corporations be dedicated to BEE initiatives that are primarily focused on training and developing small and fledgling enterprises, heavily backed by mentoring programmes. You don't want to set people up, only to leave them floundering and failing.

Coming to the public sector, our government owns a great number of mega enterprises, many of which are underperforming. If you look at the UK as an example, they sold British Airways, Royal Mail, etc. That not only rid the government of enterprises that were a headache to manage and a drain on the fiscus, but this generated extra revenue that was subsequently used in the most needy sectors of society. My wish is that we could reduce the national debt in South Africa and improve the quality of life of our needy citizenry. To achieve that, I would sell off 60 to 70 per cent of Eskom and SAA, amongst other major SOEs, and use the proceeds to improve housing, education, health services and basic infrastructure in the rural areas. I would also release a lot of the land that the state owns, again for the same purpose. The main focus would be to release the capital which is currently almost 'imprisoned' and draining away.

Of course I'm aware that a lot of our government ministers have a communist or socialist background, so they remain loyal to the dogma of state control. But it is now important to move on from some of the romantic ideas that have been disproved by history, and get realistic. For as long as we continue to cling to such dogma, we will never have our own Mark Zuckerbergs or Steve Jobs or Richard Maponyas. South Africa's entrepreneurial spirit is being held captive by dogma. In my view, the question we need to answer as a country is: Do we want to be excellent, or do we want to be average?

We also need to inculcate a culture which awakens a hunger for excellence amongst our general populace. We must inculcate this hunger not just amongst ourselves, but even amongst the next generation. Like Singapore, we must create a nation for whom it doesn't really matter how woeful our situation looked in the past: the present and the future must become our driving vision where we work towards excellence. We must create a nation that despises mediocrity.

Of course every normally functioning society has an achievement scale of 10-70-20, where ten per cent are superior performers, 70 per cent are average and 20 per cent under-performers. History has taught us that once these scales are skewed or all over the place, a society is so dysfunctional that is not sustainable.

I have also observed in certain government departments an almost fanatical and counter-productive implementation of BEE and EE. Recently I was at a particular government department where there were 11 African males, all from a particular ethnic group. That is bizarre and probably unconstitutional. Such a situation leads to inbreeding when it comes to ideas and creativity. Diversity is the strength of this country. Even the national coat of arms states that our diversity is our strength as a nation. We must never forget that when implementing AA and BEE.

I also wish there were more consultation between the president in particular, and business entrepreneurs and thought leaders from across the entire spectrum of South African society – not just business organisations, but individuals who have demonstrated both their capacity and commitment. During apartheid you had Presidential Business Advisory Councils that met once every quarter; the president (and certain cabinet ministers) sat down with top business leaders and job creators to discuss policy and regularly review progress. This allowed business leaders to point out the serious practical consequences of a policy that had looked good on paper to bureaucrats. I would argue that the recent self-inflicted catastrophe around our new immigration laws, which have greatly harmed the tourism industry, would not have occurred if such a consultative forum existed.

My final point is that our government is just simply too big for a country and economy of our size – it is almost ridiculously big. A country like South Africa has no business having 42 cabinet ministers. My humble view is that this bloated executive is not only an unnecessary drain on our fiscus, but it also creates policy confusion and, at times, implementation chaos. Consider, for instance, that we have three ministries charged with economic matters. Sometimes they send out mixed signals or defend their own turf, which drains resources and wastes time. Some ministries simply have no economic justification for their existence. The United States has a cabinet of 13 ministers, and the government of the United Kingdom has 25 ministers – these are massive economies compared to South Africa, their populations are also far larger. This makes us look ridiculous. A skewed situation has emerged where the only serious employment creation discernible over the past few years has come from government itself. This is not only a sign of an abnormal economic situation, it also exerts a serious drain on our fiscus and is simply not sustainable.

Leon Louw
Executive Director, Free Market Foundation

Leon Louw is the executive director and cofounder of the Free Market Foundation (FMF). Founded in 1975, the FMF is an independent public benefit organisation that promotes and fosters an open society, the rule of law, personal liberty, and economic and press freedom.

At the FMF, I would say there is no single view about BEE. While we are all ardent believers in individual freedoms and free enterprise, our views range from those who believe there should be no race-based initiatives like AA, to those who support such policies. The FMF has been grappling with this issue for a long time – we even produced our own policy document under the instruction of our Honorary Life President, Dr Sam Motsuenyane, more than ten years ago. I, for one, believe that apartheid, having been a crime against humanity, demands corrective action or, as I prefer to call it, compensation. When a government wrongs a citizen, that citizen must be duly entitled to compensation for that particular wrong. Apartheid was a crime against humanity, so its victims must be compensated. That compensation may be a once-off payment in cash or in kind. It does not necessarily need to entail lengthy processes like AA or BEE.

I have always been baffled by why people do not see the privatisation of SOEs and some government facilities as a massive opportunity for BEE. Take a simple thing like public hospitals, many of which are a catastrophe at the moment. Why doesn't government call in a few entrepreneurs – black entrepreneurs – and say to them: 'Let's turn this into a BEE business and the government will pay for the treatment of patients, but will not manage the hospital.' In other words, it's similar to government buying computers: it doesn't have to own the computer company, it just needs functioning computers! So, it simply pays for these and ensures that they deliver a service. This approach could spawn a lot of black entrepreneurs and BEE companies; we would have improved the quality of healthcare for the poor, at the same price. You could do that with all sorts of other things: you could do it with schools, and with licensing departments. The approach would be to look at every single government operation and ask: Could this be outsourced to a BEE contractor? You will be able to kill two birds with one stone, by significantly improving efficiencies while facilitating BEE.

To me this is a no-brainer. It shouldn't even require any discussion. Even from a politician's point of view it should be obviously attractive. Again, you would be killing two big birds with one stone: you would improve service delivery and become more popular with voters while achieving government's stated policy of empowering blacks economically.

Personally, I believe there should have been what I call a big giveaway at the dawn of our democracy, in a manner more or less similar to what Don Caldwell called for in his book *South Africa: The new revolution*. The ANC government inherited all these massive assets from the Nationalist Party government, all these parastatals like PetroSA, the SABC, SAA, Eskom, etc. These are the assets that the ANC government should simply have privatised, and then given the shares to black South Africans. That would have been BEE on a massive scale. Instead they held onto them. Today, just about all of these entities are in terrible shape and are a massive drain on the fiscus. They are just gobbling up wealth and making government look silly and incompetent. All of this wealth should be spent on the poor, on service delivery and education, instead of being poured into a bottomless pit. This kind of massive privatisation happened in Central European countries like Czechoslovakia. We can go and look at how they did it, we can look at what they experienced. As you know, these countries moved from communism to a market economy, and in my view apartheid came very close to communism. The degree to which the apartheid regime was communist is now very obvious, if you consider that we have one of the highest proportions of GDP in the hands of government of any country in the world. We have one of the highest proportions of tax per capita relative to GDP in the world. We inherited a regime which its opponents called capitalist, yet by no stretch of the imagination was it even remotely capitalist. You had all these massive organisations owned and run by the state, just like you would find in communist countries. Giants like Eskom – one single, huge government monster that runs the generation of electricity, its distribution and retailing. Everywhere else in the world there are separate entities for different energy modes: nuclear, gas, coal, hydro, etc. There are also different entities for power generation, distribution and transmission. You won't find an 'Eskom' anywhere else in the world. This is an anachronism, an archaic approach to power supply. It is a dinosaur from the communist era.

In my view, privatising these assets would be akin to returning the silver to the family. It belongs to the people. As the *Freedom Charter* states: the minerals under the soil belong to the people as a whole. Nowadays, everyone (young people included) assumes that the people are the government. What they forget is that, as Mandela, Sisulu and Luthuli explained in 1956, when asked what that meant: 'Ownership by the people does not mean ownership by the government, it means exactly ownership by the people.' So, returning these assets through privatisation to their rightful owners would be in line with the *Freedom Charter*.

This is also the view we expressed when Dr Motsuenyane asked us to debate the matter.

The view that, going forward, we should have a non-racial approach to BEE (as espoused by, amongst others, Dr Anthea Jeffery of the Institute of Race Relations), where the litmus test will be economic need instead of skin colour, is impractical. It would be an administrative nightmare to implement such a system. I know that even the poet and author, Don Matera, has argued over the years for AA that is not race based. His argument is that although that sounds like a contradiction on the face of it, in reality 90 per cent of the beneficiaries would be black. Still, I believe that would be impractical. In my view it is simply much easier to say that every black South African will receive Eskom shares, for instance. While some whites may well find this process objectionable 20 years after our democracy, I will be more than happy to be government's ambassador on this one. I will sell the concept everywhere, especially to white communities. I would explain that after this grand giveaway, we will do away with AA and BEE legislation. This will be one big transformation exercise, before we move on to a non-racial future. I believe that such a single 'Big Bang' event will catapult many black people into becoming serious stakeholders in the economy, which can only benefit us all. Surely even doubtful whites will understand that. Thereafter we can move on from race-based initiatives into a completely non-racial dispensation.

Whether these SOEs are worth anything today, given the terrible state they are in, my view is that it is a question of accounting. Surely there is some underlying value there that can be unlocked once these entities are properly managed. And, believe me, once these assets have been given to black citizens, the new shareholders will demand value creation and operational efficiencies as a priority, just like any other shareholder would. The colour of the CEO, the executive or even the board would be completely irrelevant. All shareholders want delivery and performance. The point I always make is that the biggest investor on the stock exchange is the PIC (Public Investment Corporation), which is 95 per cent black and never questions the race of a CEO. It never goes to a company's AGM and demands that there be a black CEO. So, when the rubber hits the road, no one is actually racist. People just want to see performance, and this applies to all spheres of life. Similarly, parents do not care what colour the teacher is, they care about the quality of the tuition.

It is my hope that more black leaders will insist on this approach going forward, because unfortunately in South Africa, it still matters what race the person is, who comes up with a suggestion. Any white person who puts forward this suggestion will be misread as pursuing an anti-transformation agenda, when in reality this is the ultimate grand transformation exercise. Making such a call requires people to have no political agenda. I know that politicians in government want to hold onto these assets because they are vehicles for cadre deployment and, at times, serve to enrich friends and associates. It would indeed be a tall order to expect the current crop of politicians to make this call. Civil society must therefore start making this demand: 'Let the assets of the people be returned to the people.' Hopefully with the massive realignments taking place within the trade union movement, new emerging unions will stand up and make this call. As a starting point, those trade unions which are active within these entities could insist on being shareholders, as one would find in certain Western countries like Germany and Sweden, or even Japan. That would be the beginning of a new revolution which will ensure greater transparency and better governance.

Some of the current BEE programmes are based on fallacies. Take land redistribution: the impression is created that the security guard at the gate will somehow benefit if they take some white farmer's land. It is a lie, it is a fraud: no black person is going to benefit from that. A few hundred black farmers will be put on the land, they will not be given title, and they will remain tenant farmers, exactly the way Verwoerd thought blacks should be. That means this government would be implementing Verwoerd's land policy to the letter, and all the so-called redistribution will not see a single black person owning a piece of that land. This explains why most redistributed farms are now lying idle. It is a fallacy that large numbers of black people want to be farmers. Compensation for land dispossession? Surely they would want that. As I stated earlier, apartheid in all its manifestations was a crime against humanity, therefore compensation is required.

Let's look at our love of impressive-sounding policies and programmes which are introduced with pomp and ceremony. When the National Development Plan (NDP) was introduced, my emotional response was: not another one! This will go the same way as Asgisa and so many others that have come and gone. What we need is a new paradigm, not a new document. We need a paradigm that will see us creating a high-growth, investor-friendly, job-creating economy. The sense is that the initial excitement surrounding the NDP is already petering out. Certainly in recent meetings I have held with government officials on various economic policy matters, not once was there any mention of the NDP. It almost looks like the rapidity and frequency with which new programmes are introduced, has left the bureaucrats punch-drunk.

Another thing I wish politicians would desist from doing, is seeking to score points on the back of denying that there has been any transformation whatsoever as regards the fortunes of their fellow black South Africans. There has been significant growth in the black middle class: it is now actually bigger than the total number of whites in this country. Black property ownership has grown by more than 50 per cent in the past 21 years. This denialism (mainly by the governing party) is bizarre, as the message to the voters is: 'Vote for us because as your government we have failed to give you a better life! Your life is still as miserable as it was under apartheid, so you still need us in charge.' Yet there are tons of stats that prove that there have been significant positive changes in the lives of black people. I listened with disbelief to the most recent State of the Nation Address by the president, whose message seemed to be: 'Nothing has really changed, white monopoly capital owns everything, whites still own all the land.' The race card gets played every time. I would expect the government to blow its own trumpet on this issue, but that doesn't happen. In what smacks of the 'swart gevaar' tactics used by the apartheid government, the message is: 'Your life is still terrible, so you need us. If you change us as your government, your life is going to be even more terrible.' Such denialism even negates the successes of black enterprise. To me, this is cynical and manipulative. In my view, many black people have grabbed freedom enthusiastically and made huge strides. I am puzzled why there is no celebration of these successes.

Looking to the future, the first thing I think government needs to do is to start by removing all the regulatory measures that are destroying black entrepreneurship and advancement. In other words, it should undertake a full impact assessment study of impediments to black enterprise development. By way of an example, look at the new liquor policy which proscribes selling liquor within a certain radius of residential areas. That will effectively wipe out all township taverns, thus threatening the livelihood of millions of black citizens. Similarly, the recent debacle around new immigration regulations has had the effect of almost destroying the only industry in South Africa that has been growing consistently for the past 20 years: tourism. It is almost as if there is a tendency to introduce regulations solely because they sound great on paper, without assessing their full impact.

Secondly, where government has provided land, people should receive freehold title, not these ridiculous leaseholds which are demeaning and insulting, and are reminiscent of the Verwoerdian era. Go to the townships and see for yourself that blacks still do not own the land. Give them title deeds, every single one. That way, about ten million existing property owners would become empowered, the land would become an asset and collateral would be unleashed into the marketplace. Dead capital would become living capital, there would be millions of black landowners, and the size of the Deeds Registry would triple.

Another thing to do would be to stop downplaying black ownership of companies on the JSE. Recent studies have confirmed that blacks own about 40 per cent of the companies listed there, so to state that they merely own three per cent is ridiculous. Again, it speaks to a propensity by the powers-that-be to deny the economic strides made by blacks.

I still believe we must implement the big giveaway of parastatals, departments and agencies. That will create an explosion of black entrepreneurship that would be so dramatic, people won't know what hit them. I deem the so-called BEE and AA programmes to be fraudulent in that they create a cosmetic impression that somehow blacks are benefitting. What is happening is that it evokes terror amongst whites and foreign investors, and has created a whole new group of whites who have learnt how to turn it to their advantage and make money off of it. It is, in fact, destroying growth and wealth.

And, lastly, we do not need the NDP. As I mentioned earlier, we need a new paradigm. We need government to adopt an economic philosophy, which is really not rocket science. Just take a look around Africa: Which African countries are growing fast? Sub-Saharan Africa is now the highest growth region in the world, outperforming Asia, South America, and even Europe. How? It is happening in all the countries that are liberalising and privatising. Yes, those words are deemed unmentionable in South Africa. Look at Ghana, Nigeria and Rwanda: Rwanda has seen radical liberalisation, creating a one-stop-shop where you get into business within a few days. In South Africa it takes months. Mauritius is now the 8th freest economy on Earth, having gone from being one of the poorest places to one of the richest. In the last 20 years we could have followed in the footsteps of Mauritius, but we didn't. We must now do what is known to work, which is market liberalisation. If the powers-that-be choke on it ideologically, then come up with a new word, but it is the only thing that works – nothing else does. This formula works everywhere: it works for African countries, it works for India, Mauritius and China, and more recently for Mozambique, Tanzania, Rwanda and Ghana. These are currently the great performing economies of the world; what they did is simple, not complicated. We do not need fancy commissions, investigations or reports. What we need is for President Zuma to say: 'We are going to follow those policies which are known to work for everybody. We are not going to come up with some new magic formula that no one else has thought of.'

Lwazi Koyana
corporate financier

Lwazi, founder and Managing Director of Nations Capital, is a qualified chartered accountant with some 20 years' experience in the investment management and corporate finance fields. He has overseen almost all of the R8bn worth of transactions that Nations Capital Advisors has been involved with, either as lead or co-advisor with an alliance partner since its founding.

~~~~~~

At the dawn of our democracy, the medium- to large-scale business enterprises were almost exclusively white. Black business in the townships and rural areas was largely confined to small enterprises, like a little shop at the corner or, if you were lucky, perhaps a supermarket or petrol station – and that was it. Therefore, my understanding of BEE was that it sought to redress this situation by ensuring the graduation of black businesses into medium- and large-scale enterprises. From where I stood, my expectation was that BEE would ensure that black people began to move into export, manufacturing and financial services (not just as insurance salespeople!) and would become stockbrokers, fund managers, corporate financiers and actuaries, to name a few. But, more importantly, it was my expectation that those black people who were already active in particular sectors would be the first to be empowered to graduate into the big time. What has subsequently transpired, however, is what I refer to as a major wide-scale misalignment of skills. So far, BEE has (rather strangely, in my view) been characterised by situations where for you, instance, find a medical doctor moving into the mining sector or a sports personality moving into the healthcare sector, a teacher doing a BEE transaction in the energy sector, and so on. What this has led to is a situation where many participants in such transactions move into areas that are outside their competencies. As a result, they are then not able to play any meaningful or even transformative role within these new relationships. Essentially, what you find is a waste of skills and talent, as people become shareholders in areas where they are out of their depth. That does not necessarily mean that people cannot learn new skills, but if the foundation is not there, the learning curve is going to be very, very steep and expensive.

It is my belief that this misalignment of skills has played into the hands of established big business which may well have been resistant to BEE at its onset. My observation is that these resistant established businesses would prefer to do transactions with people who are not yet experts in particular sectors, because those people would not be able to make meaningful and transformative contributions or perhaps even question certain practices within those industries.

Therefore it becomes attractive, for instance, for an established energy company to do a transaction with a medical doctor, because however bright the doctor may be, it will still take him/her quite a number of years to become *au fait* with that particular sector. In such a scenario, the established business simply ticks the right box in terms of BEE compliance, while ensuring that the status quo remains unchallenged. This is little more than a very sophisticated level of tokenism. And many of our people fall into this trap, essentiality because participating in such relationships may well be more lucrative than their original areas of expertise and profession. In fact, I would go further and say that many established businesses are generally not interested in doing transactions with black people who are already established in their own sectors, for the very reason that such people may well be 'problematic'. In my view this is a very big and somewhat sinister game that some established corporates play. Apparently, the only way in which they can protect their territory and ensure that emerging black players do not encroach on their domain, is to practise this massive misalignment of skills. I know some may well argue that this is a rather cynical view, but I have been in the game long enough to have seen it all.

Established corporates' tendency to go out and seek partners who have no understanding of the business creates another problem, in that the partner they identify often does not have any ambitions for that particular sector. Such a partner's intention is to exit at some future date with a pile of money; he has no interest in transforming the sector or influencing its direction, values and practices, unlike what would have been the case if they had done business with an expert. This created a situation where virtually all sectors in our industry remain as they were 20 years ago, in terms of their culture, practices and outlook. And, more importantly, if they do a transaction with someone who is already in that sector, such an individual already has a far more long-term outlook and would be very keen to open up opportunities for the next generation of similarly skilled black professionals. Regrettably, the majority of short-term partners are not interested on legacy issues, but are only waiting for the big payday.

This poses a challenge to us black professionals to have a high sense of discipline and the capacity to decline invitations to participate in areas outside of our core competences and skills, for the sake of ensuring genuine and transformative BEE. This is our patriotic duty, irrespective of whatever financial reward we might be foregoing in the short term. Otherwise we are becoming partners in our own disempowerment and in the bastardisation of black economic emancipation. I am not saying we must not take advantage of the opportunities which come our way, but let us at least all be aware of what we are getting ourselves into. Also, I would like policy-makers to be aware of these tricks of the game, and so I would want lobby groups like the BMF and Nafcoc to create greater awareness so that their members don't just walk blindly into these traps. You cannot transform an industry that you are new to – period.

For me it is lamentable that, even at this stage, 21 years post-democracy, we still have not transcended the perception of some of our white compatriots, that BEE by its very nature means the disempowerment of upcoming generations. I have observed on many occasions that there is still a belief that black economic empowerment equals white economic disempowerment, that this is a zero-sum game. So people spend a lot of time and energy trying all sorts of schemes to protect themselves against an imaginary enemy. One almost witnesses a siege mentality in certain corporate corridors of power. This becomes even more tragic when one considers that most of today's corporate leadership are supposed to be more liberal in their outlook than the crop of leaders who were in charge two decades ago. But I fear that many in the current crop have also succumbed to their primal sense of self-preservation – the rather unfounded fear that BEE may well decimate their legacy. So what happens at times is feet-dragging and short-termism, which almost game the system.

My view is that some companies' easy argument of 'once empowered, always empowered' is influenced by a shotgun approach to BEE. Having done a BEE transaction with a black partner who has no background in that particular sector, as I indicated earlier, and that black partner having cashed out with handsome profits, a company believes it has done its duty and should therefore be pretty much left alone to continue with 'business as usual'. That there was no transformation within the organisation itself, no skills transfer, no value added to the economy or new employment opportunities, etc., is the least of their worries. And this is regrettable, because BEE was not supposed to consist of one night stands – it was meant to go much deeper than that.

This, in my view, also explains why in terms of black representation on the JSE we seem to be going nowhere. Yes, deals are being done, some people are cashing out and making tidy fortunes for themselves, but once these deals have been unwound then we're back to square one. In the meantime, many companies feel that they have discharged their BEE responsibility and must therefore be left in peace. I personally reject the 'once empowered, always empowered' argument. BEE was not introduced to facilitate transactions at the end of which a few people end up with tidy sums in their pockets: it was designed to ensure that we create an economy in which all citizens have a meaningful share. And for as long as we have not reached that goal, we cannot stand up and proudly proclaim: MISSION ACCOMPLISHED, as some corporates are doing already. Such celebrations are premature.

It is only once we have created an environment in which a number of black-owned and black-run organisations are major players on our stock exchange, that we can begin to accede to the request that 'once empowered must equate to always empowered'. Today, as I write this, large black-owned and black-run organisations are conspicuous by their absence in JSE listings. Therefore, as far as I am concerned, it is definitely not yet a case of mission accomplished.

And this brings me to my next point. It was my original expectation that in tandem with BEE transactions, would be active support for, and the nurturing and growth of, black business – specifically black-owned and black-run businesses. That simply has not happened. The record is quite woeful. What pains me more in this regard, is that our public sector – which I would have expected to be at the forefront of a campaign to develop black business – has a very poor record of doing so. There appears to be no vigorous and consistent drive in the public sector to single out and support black enterprise.

Another major expectation which I had at the start of BEE was that what were fledgling businesses at that stage, would have by now graduated to the big time, but that has not been the case.

That is why, going forward, I would like to appeal especially to our government to use its procurement muscle to empower black companies and black professionals. Government, as a major procurer of goods and services, must now make a distinction between black companies and black-empowered companies, and must first seek to do business with black companies. This is a very important distinction. To illustrate my point, let me paint this picture: an enterprising black fellow with the necessary skills and track record in a particular industry approaches a government department and makes a proposal to become a supplier of a specific product. He makes a compelling case, and since government in principle is committed to empowerment, this fellow is given an annual contract of, say, R20m. He is elated and gets into serious debt beefing up his operation. (By the way, note that the R20m that is to be spent on him is nothing, if you consider that the total procurement budget in that particular scenario may be R10bn or R20bn.) Anyway, our young black entrepreneur goes hammer and tongs into operation. Perhaps over the next three years the spend on him increases to R150m. Then he begins to eat into the big boys' pie. The big boys realise this is becoming a serious problem, so they sell 10, 15 or 20 per cent to a BEE grouping which most likely consists of industry outsiders. Suddenly the big company is now an 'empowered' company. They come back with those credentials and make a case for increased business from the government agency. Government is impressed and starts giving them more business now that they are 'empowered'. Suddenly our enterprising black fellow is on the back foot. He is a David competing with a Goliath who has just taken steroids! He stands no chance. The spend on him begins to dwindle to a trickle, and eventually he collapses. We have witnessed numerous examples of such scenarios over the past two decades. We have even read in the newspapers of situations where government officials point major companies in the direction of a specific BEE partner, having already positioned the BEE partner ahead of time and negotiated their own cut. Some have been dragged to court over such machinations.

What happened to this young entrepreneur (as per my earlier example) is a terrible and cruel irony – a black enterprise has just been wiped out by … wait for it … BEE! I believe it is no exaggeration to say that BEE has, in many instances, turned out to be the enemy and destroyer of black-owned businesses. It is vital that a distinction be made between a black-empowered company and a black company. To me it is no accident that, as we stand today, there are no major black companies to speak of. My initial expectation, that BEE would lead to the creation of black behemoths, and that government would be leading the charge, has tended to produce the opposite result. Let me illustrate this point even further: despite all the pronouncements that have been made publicly, government continues to be very sloppy in paying timeously. I have lost count of the number of black enterprises that have folded simply because payment is not forthcoming. Remember, these are enterprises that do not have huge resources or hefty balance sheets. They therefore run into serious cash-flow problems, banks call up overdrafts, promising young entrepreneurs end up with massive judgements against them from their own suppliers, and their credit records are ruined. You see big dreams and great potential going up in smoke. What makes it even more heart-breaking is that such young enterprises die at the hands of the very party that was supposed to see to their growth and survival.

My other observation as a financier is that we have now arrived at a rather dismal point, where it looks like the only institutions that are still willing to consider funding BEE transactions or enterprises are the PIC, National Empowerment Fund (NEF) and, to some extent, the Industrial Development Corporation (IDC). The other players have quietly tip-toed off the stage, leaving us, as corporate financiers, high and dry. And even these development funding institutions have been ultra-conservative. One example that comes to mind is of the black fellow who first set up the Chesa Nyama operation: when it became a runaway success, he decided to go to these development funding institutions to fund his expansion plans and help alleviate his cash-flow constraints. He realised that in order for his operation to become commercially viable, he needed to achieve economies of scale through rapid expansion. All of them turned him down. He ended up selling his business and concept to a white entrepreneur who was able to raise expansion capital without breaking a sweat, and rolled out around 90 of these franchises nationally. Two years later he sold them for R96m!

Risk tolerance for start-ups in our country is atrocious. Many institutions will easily fund you if you want to buy a piece of a blue chip company. But if it is a startup – even if its potential is self-evident – funders will most likely slam the door in your face. It gets worse if you are a black entrepreneur. The venture capital culture in our country is virtually non-existent, so it is no wonder that unemployment is ravaging our nation.

The last point I want to make is a message to my black compatriots who exit a BEE transaction at its maturity. Usually, their major focus becomes cashing out their chips. They do not seek out new, fledgling and dynamic BEE successors to the transaction, to ensure continuity and legacy. So what happens is that the established company is once again leading the effort to seek new partners who meet its own criteria, and they will most likely again be newcomers to the industry. In this way, the cycle of non-transformative BEE is repeated endlessly. Instead of the exiting guys being very active in identifying deserving successors and giving them the benefit of the knowledge and experience they gained during their tenure, and helping them to hit the ground running, our black compatriots will just cash in their chips and move happily into the sunset.

In my view, those of us who have been empowered also bear the responsibility – in addition to what I mentioned earlier – to ensure that empowerment and skills acquisition don't stop with us. We have to pave the way for a new generation, and we have to help that new generation to settle in even quicker than was the case with us.

Mandla Malinga
prominent Soweto social entrepreneur

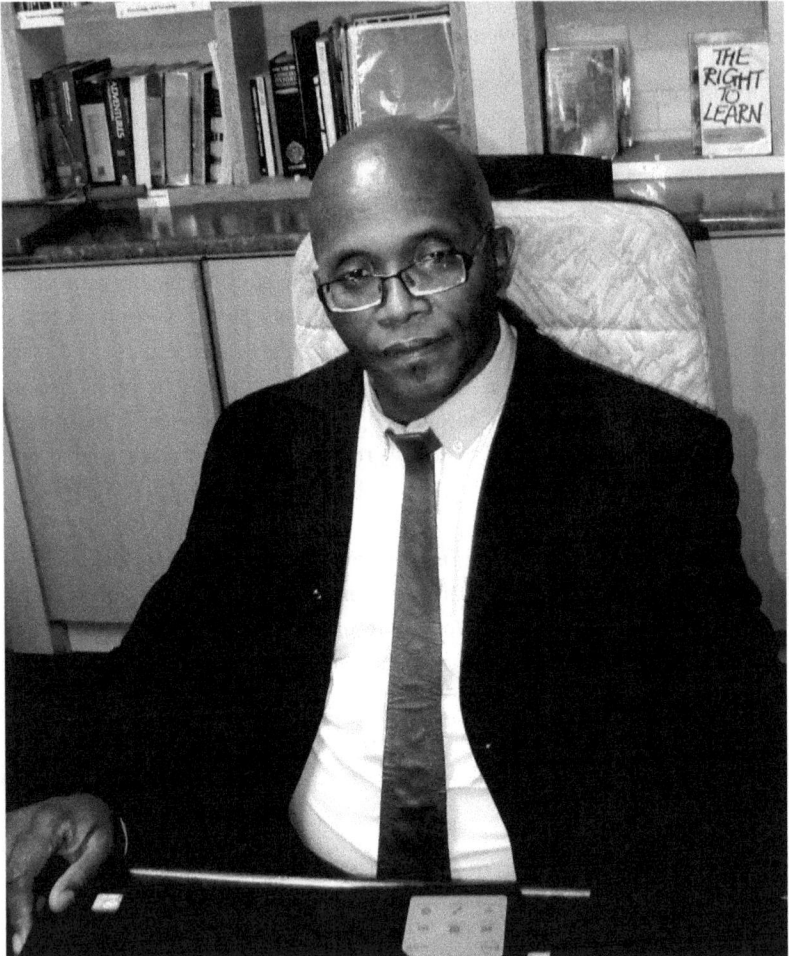

Mandla Malinga, a graduate of Wits University in Social Sciences, is a founder of African Dream Campus, a Soweto-based training and skilling facility which, for the past eight years, has been offering Service Education and Training Authority (Seta)-accredited skills development and empowerment programmes for the Soweto community. His facility emphasises an integrated approach to skilling and empowerment, offering both 'hard' skills like carpentry and artisanry combined with 'soft' skills like personal motivation and business etiquette. He is also an active community leader, serving on various local business bodies like the Greater Soweto Business Forum, the South African Spaza and Tuck Shops Association (SASTA) and the Motsepe Foundation, to mention a few.

When BEE was first spoken of and later introduced as official policy, it was very exciting, especially given our history of oppression as black people. It was my understanding and expectation that, as previously disadvantaged people our new democratic government was going to prioritise improving our lives in a variety of areas, starting with education, skills and business, amongst others. This was going to help us as a people gain our rightful place in society. I would say our expectations were pretty high, and I think deservedly so.

In our context, the term 'empowerment' brings to mind an active reversal of the disempowerment that had been deliberately brought about by colonialism and apartheid. Because our disempowerment as a people had infiltrated every aspect of our lives, our expectation was that empowerment would also begin to be visible in every aspect of our lives. For me, it is the education and skilling part that I was excited about, because apartheid had principally emasculated our people in this area. A lack of knowledge and skills is the ultimate disempowerment. Apartheid, by depriving us of education and skills, intended to make 'half humans' of us. It almost succeeded in making useless chattels out of us, by working to ensure that we were lacking in worldly knowledge, vision, sophistication, technical know-how, and employability, etc. That was its mission, and by the dawn of our democracy, that mission was almost accomplished. Therefore, from my point of view, I just could not wait to see an aggressive reversal of the rot that had set in. When he introduced Bantu Education, the then Minister, Hendrik Verwoerd, stated that the purpose of this system was to educate us black people so that we would become fairly proficient at rendering basic forms of labour – no more and no less! No engineers would come from the ranks of our people, no scientists, no intellectuals … only gardeners and maids. You can't be clearer than that! This was a harsh, in-your-face no-holds-barred articulation of apartheid policy.

As a result, my expectation was what I would call a 180 degree departure from the policy articulation from our government, yet it was equally frank, in-your-face, no-holds-barred: we wanted to train our citizens to be world-class engineers, scientists, artisans, mechanics, etc. because that's what the economy needs right now! To clean a deeply ingrained stain, you have no choice but to take aggressive, definitive measures.

As I said earlier, the irony in all of this is that apartheid's vision when it came to educating and skilling blacks, albeit evil and sinister, was nonetheless very clear. But I get a feeling that at present, our democratic government's policy on skilling and educating its populace seems unclear and, at times, all over the place. My fear is that this is having a devastating effect on particularly the poorest of the poor, the black people who need to be pulled out of the cycle of poverty. It pains me greatly to witness this.

I believe any education and training system must be tailored to meet a particular country's needs. In my travels around the world, I have observed that successful countries tailor their systems to meet their particular needs at certain points in time. Even the apartheid regime did this – it built an island of highly skilled and well-trained whites in a sea of cheap black labour, because it was precisely the regime's intention and policy to do so. You educate and train your citizenry as a nation to achieve specific social and economic objectives. There's no point in training superb poets and philosophers when your country is in desperate need of artisans, for instance. Doing so, constitutes a colossal waste of both human and financial resources.

Frankly, it really frustrates me that in my country I just cannot figure out what exactly our model is. It may sound almost mechanical to say this, but a country's education system must help to produce the type of citizen the country needs in order to grow and be economically prosperous. That is the hallmark of all successful nations. Doing this also sees to the economic empowerment of a citizenry. You don't educate and train people to confer fancy yet socio-economically mismatched certificates, diplomas and degrees on them – especially not in a developing country like ours. I would contend that even if yours is a highly developed nation, the minute you start training people merely for the sake of it, you will quickly lose your edge in this extremely competitive global environment. So, when I take stock of where our country is, socio-economically speaking, and what is needed, and I look at what is happening in our education and training system, I just can't marry the two.

Last October, as I read a report on the state of our education, published by the Department of Basic Education, I almost collapsed in despair. The matric class of 2013 had 562 112 full-time candidates; 439 779 of them passed, meaning the pass rate was 78.2 per cent. This looks great at face value and fools many into thinking: 'Wow, great stuff, progress!' But it is illusory. If you go back all the way to the time when that particular group started its schooling, your joy gives way to shock and horror. When the cohort started, there were 1.2 million of them! In fact, many stuck it out until grade 10, when there were still around a million learners in the system. Then, between grades 10 and 12, a staggering half a million suddenly dropped out and just 'vanished' from the system!

I'm sure that a more or less similar cycle is repeating itself year in and year out.

So every year we have these throngs of 'lost souls' who are dumped into poverty, despair, and perhaps a life of crime and other anti-social behaviour. This statistic by itself must say to all of us that something is very, very wrong here. Instead of creating an army of well-trained and capable citizens who can contribute to the growth of our economy and the development of our society (as we all expected a new democratic government would ensure), we are spawning hordes of roaming, lost souls who are most likely bleeding rather than building the economy. My view is not that they dropped out of the system, but that the system dropped them. I don't care if the new South Africa sees to it that every gravel road is tarred in every inch of our land, but this statistic alone angered and terrified me. We are talking about people's lives here – their hopes, the hopes of their families and the dreams of a young nation are all going up in smoke. These lost souls won't just miraculously disappear into thin air in a year or two – they will be haunting us as a nation for generations to come. But, more importantly, they will be swelling the ranks of the angry and disaffected, making the threat of social upheaval more real every year that the situation remains unresolved.

That is really is where my major disappointment stems from. For me, good education and training are ultimately the vehicles which work towards empowering people in a permanent and sustainable way – not just enabling a few to buy shares in some established big white companies, or some filling top positions in these companies or serving on their boards. To me that is NOT BEE. That is simply the success of a few, and we celebrate their success, so good luck to them. But what about the rest of the populace? Surely the struggle was not about allowing a few to just squeak through into the lap of luxury. It was about ensuring that the ordinary Sipho or Tshepo or Tumi has a better chance in life than was the case during apartheid. So I work here with the Siphos and the Tshepos and the Tumis. They come to me and say: 'What do we do now? Our lives are either stuck or they are just sliding down. What do we do?' Surely we wanted those citizens who, unlike us, were fortunate to grow up in an apartheid-free environment, to have higher hopes and greater achievements, not less. It can be heart-breaking at times.

Another incorrect assumption we make is that every child is automatically ready to follow the traditional model of schooling, in other words, to obtain a matric certificate as the end goal. Dr P. Normand, a clinical psychologist, published a study which estimated that approximately 10–30 per cent of South African children have learning difficulties of one form or another. Most learning disabilities – including reading disorders, concentration difficulties and language problems – are more prevalent in boys than in girls. So therefore there are children who, through no fault of their own, are simply not in a position to complete their mainstream schooling.

But that does not mean they should be cast out. New, innovative and appropriate ways need to be developed to ensure that they, too, become productive citizens. They must not just be thrown in at the deep end to sink or swim, as has been the case thus far. And I must say I was heartened to hear that our government is now considering a Grade 9 school-leavers certificate for those learners who do not wish to proceed to matric. This development needs to be applauded, but it must not be used as a legitimate way to cast these pupils out, because if we do that we won't have solved the problem. We will simply be formalising the dropping-out process. We need to be certain that no school-leaver becomes a lost soul.

Of course the story does not end there. Even those black pupils who eventually do get degrees are not necessarily home and dry. A recent survey by the DTI has established that black graduates are three times more likely to be without a job than white graduates.

I have always contended that to speak of BEE in an environment where people are not acquiring the tools to join the employed, is truly building castles in the air.

Coming to skills development, I believe the government's introduction of the South African Quality Assurance (SAQA) framework was a major step in the right direction, because it is an holistic approach; when you train a person you train them in numeracy, literacy, business, life and marketing skills, and give them in-depth training in clothing or furniture manufacturing, depending on the type of training. However, as soon as we are done with them, within a matter of six to 12 months they have an idea how to run a businesses, as well as the skills to draw up their own plans.

A study published by StatsSA last year (*Employment, unemployment, skills and economic growth: An exploration of household survey evidence on skills development and unemployment between 1994 and 2014*), looked at how various population groups had progressed in terms of skills development. This research painted an extremely distressing picture of how particularly Africans had fared over the period in question. Blacks had only experienced a three per cent improvement in skills development, whereas for whites it was 18 per cent, Indians 22 per cent and coloureds 11 per cent.

These numbers are shocking. My point overall is that it does not matter from which angle you look at it, the picture always ends up looking the same: we are failing our people very badly in terms of skilling them so that they are able to fend for themselves.

The economic think-tank, African Economy Outlook, conducted a survey among recruitment and temporary work agencies in nine African countries. It found that such agencies generally struggle to find suitable candidates to fill vacancies, even if such candidates have a tertiary qualification. The findings showed that the problem is more prevalent in South Africa and Tunisia than in countries with much lower incomes, such as Kenya, Ghana and even Niger. Essentially this means South Africa and Tunisia produce graduates with industry-irrelevant qualifications. And remember – the youth rebellions that toppled governments in North Africa, during the so-called Arab Spring, started in Tunisia. This is a scary feature to have in common.

One of the difficulties facing local social entrepreneurs in particular, is an extremely bureaucratic and often less than empathetic approach from local government officials. Some of them seem to be more interested in ticking boxes than realising that we are engaged in a much bigger effort here, trying to reconstruct a society that was deliberately ravaged by apartheid. It is not uncommon to be met by a 'why-are-you-disturbing-my-peace' attitude from officials, instead of a 'how-can-we-help-you-help-us' approach. It makes one almost feel that many of these officials need some conscientisation on what exactly the bigger mission is. Thankfully, some still have a constructive attitude, but I just wish there were many more of them. One almost gets a sense that our government is fascinated by the education models of other countries. It then imports them and seeks to replicate them here. In the process, the experience of local, experienced educators and trainers is generally ignored in favour of a 'global' model which has seemingly left us stranded in the middle of nowhere.

But you may say, quite correctly, that we should not throw out the BEE baby with the bathwater. So, what do we do now?

Looking ahead, I would propose an indaba between industry and education policy-makers and ministries to develop a new education model. It is getting us nowhere to have policy-makers develop grand, well-thought-out models when, at the end of it, all they produce are people who are not deemed employable by industry. I know that sometimes our politicians have a tendency to be territorial and that they may retort that they will not be dictated to by industry. But in the main it is industry that employs people, and if industry believes the wrong kind of products are emerging from our education system, it will simply import labour from other countries, while our own people languish in poverty.

I don't think it is enough to blame the current shortcomings of our education system on apartheid. Certainly not when a new democratic government has been in charge for 21 years. We already have a full generation of matriculants who started their education during the tenure of our current democratic government.

My view would be that we need to create a mechanism to capture these lost souls as a matter of extreme urgency, not just because it is good for them, but also because it is good for the country since surely they are a drain on South Africa's resources as things stand. These lost souls haven't disappeared into thin air – they are living amongst us. They cannot be wished away.

Mzwanele Manyi
President, Progressive Professionals Forum

> Mzwanele Manyi CM (SA) is a chartered marketer and Harvard Business School alumnus with a background in Economic Geology. He is the immediate past president of the BMF and is also Executive Chairman of his own company, Afrotone Investments. He is also the founding president of the Progressive Professionals Forum (PPF). Mzwanele has extensive corporate experience at executive level of blue chip companies and multinationals. He is also a former Director General and former Cabinet spokesperson who has served on various boards.

The introduction of BEE in this country was based on the realisation that we had a skewed economy that essentially belonged to white people, with black people barely visible on the radar. BEE was supposed to give economic realisation to the spirit of Codesa and national reconciliation, amongst others. More importantly, it was designed to fulfil certain constitutional imperatives. If you look especially at section 9 of the constitution, it allows for what I would call positive discrimination. Even when it comes to procurement by way of a specific example, the constitution is very clear (see s217) that mechanisms have to be put in place to enable previously disadvantaged individuals to render goods and services to the government. There is a tendency amongst certain people to cherry pick specific provisions of this section, as if the only considerations which government need take into account prior to procuring services from a supplier, are price and efficiencies. But certain subsections indicate very clearly that special considerations can be put in place to accommodate individuals from a previously disadvantaged background. This was done precisely because of the reality that many black entrepreneurs do not have the resources to compete purely on price, given their background. As a black entrepreneur you are likely to have difficulties in securing favourable credit terms, your balance sheet is likely to be weak. Therefore these are serious constraints in terms of your ability to compete with well-established players in a particular sector. It was with these constraints in mind, and in line with the spirit of our constitution, that these special considerations were implemented to accommodate previously excluded players. I would therefore argue that the current procurement laws, as reflected by the *Preferential Procurement Policy Framework Act*, with their emphases on price as a major consideration in a procurement situation, could well be unconstitutional and need to be tested in court. If price becomes the only criterion, then automatically a whole lot of black players are excluded from accessing government business. And, unfortunately, certain key players who are representative of established business have been selectively emphasising the price component of this legislation, without taking into account that it makes provision for special measures as initially envisaged in our constitution. Some established business players, in a very cynical move, use a loss lead strategy where they undercut black players on price, in order to gain a foothold when it comes to doing business with government. This piece of legislation has unfortunately turned out to be disempowering to black enterprise. The aspect of this legislation that puts 90 per cent of the total points on price is, by its very nature, exclusionary of black enterprise, and deserves to be challenged for being unconstitutional. Indeed, I would even go so far as to say that I don't get particularly excited these days when I hear that there are huge public works programmes whose budgets run into trillions of rands, because I know very well that many black players are simply going to watch and salivate from the sidelines. It almost always ends being the 'good old boys' who get the lion's share of this type of business. The tragedy in all of this, in my view, is that it is these massive projects that were supposed to be the vehicle for creating a vibrant black entrepreneurial class, especially given the reality that established white business appears not to be interested in facilitating the creation of such a class.

To illustrate this point further, let me cite another example. The CIDB (Construction Industry Development Board) is structured in such a way that it almost exclusively empowers established business, excluding fledgling black enterprise from becoming meaningful players in the construction sector. To me it is mind-boggling how policy-makers and regulators could have agreed to that. For instance, if you want to build a bridge for the government as part of the public works programme, the CIDB requires that you submit very strong financial credentials. You therefore need to have a massive balance sheet, an impeccable credit record, a number of engineers in your company, etc. Again, this by its very nature sees to it that black players are left on the sidelines while (in a tragic irony) those who benefitted from apartheid are handsomely rewarded for having been such beneficiaries. These scenarios make me conclude that almost in a bizarre fashion we have done a meticulous job of putting in place structures and mechanisms that will keep blacks on the periphery of the economy. We have put in place well-functioning disabling mechanisms. Even the *Public Finance Management Act* has disabling elements. To illustrate my point: if, as a government official, you haven't fully exhausted your budget in a given financial year, according to this law you are either lazy or incompetent or both. The fact that you may actually have saved the government some money due to improved efficiencies is overlooked in the process. The emphasis is solely on spending, even in circumstances where there is wanton wastage.

My view is that during the Codesa negotiations for a democratic South Africa, we as black people were so obsessed with 'one man one vote' that we completely overlooked the economic issues. I also think that our general tendency as black people towards humanism, compassion and *ubuntu* led us to assume that our white compatriots were going to openly embrace us and welcome us into their world of privilege by making space for us to come and settle amongst them. We were too trusting, and consequently we were taken advantage of. That is why today we are now facing a volatile situation that is threatening to erupt into social upheaval. For instance, the fact that in the last national elections one million people voted for a new, untested political party whose main motto was 'radical economic transformation', says a lot about people's disillusionment. It is my sense that people on the ground are sick and tired of waiting for economic emancipation that is simply not materialising.

I'm also of the view that many of our white compatriots have betrayed the message of Mandela. Here is this man who was once a firebrand, and even moved the ANC from being a peaceful resistance movement into adopting a military strategy. But, after 27 long, tortuous years in prison, instead of being even more of a firebrand and harbouring bitterness, he came out preaching reconciliation. His message was not just a simplistic 'let's forget about the past and all move back into our boxes'. His message was 'in order to build this nation, let's stop being at each others' throats and use all our energies to help one another build a fair and equitable society'. And it is this part that many of my white compatriots – especially established white business – seem to be ignoring. So, BEE and AA and all these other processes were designed to help those who were victims of apartheid become rightful citizens of this country. The games being played to outsmart and thwart BEE and AA are, in my view, a grand betrayal of Mandela's vision.

Another feature in our new democracy that continues to puzzle me, is that when some of our people are appointed in senior positions in the public service, where they are supposed to facilitate the economic empowerment of black people, somehow they undergo a metamorphosis as if they no longer understand the problems and constraints facing black business. When you meet them sitting behind their desks, you have to make your case from square one, as if they do not come from the very same background as you do. It is almost as if high office blanks their memory of where they came from.

It is also quite disappointing that when one raises these issues in various public forums, there is a tendency to rush to label and pigeonhole an individual, instead of doing introspection about whether there is any merit in the issues being raised. The sad fact in all of this is that many high-calibre thinkers in our communities are effectively sulking and have decided to disengage from any public discourse. You thus effectively have a demobilisation of black intellectual capital in our country. That is why we formed the PPF, which aims to reverse such disengagement from policy issues – especially on the part of progressives. We wanted to have a collection of highly skilled professionals who would also develop policy proposals for government and present a counter view to a space that is now dominated by expertise from established business. Our clarion call to black professionals in particular is: 'Do not disengage, stop sulking, do not despair. Come join us. Let us make our voices heard by presenting well-thought-out, scientifically sound, data-based policy proposals to policy-makers.'

There is also a tendency on the part of policy-makers to readily accept 'free' advice from established business, sometimes to the total disregard of views from struggling black business. Usually this 'free advice' comes at huge cost to transformation, because it tends to be skewed in favour of established business. And let's be frank: some high-ranking government officials have been 'captured' by the corporate world, hence their haste to lend an ear to established business. Corporate capture comes in many forms, like the ability of international markets to punish the South African government for any policies they don't like; many large companies have, for instance, basically relocated their massive treasuries to outside the borders of the country and simply hold back direct fixed investment if they are unhappy with certain policy issues.

The corporate capture of our leaders does not merely imply that they are captured for their own personal gain. Sometimes this phenomenon manifests itself in the form of the power to intimidate government leaders. This can be illustrated by what recently happened when the DTI announced that if a black entrepreneur does a BEE transaction as an individual with established business, that will be rated higher than the usual 'fill-up-the-bus-with-blacks' approach to BEE. That sparked such outrage from the corporate world that, within less than a week, the DTI had beaten a hasty retreat from a position that was designed to facilitate the creation of black entrepreneurs. If the department had not retreated on that issue, we would have been well on our way to producing black Brian Joffees, black Anton Ruperts, etc. So, a good policy suffered a quick and merciless death, because established business caused an uproar which proved to be highly intimidating.

Many of our leaders have become cowed, unfortunately. Perhaps it would be better if our leaders took the populace into their confidence and conceded where they have been hamstrung, instead of promising things that they pretty much know will never materialise. Then our people, mindful of how they resisted apartheid, will explore their own activism for economic justice. Our people also can see that 70 per cent of GDP is generated by the private sector, which is still almost entirely white. We know that when that 70 per cent roars, our leaders cannot ignore the noise. But our leaders have to begin to heed the people because if they don't, in a few years' time there will be an uprising in this country because a privatised version of apartheid will have been returned. Yes, a few black individuals will have done extremely well for themselves, but the vast majority will be trapped in poverty, and they will be seething.

I must admit that looking at recent policy documents issued by the ANC in preparation for its National General Council, one gets a sense that a more introspective attitude may be emerging. That is to be encouraged. The real test, however, will be whether people's inputs will be taken seriously.

My final message to my white compatriots is that they need to migrate from the 'wanting-to-own-it-all' apartheid-induced point of view. The majority of people in charge of the economy today grew up when it was widely accepted (and even taught at universities) that black people are inferior beings. Therefore there is still this mental block which prevents them from being comfortable with blacks being co-owners of the economy and aspiring to enjoy the finer things in life, beyond just water and bread. In my view, this mentality is behind all the games which corporate South Africa plays in order to outwit transformation. It can almost be labeled institutionalised racism. At times it manifests itself with corporate South Africa being comfortable with a black executive being in charge of human resources or government liaison – the so-called soft functions within a company – while many remain skeptical about appointing a black financial director, let alone a black CEO. On many occasions you find those black entrepreneurs who have graduated into the big time handing over the day-to-day running of their operations to white executives, yet again reinforcing the stereotype that black executives cannot handle complex organisations. We have to face these harsh realities in order to exorcise them from our psyche.

I appeal to my white compatriots to see the wisdom of owning say 30 per cent of a massive South African economy, rather than 70 per cent of a small economy that may well end up in ashes in a few years' time. It is important for every South African citizen to almost desperately want the economic advancement of the destitute, because then you end up with the majority having a stake in the economy. You end up with a vibrant middle class that will be buying items and making all businesses prosper even more. The masses would then be ready to defend this economy, instead of being ready to burn it to the ground.

Peter Vundla
black advertising pioneer and prominent entrepreneur

Peter Bunguza Vundla is Chairman of African Merchant Bank Capital. He is the founding Chairman of South Africa's first black advertising firm, HerdBuoys, and has been the director of many listed companies over the years. Currently, he is Chairman of the *Mail & Guardian*, a member of the Unisa Council, and a director on the boards of the Mapungubwe Institute for Strategic Reflection, Wesbank, Business Against Crime and Special Olympics South Africa.

~~~~~~~~

I think what really spurred us to found the first black-owned advertising company in this country, in April 1991, was that we could see democracy looming on the horizon. That gave us hope and an added incentive. We could see that that those impediments to black business development which had been entrenched all along during apartheid, were on their way to dying a slow death. I am using the term 'black business development' because there was no BEE at that time. As the founders of HerdBuoys we were very gutsy but, more importantly, we had been involved in advertising for many many years and had practically reached the glass ceiling. We were not opportunists who sought to take advantage of the unfolding political changes, but we had had enough of seeing white youngsters, whom we had trained, being promoted over our heads.

The industry at that time was dominated by white people who defined us as maids, gardeners, petrol attendants, and so on. So, additional to our business ambitions, we sought to fight this stereotype of black people only being fit for menial tasks. We sought to redefine black people to fit into an intellectual and a creative space; people who could also be thinkers of finer concepts and create captivating campaigns, visuals, graphics and sounds. And so it wasn't just business as usual or a case of solely wanting to make money, or anything like that. We saw this mission as an affirmation of black talent, broadly speaking. We were truly motivated by a huge patriotic passion. Money was going to be just the cherry on top.

As I said in my book, *Doing time* (Jacana Media, 2013), our hopes were almost dashed right from the get-go, as we couldn't get funding from any institution or bank. The odds seemed to be stacked against us. We even we went to our future competitors for funding! Finally, we ended up partnering with established white agencies with whom we formed rather uneasy (but mutually beneficial) alliances.

We had a track record in the industry, yet no funding! Unlike today, there simply was no BEE programme to ease our way into business. Of course, contrast that with the current state of affairs, where some individuals with no track record in any particular business quickly jump in and opportunistically set themselves up, only to wake up with a contract or tender the next day. That is the major problem with many so-called black entrepreneurs today. When you dig deeper you find that many are just project managers running their operations from laptops. When we started HerdBuoys, we were hardcore entrepreneurs who knew the industry from every angle. We went many months without paying ourselves salaries, literally living from hand to mouth. But we felt the mission was worth the sacrifice. Interestingly, the irony in all this is that when we were eventually up and running, we were the most integrated advertising agency in South Africa – integrated in terms of race, language, gender, and so on. When someone walked into our offices it was almost as if they had walked into a different world, an oasis of non-racialism surrounded by a sea of racism. HerdBuoys looked like the new South Africa before the actual new South Africa was officially born!

Then came BEE as a new approach in South African business. Interestingly, for us at HerdBuoys it didn't make much of a difference: we were already in business and were proving ourselves of value to our clients, especially in helping them to understand and penetrate the black market. By then, white corporates had long been convinced of our value to them, and we were already doing roaring business. BEE simply enabled our clients to claim kudos and score BEE points from doing business with us. Otherwise, they had already been benefitting from our expertise. Some transforming government agencies and SOEs like Transnet began to approach us, because they saw us as torchbearers for a transformed industry. These almost became the golden days for us at HerdBuoys. At one stage we had an incredible success rate: out of ten sales pitches we made, we were bagging eight!

Coming from the past to the present, of course BEE has taken a rather disturbing turn of late. Remember when we set up and served on the BEE Commission and sought to define BEE, we defined it in much broader terms than just obtaining shares in white-owned companies. When you look at the commission's report, we spoke of many other initiatives; it was a fully integrated approach that aimed to facilitate the creation of a broader black entrepreneurial class and to uplift as many people as possible from poverty. We spoke of empowering women, of rural development, and of setting up risk-funding mechanisms and a BEE regulator, as well as a procurement agency within the treasury, amongst others. As a commission, we were very clear that we did not want leaches, people who would suck the economy and industry dry in the name of BEE. We wanted to facilitate value creation. Sadly, many of our recommendations were subsequently ignored.

We were talking about genuine black enterprise development, not opportunistic tie-ups. Unfortunately, all we have done is to hitch our wagon to established business such as Sanlam, and others. We have not created new businesses, we have not created jobs. We have become almost obsessed with shareholdings on JSE-listed companies.

With all of this unfolding, some established companies decided to game the system. When I was Chairman of the Business Working Group advising President Mbeki, we conducted research with the University of Pretoria to gauge the progress of BEE across the seven pillars set out in the BEE Commission Report. What we found was that even with low-hanging fruits as such as CSI, compliance was around eight to ten per cent. Companies were lying in their annual reports about their expenditure on CSI, faking the numbers, let alone being honest about other aspects of BEE like management diversity, ownership and enterprise development. That study was so revealing and it was supposed to be a continuous undertaking. We had agreed with President Mbeki that we were going to do the study annually, but then came the ANC Polokwane Conference with its momentous changes, and that was pretty much the end of this approach to monitoring progress on BEE on a yearly basis.

Going forward, the first thing we need to fix is the leadership, both in government and in business, and here I am throwing down the gauntlet to black leadership. Unfortunately, what is evident nowadays is leadership who are really there only for themselves, to be close to the high offices and get tenders, and go to trade missions etc. for the purposes of self-aggrandisement. You hardly ever hear talk of growing black entrepreneurship. We need a major return to selfless leadership; to people who see their mission as empowering the nation, not their associates.

Yes, there are encouraging noises from certain government quarters, like the need to develop black industrialists. But it needs to move beyond slogans. What we need are fully developed and well-managed programmes. If we fail to do these things, this country will go back, in terms of economic representivity, to what it was 20 years ago – with blacks being on the sidelines once more. We cannot afford to see the dream of economic transformation dying. Otherwise, what was the struggle for? BEE represents seriously unfinished business. With youth unemployment above 50 per cent, our youngsters will turn on us one of these days.

Of course there are pockets of very encouraging initiatives being undertaken by some sectors of black business. Here I want to cite the Shanduka Black Umbrella Programme which does incredible work. We need this model to be replicated throughout the entire country. How they help to establish, nurture and incubate black businesses until they are ready to set off on their own, is an inspiring piece of work. Kudos to them!

Also, going forward, I see one major thing that needs to happen as of yesterday: the creation of a black risk-funding institution; a bank whose focus will be to fund black entrepreneurs, with a strong developmental focus or approach. And we need to ensure that it is headed by hardcore bankers with proven track records, like Kennedy Bungane or Sim Tshabalala. Properly incentivise them and then unleash them to carry out the mandate, without political meddling anywhere. That, in my view, should be the next big step.

Richard Maponya
prominent black entrepreneur

BEE killed self-reliance, says Richard Maponya

(Reproduced with permission from Business Day Live (Barron, 2012, http://www.bdlive. co.za/business/2012/12/09/bee-killed-self-reliance-says-richard-maponya)

ONE of South Africa's greatest entrepreneurs, Richard Maponya, blames the country's lack of entrepreneurial activity on black economic empowerment (BEE).

He says BEE fostered a culture of entitlement and expectation that has robbed matriculants and university graduates of the incentive to start their own businesses.

Mr Maponya, 86, was raised in Limpopo and trained as a teacher before starting small grocery stores in Soweto in the early 1950s, which became the foundation of a remarkable business empire.

Nothing symbolised his success more than the 65 000m^2 Maponya Mall he built in Soweto in 2007, which was recently voted No1 shopping centre in Gauteng and number two in South Africa.

Mr Maponya recently won the 2012 Africa Entrepreneurship Lifetime Award presented in Ghana by African Leadership Network and philanthropic investment firm Omidyar Network.

His observations about the deleterious effect of BEE on the spirit of entrepreneurship in post-apartheid South Africa echo those of another local business giant, Sam Motsuenyane, who, like Mr Maponya, built his business empire in the teeth of a system designed to suppress black business in urban areas.

Mr Maponya says that while BEE was designed to empower black people, it has, in a sense, done the reverse by taking away the incentive to start their own businesses.

"Our youngsters are growing up with the idea of having everything for free. It's an entitlement attitude. That sense of entitlement has killed the initiative of our youngsters."

While BEE has promoted it, he says the entitlement culture was borne out of an attitude that began growing from 1976.

"Our youngsters believed that when the ANC takes over, we are going to grab whatever belonged to a white man and give it to the black people."

As a result, when 1994 came along, the "do-it-yourself" attitude that had driven his generation to start businesses was largely absent.

He agrees that BEE was necessary, however, even if it did have negative unforeseen consequences.

"BEE was created to empower the majority of our people, unfortunately it was abused and misused so that it empowered the few who were connected."

It has left a sense of resentment and "a feeling that the government owes us".

He says BEE in its present form should be scrapped.

Even preferential procurement, a central pillar of BEE, has only helped "the very few who are connected. It has not helped the majority."

Those who, in spite of BEE, are motivated to start their own businesses are being held back by excessive red tape, he says.

There was a lot more red tape when he started in business, but he succeeded because "I never took no for an answer. I wanted to achieve what I wanted to achieve".

Young people no longer have that never-say-die attitude, he says.

"They think government must do everything for them. That's the problem. Also the empowerment thing where you are given so many shares.

"You don't really create anything. You are allocated some shares in an organisation that has been going. That doesn't create a single extra job.

"We need to cut the red tape and educate youngsters to have the self-confidence and desire to start up things on their own."

The other serious obstacle in the way of those who would like to create businesses is a lack of collateral.

"We have thousands of young people matriculating and graduating, and when they want to go into business they have no collateral to put forward."

He says government funding mechanisms have largely failed.

"This is something I talk about to parliamentarians every day. We have thousands and thousands of youngsters who want to get into business and just cannot access funding."

Politicians tell him they are "working very hard to achieve that. And then they refer you to a minister who is heading that kind of area and you find the minister doesn't walk the talk."

Mr Maponya has recently set up the Maponya Institute to educate young people to start and run their own businesses, "so that when they matriculate or graduate they don't just look at being employed".

He saw the idea working very well in Brazil, he says.

"Fifteen years ago, they were in a similar situation to ours. Very fortunately they had a president who was a trade unionist and knew the sufferings of the people on the ground."

Under Lula da Silva's leadership, the Brazilians established training institutions "right throughout the country. It worked so well that they told me that in ten years they empowered more than 24 million people whom they uplifted to a middle-class status. I found it working like magic and thought if we could have something like that we could address our unemployment."

Mr Maponya says that in South Africa trade unionists are not concerned about the sufferings of the unemployed.

They represent the interests of "people who are already empowered, as you can see if you look at the Marikana thing, which has thrown the whole country into terrible disarray.

"Everybody now is making demands that industry cannot meet. They don't realise that by doing so they are creating a situation where only a few will be empowered and the majority will be left poor."

If business chambers had been more proactive and shown more leadership "we would have had hundreds of thousands of young people starting things on their own".

Mr Maponya was the founding president of the National African Federated Chamber of Commerce and Industry (Nafcoc), which was started in 1964 to serve the interests of small businesses. He blames the difficulties facing small businesses on the fact that this and other business organisations have not championed their interests strongly or consistently enough.

He suspects that BEE, and above all a tender system which rewards loyalty, has created a situation in which too many business leaders feel they have too much to lose if they make trouble for the government.

"I am very, very sceptical about this BEE thing."

If government cut red tape, provided accessible funding and a more business-friendly environment for entrepreneurs, then "BEE would not be necessary at all", he believes.

"The need for that kind of thing would fall away completely. There would be thousands of youngsters who were self-initiated and creating jobs and opportunities.

"In no time we would have people living in a wonderful country."

This article was first published in Sunday Times: Business Times

Sandile Zungu
entrepreneur and Deputy President,
Black Business Council

A qualified mechanical engineer with an MBA, Sandile Zungu is the founder of Zungu Investments Company (Pty) Ltd (Zico), which has diversified interests in manufacturing and services. He is the current Chairman of EOH Holdings and Non-Executive Director of Grindrod Limited and Novus Holdings, all listed on the JSE Securities Exchange. He is a member of the BRICS Business Council, Vice President of the Black Business Council and also serves on the Presidential BEE Advisory Council. A council member of the University of Cape Town (UCT), he also serves on the advisory board of the UCT Graduate School of Business.

My thinking even before the dawn of our democracy, which by no means I would claim was ground-breaking, was that our political liberation as black people was a given. The sheer force of our numbers as the disenfranchised was making that more a question of 'when' than 'if'. The intriguing question to me, was: 'What about economic power?' That is what had been consuming me all along. My approach was – even when we had finally assumed political power – that failure to also acquire economic power would threaten the stability of a new, democratic order. It was always clear to me, as I'm sure it was to many of my fellow South Africans, that even at the height of political power, our new democratic order was going to have its bluff called on economic issues. Again this, in my view, was a matter of 'when' rather than 'if'.

So I began to feel that, once our new democratic order had been established, those of us who could do so, had the responsibility to accelerate black participation in all sectors of the economy. Where possible, we had to own industrial operations, banks, commercial farms, we needed to manage businesses across the board and become involved across the supply chain of practically every economic activity. This, in my view, meant more than just owning shares in already established enterprises; it meant being involved in the guts of those operations, in the engine-rooms of production. We needed to be involved in every facet of business activity. This was more than just ticking boxes on BEE scorecards, or being active in so-called softer areas such as CSI.

It was clear to me that, even if we survive the scrutiny of the current generation on these issues, forthcoming generations (our grandchildren and their children) would cast a probing eye on whether we hadn't dropped the ball in this regard. I also saw BEE within the broader context of the African Renaissance and the dawn of an African century. President Thabo Mbeki was very clear in articulating this vision, and my view was that we needed to ensure that the project was not compromised by our lapses on matters economic. An African Renaissance in the absence of black economic emancipation would be illusory. I also saw this process as a grand gathering of achievements at the height of what is clearly emerging now as an African century. This grand gathering needed to be characterised by a collection of achievements – in the areas of politics, culture and human rights, but also in respect of the economy. Therefore, to me, BEE was an integral part of the African Renaissance.

At the dawn of democracy we had the responsibility to ask probing and perhaps uncomfortable questions, knowing very well that if we did not do that, coming generations would be severe in their judgement of our efforts. We had to ask questions such as the following: Do black people own any land in this country of their forebears? Are they involved in industry? And we had to ask these questions not because we sought to exclude our fellow South Africans, but simply because we knew that our democratic project would not be complete until the colonial and apartheid legacy was reversed.

To me, the questions that needed asking on the economic empowerment front were not to be confined to who owns pieces of this or that industry. Let me expand on this by using an example: I think it's been by God's grace and through the toil of our people that we now have major black players in the platinum and coal industries, amongst others. And we celebrate these strides. As black people today, we may own chunks of major corporations – some listed here on the JSE, others listed on international bourses like the London Stock Exchange – but the question is: Do we as black people control any particular value chain? Even a single one, for that matter? Personally, I would argue that if you look at a range of products across the economy, there is not even a single value chain controlled by blacks. And that is, in my view, a serious indictment on the state of BEE.

Let us, for instance, look at the value chain of a loaf of bread. I'm using bread as an example because it is our people's staple food. If we look at the land where the seed of wheat is planted, who owns the land? Who plants those seeds, who are the commercial farmers that actually produce the crop on a very large, world-class scale for local use as well as for exports? Are any of our people part of those huge commercial farming operations? The starting point of the value chain is where the planting happens, with the ownership and working of the land, to flour mills and the bakeries where the bread is finally baked. Where are black people involved in producing this most ubiquitous of staple foods? They are not there. All the major players in this particular value chain are definitely not black owned. Yes, a few major companies here may have black executives doing a great job. A few may have sold chunks of their shareholdings to black investors, but can it be said that black people own and/or run this entire value chain? No. Let's move on to the retailers, to the Shoprite Checkers and PicknPays of this world: Where are the black people? Yet who are the ultimate and majority consumers? Blacks! At home, at school, in hospitals, in prisons, etc. In Soweto, millions of loaves are sold every day. Now, you can take bread as a microcosm of the entire economy of this country. Take textbooks, take the needles used in syringes in hospitals, take cars or taxis – if you look at the value chain, where do the taxis come from? Toyota in Japan. They are assembled in Durban at the Toyota factory, but who owns that assembly plant? If we look at support industries for taxis: insurance, tyres, gasoline, panel-beating – black people are not there, yet they are the ones who are transported in these vehicles on a daily basis. And I am raising this point not because we seek to exclude any other racial grouping, but because surely if black people are now liberated and are supposed to be fully involved in the entire spectrum of economic activity, then we need to ask tough questions if they remain conspicuous by their absence.

For me, we cannot be satisfied even with 50 per cent ownership of the economy in black hands when we are not represented in at least the value chain of one significant product or service. Right now, our involvement in the economy is patchy and erratic. I think it almost poses a challenge to black entrepreneurs, thinkers and leaders to admit that it is far too soon to be complacent. The mistake we made was that we probably have a compartmentalised approach to BEE. If you look at BEE from the angle of a single link in the chain, you might get excited and feel that perhaps it's mission accomplished, but once you widen your view and look at it from an integrated perspective, the picture changes completely.

We as black entrepreneurs need to begin to look at BEE from an integrated perspective. Instead of just looking at a single company or even sector and saying we want control or representation there, we must look at value chains. Historically, some communities achieved great economic success by following this approach, and now they hold massive sway on certain value chains. I do not wish to sound paranoid, but it is a question of risk management, too. We must avoid being vulnerable, or, in certain situations, being held to ransom. And let us not delude ourselves – sometimes the economy can be used to hold a people to ransom by those in control of critical value chains. As a transforming society which is trying to bed down our democracy while redressing past injustices, we must have no illusions that the entire universe is rooting in unison for our success. Sometimes I think we, as a newly liberated people, are too trusting, too naive, by assuming that there is fairness and goodwill all round. It isn't necessarily so. Our not being in control of critical value chains makes us extremely vulnerable as a young democracy, not only to external forces which may have less than supportive intentions, but sometimes also to internal forces. I am not alleging that there are conspiracies being hatched against us as a people, not at all. But right now, economically speaking, we are sitting ducks to any forces that might want to punish us because they may not like the stance we as a country take on this or that issue. We cannot repeat the mistakes of our forefathers who were very trusting and ended up being taken advantage of.

Yes, it is admirable that we now have more black CEOs and more black chairmen of major companies, but that is far from enough. Those of us whose interest in matters economic goes beyond merely the commercial, need to think harder and sharper. We need to cast our net wider and ask ourselves bigger and broader questions, beyond just tying up the next transaction or being appointed to the next board.

As things stand on BEE right now, I see pockets of excellence here and there, but also massive gaps and gaping holes. I don't see a nice, clear picture or any shape at all. The time has come to really talk about the bigger picture we want to see emerging at the end of this process. In fact, I would go so far as to say that BEE right now has lost steam and appears to be adrift at sea, prone to having its direction changed by the currents or whichever powerful winds are blowing. It is alive, but seems to be going either in circles or zigzagging without any clear direction. It needs to be revitalised in terms of purpose and vision, and the responsibility is ours as black leaders to breathe life into it once more. Naturally we must not forget to give credit to our political leaders who have been bold enough to push this process into the national economic discourse, sometimes against fierce resistance. President Mbeki saw to it that laws were passed to kick-start the process. President Zuma has moved it beyond the mere tradition of shared dealings and AA, into insisting on the creation of black industrialists. But our leaders have all sorts of national issues to deal with, so it becomes incumbent on us to re-invigorate this process, to help it build up steam. We must remember that this process is also about citizen activism: if ordinary citizens feel that the process is going in the wrong direction or has been hijacked by sinister forces, they need to stand up and shout.

We also need to ensure that organisations like the Black Business Council, the BMF and Nafcoc remain energised so that they can be vigilant at all times and safeguard the process against drifting off course. Even outside of organised business we need to have thought leaders who will say: 'I don't want to be constrained by organisational structures, I want to make my point.' We need to encourage such outspokenness, because this process needs to be inspired and continually re-energised by every available resource. We also need to guard against demonising those who are detractors of BEE. We need to allow space for people, be they from the right or the left, so that they feel free to articulate their views.

As a member of the current generation of South Africans, I believe we are in a very privileged position in that we have the time and space to establish a new rallying point for the broader African Renaissance project; to inspire and galvanise not only black people on the continent, but throughout the entire diaspora. We should not be intimidated by the challenges we face, or worse, feel we have to lower our aspirations. No, we have to up our game and step up to the plate. For me, BEE has to be located within this broad agenda. What is the end game? For me, the end game is black people, throughout the world, re-asserting themselves so that black people – whether they are in Africa, the Americas or wherever – can begin to take their rightful place in economic activity. And, more importantly, once we have asserted ourselves not just in global political affairs but in economic ones too, we can begin to infuse our own perspective, thereby enriching the world with our unique concepts such as *ubuntu*, amongst others. Black people must have greater sway in economic matters, and must achieve ownership and control of certain value chains in their entirety, yet it is about more than that. It is about us taking our rightful place in the community of nations and influencing world thought. That is why I personally am exhorting even greater efforts on the part of black entrepreneurs, instead of resting on our laurels. The mission is bigger than just monetary benefits. If we assume this particular stance, I am confident we will be judged kindly by history. Our grandchildren and their offspring, at the turn of this century, will look at us with admiration. But if we drop the ball now, we will earn nothing but their scorn.

Thami Mazwai
Black publishing pioneer and academic

Dr Thami Mazwai is a former journalist, editor, entrepreneur and small business academic and practitioner. He is Resident Executive at the Wits Business School, advising on small business support and is on the Black Business Council with a particular interest in small business development. He is former Director of the Centre for Small Business Development (CSBD) at the University of Johannesburg. In January 2013 he was in Russia as part of a panel of experts looking at methodologies to integrate small business into the value chains of the BRICS countries. He is currently head of consultancy firm, Mtiya Dynamics, that specialises in the area of business enterprise development. He was a member of the Skills System Review Technical Task Team of the Human Resource Development Council of South Africa, chaired by the Deputy President, whose secretariat is Department of Higher Education and Training.

My interest in matters economic in general, and black economic advancement in particular, started in a rather strange manner. It all began while I was serving a two-year jail term as a political prisoner around 1982 and 83, for having refused to testify against a fellow student rebellion leader. As Category D prisoners, we would be taken to clean the cells where the more senior Group A category prisoners (like Aubrey Mokoape, Strini Moodley and others) were interned at Victor Verster. Category A prisoners had earned the right to receive certain publications and reading material, so every time we went there to clean the cells, there would be this pile of *Financial Mail* magazines. Being mainly focused on business and economic matters, the magazine was probably seen as not militant or harmful by the authorities, which explains its ready availability to Category A prisoners.

So I stole some copies of the *Financial Mail* to go and read in my cell – out of sheer curiosity, at that stage. All of a sudden the world of business opened up in front of me. As an activist journalist all I had ever been concerned about was writing stories on the fight for the political liberation of black people in this country. But as soon as I opened those copies of the *Financial Mail* (I ended up stealing and keeping about 20 of them!), something inside my head began to say: 'But here is the power.' It gradually began to dawn on me, as I kept reading various reports and stories, that even if we ultimately gained political power – which was the reason for our involvement in the struggle – that would be where the true power lay. Of course I was familiar with economic concepts, because at that time I was a distance-learning student with Unisa. But until then, to me, all matters economic and business-related had been remote and academic. The *Financial Mail* was bringing it all to life, and I saw power there. There was no doubt in my mind that the people who were frequently at the centre of the magazine's stories were just as much movers and shakers as the politicians were. I began to develop a view that, as black people, we needed to begin to elevate the struggle for economic power to the same level as that for political power.

When I was eventually released from prison, I went back to working for the *Sowetan* newspaper. By then I had already been inspired to kick off a number of vigorous business and economics-related dialogues amongst our readers. My editor allowed me to start a business section for the newspaper, thanks to my argument that people must start looking at empowering themselves personally, while also empowering others in the black community. When my editor, Aggrey Klaaste, started the nation-building initiative, I linked the economic empowerment wing to it. This narrative, of economic empowerment as an integral part of the nation-building programme, began to get stronger and stronger and I stuck to it until 1992 when I was recruited by the then fledgling *Black Enterprise* magazine, which was owned by the insurance company, African Life. Also at that time I needed a change of scene as I had recently suffered the tragedy of my then wife's death.

I found *Black Enterprise* to be too stuck in glorifying informal trade and street-level enterprise. That was fine, but it wasn't good enough, in my view. The magazine wasn't casting its net further and wider, or portraying the visions and aspirations of black people being part of the upper echelons of economic activity. I changed the magazine's editorial approach completely, from being focused on the owners of little corner shops, to take a much more ambitious perspective. It attracted an even wider audience and was admired by many for its more ambitious approach.

Around 1993, African Life decided to divest itself of the magazine, so I decided to buy it and we formed Mafube Publishers as its owner. We did fairly well and even secured the contract to publish the in-flight magazine, *Sawubona*, of South African Airways, which was beginning to push BEE as its policy. Perhaps we began to be a little too successful for some conservatives within established business, because when our contract was renewed, there were howls of outrage from the conservative media. That the previous white publishing house had held the contract for 17 years was conveniently ignored by these howlers. We were just besieged. To see old interests pouncing on a new supposedly upstart operation like ours was sobering indeed. To be a new black entity trying to shake the old order was simply too much for some.

This created an environment where I, as a fledgling entrepreneur and journalist, spent too much of my energy fighting fires and all sorts of distractions, instead of being able to capitalise on our growth. Consequently many mistakes were made in the process, and this ended up costing us dearly. Although the then CEO of SAA, Coleman Andrews, tried to stand his ground and defend us, essentially because the quality of our product was widely admired even by our detractors, he was embattled. We eventually lost the SAA contract, and that sounded the death knell for our publishing house.

As our publishing company folded, I decided to follow my passion for enterprise development and joined the Faculty of Small Business Development at the University of Johannesburg (UJ). I still wanted to pursue the ideal of empowering our people to start their own viable entities. I remain forever thankful to the Vice-Chancellor of UJ, Prof Ihron Rensburg, for buying into my vision and enabling us to really get this unit going.

I had been with UJ for five years when my contract ran out, and unfortunately I was of retirement age. Next I went to Wits Business School for a year, before starting a company called Mtiya Dynamics, which really is still focused on my passion: developing business enterprises.

In terms of where I now stand on matters relating to the economic advancement of black people, I still hold firm to the view that we will only achieve economic liberation when a large number of us own and run our own businesses. Nonetheless, one cannot say that people who received shares in established white companies were wrong to do so. That was another dimension of empowerment: it does not manifest in a single formula, there are numerous approaches, and it's not a zero-sum game.

Working at UJ had brought me very close to the issue of developing small enterprise, and to do a lot of research on the topic. Indeed, even my doctoral studies were in this area. Of course, I also had access to research by other academics, along with the vast resources of the university. This enabled me to marry science with my passion. And, I have to say here, my wife is a great believer in this. She always says to me: Put science behind your passion!

When I look back on my life, there are two people who I would say have had a seminal influence on me. The first is Percy Qoboza, the doyen of black anti-apartheid journalism, who suffered frequent incarcerations and instances of harassment in the 70s and 80s, before his death in 1986. This is the man who made a journalist out of me. The second, of course, is Ihron Rensburg, UJ's

Vice-Chancellor, who created an academic and research space which allowed me to dig deeper into my other passion – developing black enterprise. These two are the architects who made me a journalist who is passionate about black enterprise – that is how I see myself.

There are a few key learnings that emerged from my work at UJ with regard to BEE and black enterprise development in the townships in particular:

- Townships, as conceived by apartheid architects, are more than just physical black urban settlements. They had a certain sociological and psychological construct. In other words, they were intended to develop and mold a particular kind of a black person. They had a central and continuous message for residents: 'You are not home here. You are just a temporary sojourner. You could be thrown out tomorrow.' They had the design and architecture of impermanence. Residents were never supposed to feel at home, or even to begin to be ambitious about building greater things. And this is a major impediment because, with the advent of democracy, suddenly the message had changed to say: 'Well, this is your home. You must make the best of it. No one is coming to kick you out of here.' And unfortunately the entire township infrastructure was built essentially for tent towns – something which continues to be a serious impediment to business development. It's a headache for government. Some of our entrepreneurs have become psychologically arrested in this mindset of impermanence – a mindset of subsistence and survival ... because, presumably, you might not be here tomorrow. This is one example of a town's physical architecture messing with people's minds. It shows what kind of challenges policy-makers face.

- The second component to this township challenge is the almost accepted view that township business must grow and develop parallel to established big business. In other words, small (almost subsistence-level) business must be confined to the townships, while big, established business operates in developed areas. To expand on this point: small, menial business activity is for black entrepreneurs, and big, complex commercial activity is for white established business. There is no talk of a symbiotic relationship between fledgling black enterprise and established white business. That means we don't have an integrated strategy that sees the development of black business in the townships happening as a joint and mutually beneficial effort with white business. We need to address these parallel subsystems which were obviously developed by successive apartheid regimes. Accepting these subsystems as they stand will lead to uneven and poor development for both established white business and fledgling black businesses in the townships.

These contradictions are not confined to urban areas. Even in rural areas, such parallel systems continue to exist, thereby constraining economic development. For instance, instead of hiring an established company to provide food for learners in a rural school, why aren't we recruiting locals who obviously are familiar with local dietary preferences, who can form co-operatives and cook for the children and serve them the food, while ensuring that health and hygiene standards are adhered to? Our current approach is to say: 'No, this project is too big for the local mamas, let's go and give it to Big Catering Corporation.' That way, locals remain marginalised and are confined to menial projects that keep them at subsistence level.

In sum, you have a situation where blacks are mired in subsistence-level business and not graduating to the big time. The subsystems established by apartheid are seeing to that. Those who have 'graduated' to the big time have simply acquired shares in long-established white operations, almost graduating by default.

But there is hope at policy level. Like many others, I have greeted the recent establishment of the Ministry for Small Business with great excitement. I am currently working with policy-makers to tackle existing barriers and obstacles. I am hopeful that we will finally crack the code, but there is a great deal of work to be done. I've learned that this will be no easy task.

Themba Dlamini
Managing Director, Black Management Forum

Themba Thomas Cyril Dlamini is the Managing Director of the Black Management Forum (BMF). Before that he was Chief Executive Officer (CEO) of the National Gambling Board (NGB). Themba has more than 15 years' experience as an executive, primarily in the public sector.

~~~~~~~~

The BMF is not merely the midwife that delivered BEECom, it did the same with EE in this country. I always say people still owe the BMF a big 'thank-you' for being the engineer that designed what was to eventually become the *Employment Equity Act*. As a result, we have watched developments in these processes very keenly over the past 20 years.

The positive is that we have seen some encouraging (albeit very limited) movement on EE generally. In the public sector, there have been significant strides, but the private sector has been problematic. And here we are not just talking of people 'going up' in terms of their remuneration and swelling the ranks of the so-called black middle class, but we are talking of people being in charge: running key business units, influencing and at times directing a company's strategy. If you go around the world, what you find is that on average, indigenous people are in charge of the levers of the economy. It is only here in Africa, and more so in South Africa, where indigenous people are not in charge. And for us at the BMF, this anomaly is unacceptable. There is something missing here, especially taking into account that all parties to Nedlac (National Economic Development and Labour Council), which includes business, agreed and committed to correcting this anomaly. For us, this is inexplicable defiance, given the fact that people agreed at Nedlac, that this was the right course of action. Then they walk out of there and do almost the direct opposite. That is why, as the BMF, we fully support the harsher penalties that have now been introduced to correct the errant behaviour of corporates. The oft-quoted Irish coffee scenario is still very much the norm in corporate South Africa, where the top is almost exclusively white and the bottom is almost exclusively black, 21 years after the advent of democracy! The upper echelons in corporate South Africa are still mainly white and predominantly male. Whatever improvements have occurred over the past two decades have really just been a drop in the ocean. We cannot come to terms with this as the BMF.

Another anomaly we have to contend with, is that the progress of black management into the upper echelons of the public sector has, tragically, not been accompanied by wide-scale improvements in the service delivery of the institutions they head. One would have expected the delivery of services –

especially to historically disadvantaged communities – to skyrocket, given the fact that the people who are now in charge, mainly hail from those communities. Instead, I would argue that the opposite has frequently been the case, especially in the past five years or so.

We have always been of the view that those black executives who have achieved greater heights, particularly in the private sector, must play the role of midwives to other black up-and-coming talent, so as to ease their delivery into the intimidating corporate world. But we are not seeing that. Yes, it can be argued that because currently there isn't a critical mass of black executives up there, they may feel isolated or their efforts are diluted. However, if you are committed to a cause, you do not derive your strength only from numbers. Your strength must come from your convictions too. So then you begin to ask: What happened to this black leadership whose ascendancy into these high positions we, as the BMF, have been advocating for? You begin to (almost nostalgically) ask the question: Why are we not seeing new Lot Ndlovus or Reuel Khozas emerging? What has happened to the original spirit that moved these pioneers?

As those ground-breakers naturally and gradually moved off the scene, we would have expected new and more vigorous, similarly minded leadership to come to the fore. But it seems not to be happening. It is almost as if the original spirit of the founders of the black advancement movement is dying with these leaders. The willingness to challenge the status quo that characterised these leaders seems to be absent now. It is almost as if the new crop has become complacent, as if they only see their role as that of maintaining and confirming the status quo, while of course enjoying the status and perks that come with these high offices. The transformational leadership spirit seems to have died out, to be replaced by self-interest and self-aggrandisement.

This becomes an indictment on us also as today's black business leadership, in that we seem not to take responsibility for doing succession planning within our own ranks. And here we need to take a leaf out of the Jewish community, where there is a very strong sense of community. Once a successful person has retired in that community, s/he always shoulders the responsibility of mentoring and nurturing the younger generation; of infusing them with the same values s/he was bequeathed as a young person. So what you see there is a common set of values that are transferred from generation to generation, in effect ensuring a continued conveyor belt of community-conscious new talent. Also, from this community we need to learn how they realised that the most potent weapon against disempowerment and marginalisation is the empowerment of their people's minds with certain core, inalterable values. In a way you could say they decided to fortify the minds of their own people, lest those minds be colonised by external forces. Their minds and values formed an impenetrable fortress. In addition, they developed a view that said: 'We will be relentless and uncompromising in our demand for self-determination, self-empowerment and self-actualisation as a people. And we will teach our children to be like that as well. That is the only way we can ensure not only our survival as a group that has been on the receiving end of brutal racism and subjugation in history, but also our growth and development.' This view superseded even whatever personal or political differences they had amongst themselves, as is wont to be the case with any community.

In a way we, as black professionals, have not exorcised the ghosts of apartheid from our own minds. The architects of apartheid knew that the first asset of black people which they had to 'capture' was their minds. That is why we need to go back to the teachings of black empowerment leaders like Frantz Fanon, Steve Biko and Cheik Anta Diop, because their view was that we as black people needed to first take our minds back from our conquerors. They argued that once you have 'decolonised' your mind, it will always be clear to you that your first and foremost responsibility is to see to the empowerment of your own people, not just your own, individual self-promotion. Therefore, when you become a CEO of an SOE, for example, you know that your key responsibility is to ensure that the organisation delivers a superior service to your people and betters their lives, not that it becomes your personal piggy-bank which enables you to live lavishly, while your people wait in vain for services. Once you have imbibed the teachings of these visionaries, your access to state resources will become a vehicle which assists you in emancipating your people from misery, rather than it representing your personal pot of gold.

I have questioned my colleagues here at the BMF by asking whether, with all our seminars, management training programmes and annual awards, we ever touch on these subjects, or whether we merely concentrate on giving people technical skills to they can rapidly ascend the corporate ladder. Surely if we only do that, then we are producing a cadre of black executives who will only want the perks and the good life, without caring a fig for the community's needs. I argue that we now need to infuse 'values' as part of our development of black executives. Failure to do so would be a dereliction of our national duty.

Although we as the BMF are an organisation that seeks to facilitate the production of top black executives, our job, in my view, is incomplete if we fail to teach our membership the values espoused by luminaries like Frantz Fanon, Steve Biko and Cheik Anta Diop, amongst others. Failure to do so only produces self-centred defenders of the status quo. We have already seen over the past 20 years that the ascendancy of a black manager to the top echelon of a private or public sector organisation does not automatically mean that once that individual is there, he will pursue the broader agenda of black economic emancipation. Indeed, we have seen situations where once some individuals get into top private sector positions, they are co-opted into the trappings and amenities there, and completely forget their bigger mandate.

We have seen massive co-option of some of our former militant leaders and cadres who, ensconced in corporate comfort, have suddenly gone tame. They have become liberal and, on occasion, even downright conservative! As a result, you see them espousing the most conservative business dogma – almost as if they have no background in poverty and deprivation: profits are down, we must wield the axe, retrench left, right and centre irrespective of the human cost! What happened to their *ubuntu*? Given their background, I certainly expect them to think differently and out of the box, not to regurgitate Western business dogma without blinking. Again, it is because their minds have been colonised. Their attitude seems to have evolved to: Damn all this talk about *ubuntu*. Naturally they begin to enjoy the adulation of the markets and traditional business media as they unleash the axe on their very own people. In my view, the only way we can guarantee that this does not happen is when that individual, in addition to technical competencies, is also infused with sensitivity in respect of the values of black economic emancipation.

Going forward, I would like to see a situation where organisations that want to do business with government agencies or enterprises are compelled to have in their business proposals, a programme for developing fledgling black entrepreneurs. Not the oft-repeated 'rent-a-darkie' phenomenon, but a genuine black entrepreneur. The entrepreneur may not even have the requisite skills at the beginning of a programme, but as long as s/he displays passion and commitment, the bigger organisation will help that individual and their enterprise develop over the coming years. And I emphasise the word *years*. We are not talking convenient quickies, we are talking about a long-term business partnership programme that will impart resources and skills to this entrepreneur. Our people also need to get out of the get-rich-quick mentality. So no more visions of overnight riches, but rather long-term business-focused partnerships where riches may be a long time in coming, where patience is paramount. And the government must meticulously and relentlessly monitor this partnership over the years, to ensure that all milestones are met, with penalties being levied if there is default on either side. Interestingly, one minister who, to my knowledge, tried this approach was the late Stella Sigcau.

The last point I wish to make, is that one almost gets an impression that many of the policies of our government are not drafted by our own people. Our challenge, as black professionals, is to be content and knowledge generators, so that our government does not end up using alien resources who, at times, emerge with solutions that do not take local intricacies into account.

Vusi Thembekwayo
new generation black entrepreneur

Motivational, keynote and international speakers are not trained, they are born! At the age of 17, Vusi was already ranked 1st in Africa for motivational speaking. As one of the best motivational and keynote speakers he has spoken in four of the seven continents to over 250 000 people each year ... and counting! Motivational and keynote speakers around the world have come to revere his talent and delivery style. Companies and governments find him a dream to work with. His humour is the glue that binds some of his most diverse audiences in the world. A funny keynote speaker and hilarious motivational speaker, John Howard, former Prime Minister of Australia, called Vusi the 'rock star of public speaking' and global strategist, Clem Sunter, said he was 'simply riveting'.

My understanding of BEE is that is in an instrument by which black people are brought to the economic state where they deserve to be. It is about saying: 'Given the blood, sweat and tears that we have given towards building this country over centuries, we are not where we deserve to be.' And I emphasise the word: deserve. Our people suffered in building this country. Families lost fathers and breadwinners when they were slaving underground in the mines, or in scorching sunlight building roads and railways. The instrument we have chosen as a nation to ensure that these rights are wronged, is BEE.

The process of BEE has unfolded in several phases, in my view. Let me explain: there is an old saying, favoured amongst historians, that after every revolution, before a new order settles in, certain opportunities arise for some to take advantage of the situation. So, before the dust settles after a revolution, some fleet-footed individuals grab those opportunities and benefit immensely in the process. The same thing happened in our country, when after the collapse of apartheid, and before the new democratic order found its feet, certain opportunities arose and some who were quick off the mark, benefited. Those who criticise the opportunists, are missing the point. Those who took advantage of opportunities may be huge names today, having made massive fortunes, but in the aeons of time they are but a blip, an anecdote of history. To begrudge them or obsess over their gains is therefore a futile occupation. We have to move on. We need to take a broader approach – almost like historians would – and say that these things have been occurring throughout the history of humankind. Nothing unnatural or hitherto unknown in human history occurred here. In my view, this first phase was characterised by apprehension and anxiety on the part of many whites in general, and the white corporate world in particular. At that time, many had a single criterion in trying to find a black business partner: 'Can you get me a meeting with the president? If you can, here's a BEE deal for you!' Now, as a young person myself, I understand that many of these individuals, at a personal level, had suffered immensely and made huge sacrifices. I therefore do not begrudge them their fortunes at all.

Those individuals who took advantage of the chaos and confusion were able to amass for themselves massive fortunes within a very short space of time – fortunes that, on average, would have taken a decade or even a century to build up. I would say during the second phase of empowerment, around half a decade into our democracy, as the dust was beginning to settle, a certain degree of financial or business acumen began to be a requirement in accessing BEE opportunities as a black person. And once again, some did very well for themselves in this phase – especially those who had a nice combination of political connectivity and business acumen. Once more, I see this in a broader historical context and have no qualms about it.

For me, these two post-revolution phases had the following common features:

1. They required that black business partners be politically connected. Not being politically connected was almost always an automatic disqualifier;

2. They ignored certain very established black businesspeople who had succeeded despite the harsh conditions of apartheid, people like Herman Mashaba, Richard Maponya and many other black entrepreneurs with excellent track records. This, in my view, is a travesty and a wanton waste of an already established talent base.

A lot has been said about tenderpreneurs. Personally, I don't see them as a new, distinct feature of BEE – after all, tenderpreneurs utilised the same skills and tactics that were commonly employed in the two phases I mentioned earlier. For example, post-revolution BEE entrepreneurs would discuss their ten per cent cut with the chairman of the board, while today's tenderpreneurs tend to discuss their ten per cent cut with a local politician or the chairman of the tender panel. But it is essentially the same thing. So, the post-revolution and the most recent tenderpreneurs shared the following key features. A BEE partner

1. tends to create no discernible value at the conclusion of a transaction;

2. does not industrialise or engage in business operations;

3. does not create or acquire skills or competencies;

4. adds an extra margin to goods and services in order to accommodate his/ her cut. So, such a person is inflationary.

All the above traits, instead of adding to the underlying economy, are extractive. They are sucking the economy dry. The unfortunate effect of these tendencies is that they almost inculcate and glamourise a culture of bling, without adding value and without breaking a sweat. Those who are watching, wonder why they need to work hard and get little when they can work little and get a lot by being a tenderpreneur of some sort. This moves society into a state where social significance becomes a question of what glamorous possessions you have, rather than the nature of your character or the level of your skill. People begin to see BEE as a vehicle enabling you to access nice toys, rather than as a bigger process working towards the economic emancipation of the previously disadvantaged. Then corruption follows naturally, because the obsession is not with acquiring skills or adding value, but with having the means to acquire those accoutrements that define your significance in society.

In a way, I believe our obsession with trying to combat corrupt activities becomes a digression because it is the new, emergent values that make people corrupt. Many believe that in order to be taken seriously by society, they just need to own a Maserati, obtaining it by whatever means necessary, fair or foul. Then a situation arises where someone is not deemed successful, in BEE terms, if they don't own a Maserati. This explains the strange phenomenon of highly educated people being caught doing corrupt activities. It begs the question: Why would so-and-so, who has a string of qualifications, risk it all? It is because he feels under-valued in society, despite all that education. He knows that his views are likely to be taken seriously if he drives a Maserati, not necessarily because he has a PhD. On the other hand, you may find people faking their qualifications in order to access opportunities, not necessarily to be respected as intellectuals. Their focus is solely on getting that job and the perks that go with it.

As a younger generation of entrepreneurs, we watch this and learn. So we say to ourselves: 'Get yourself a fancy toy, quickly, by means fair or foul, and all else will follow.' We are being taught the wrong lessons and have become short-term in our orientation. Short-termism is a serious cancer which is spreading fast now that BEE has become equated with bling.

Short-termism is what will push our economy over the cliff.

To prevent that, we need to remember what we mean by 'society'. A society is a system of accepted behaviours. If the behaviours I mentioned before become the norm, then we're finished as a society. Deceit, corruption and short-termism will in no time become the norm, and it will doom us as a nation. Our current 'war on corruption' entails dealing with the symptoms, while the real problem is our values.

We are now at a stage where the two preceding phases of BEE transactions are coming to a conclusion and winding down. Many of that generation's beneficiaries are cashing in or have cashed out already. Recently there has been a rise in broad-based operations and community trusts, although those are not without their problems: by being too inclusive, some sharks got in there and basically raided community trusts. Many communities became very excited about the prospect of benefiting, only to realise at the end of the day that their expected fortunes had melted into thin air. So, in sum, hitherto our experimentations with BEE have been less than stellar, since they failed to address the issue of economic value-add and job creation.

Thankfully, I get a sense that policy-makers are beginning to realise that, unless we drill deeper into hardcore economic matters, beyond the glamour and the symbolism, we are going nowhere. The penny has dropped and the signs are promising. In a way I feel for our policy-makers because they are dealing with a problem that is both complex and dynamic. And we all know that the wheels of policy-making grind very slowly, no matter where you are in the world. On many occasions, by the time they introduce an appropriate solution, the nature of the challenge has morphed into something new. That is why they deserve our support, rather than our continuous condemnation.

The stricter and (in a way) more punitive BEE requirements of late are, I believe, a step in the right direction. I think many companies have been playing hide and seek for too long on this matter. Of course the unintended consequence is that the codes almost reward 'retaining' black talent rather than demonstrably developing it. But, in essence, the country needs more black entrepreneurs to go out there and create employment opportunities. Companies which would have spent vast amounts of money training black talent, or paying them huge salaries, are being penalised if such an individual leaves to start his or her own enterprise. And, in any case, hugely talented black executives would themselves be loath to leave high-paying secure jobs to start an operation where they have to curtail their lifestyle. They won't make such a huge sacrifice simply because it is the 'patriotic' thing to do. Let's be realistic about that. When I left my well-paying secure job in the corporate world to start my own enterprise, some of my friends and relatives thought I was crazy. I had to dig deeper and say to myself: 'There is a bigger issue here than my own immediate personal comfort.' Of course the worst part is that we are a nation that celebrates job security and is practically hostile towards entrepreneurship. When I was an executive, banks were beating a path to my door with offers of generous personal banking services. But the minute I set off on my own, they no longer wanted to speak to me. Culturally, we are a society that heaps condemnation on an entrepreneur who tries and does not succeed, instead of being supportive. People would rather see their super talents and brains vegetating in posh corporate offices than being out here, eking out a living.

The black community's role can also be very counter-productive, in that it almost holds black talent 'captive' in the corporate sector. Many of my friends who are hugely talented and visionary fellows, should be out there creating new and fantastic services and products, but their excuse, without fail, is: 'I am afraid of failing. The consequences are too ghastly to contemplate. Should things go wrong, I will lose my credit rating. I will be blacklisted and be cut out of getting any form of credit for seven years. I will be universally condemned by my family for having been self-centred instead of thinking about their welfare too. No ways, I'm staying here in this big corporation.' Our culture does not celebrate start-up entrepreneurs – we do that only once they have attained stupendous success. But until then we see them as weird, reckless and crazy. Black people in particular, possibly because of the psychological effects of apartheid, are almost hard-wired to think in survivalist terms. We are not hard-wired to want to build great things that will live on long after we are gone. We just want to survive, to not sink. Even our friends and relatives caution us against setting off on our own: 'You're fine now. You are going to survive. You are going to live well. Why do you want to now risk it all?' We have to exorcise our people of this spirit which is holding us captive. As black people, we need to change the narrative amongst ourselves in favour of a new narrative that says risk is okay; failure teaches you something and so it is also okay. If we want to rise as a people, we must not look at riding on the coattails of others and insisting that they give us a piece of their pie. Let us go out there, take risks, rise and fall, learn and create our own pie.

Going forward, I believe our starting point must be that of humility. Humility from all round: politicians, academics, corporate South Africa, etc. We need to migrate from a perception that some sectors have a monopoly on wisdom. We need a common meeting point that will hopefully produce a new accord.

The second point is that we must all accept that we are in this for the long haul. All of us want to see results yesterday. We must come to terms with the fact that, for this thing to work out right, it must be given time.

The third point to make especially to some members of the white community, is that it is important not to see BEE as only a win-lose initiative, namely that if it works out well for black people it can only mean whites will suffer serious losses. Too many today continue to label BEE as the enemy. They invest all their energy in fighting the process tooth and nail, and celebrate with glee when it fails or when individuals stumble. I would urge my white compatriots to embrace the Theory of Abundance, as espoused by Peter Diamandis, namely that there is enough for all of us. BEE can and should be a win for all.

The fourth point is rather controversial. In a transformative exercise of this nature, at times democracy can be an impediment. That is why, when China decided to make a u-turn from communism to capitalism, the country was so successful. The Communist Party did not have to call referendums, it merely told the people: 'We aren't going left anymore, we're going right – like it or lump it.' South Africa is a democratic country, and our march towards the economic emancipation of black people will be characterised by strides forward and steps backwards, by trial and error, glee and glum. It is going to get a little messy, let's accept that. Our politicians have to be continuously thinking of the next elections, and unlike China's leadership, they can't say to people: 'We know you are going to hate us now, but you will love us in 50 years' time when it all comes together.'

In conclusion, in my view the most important thing is that we need a culture of patient capital. The fact that we do not have it, is the single most important thing that is keeping us hamstrung in a broad economic sense, not just from a BEE perspective. We have these large financial institutions which boast to all and sundry that they are the most secure institutions in the world. Essentially, what they are saying is that they are the financial institutions that take the least amount of risk in the world! They are saying: 'Dear investor, if you give us your money, we are going to sit on it and we won't give it to some wild entrepreneurs with crazy ideas.' Now how do you marry that with a country that is on record as being the most unequal in the world? Or with a country that has one of the highest youth unemployment rates in the world? Or consistently has the highest unemployment rate in the world? Many of our financial institutions take pride in hoarding capital and starving entrepreneurship in this country. My argument is that if we say we are developmental, by definition that infers higher risk-taking. Tragically, this 'developmental' language seems to be confined to government, with financial institutions overwhelmingly silent on this. It is almost as if they are deliberately distancing themselves from this imperative, as if a First World financial institution mindset is operating in a Third World context. Something isn't jiving here! And the biggest irony is that our banks are more aggressive and entrepreneurial on funding short-term consumerism. If you want to buy a TV set, they have the money for you. If you want to start a shoe factory ... Sorry, they don't do factories.

It goes even further. When you look at the developmental funding institutions (DFIs) we have, with the greatest of respect to them, be they the IDC (Industrial Development Corporation), NEF (National Empowerment Fund) or Development Bank, they do not employ people who are entrepreneurial thinkers. Their bias is towards hardcore commercial bankers. These institutions are therefore populated by people who have been trained and are grounded in a risk-averse mindset. Let us remember: all institutions and organisations are made up of people, not just bricks and mortar. It is people, with their mindsets and biases, who make an organisation. That is how a commercial bank mindset manifests itself at a developmental institution. In that scenario you end up dealing with people who are just ticking boxes, not changing society. So you're back to square one. For me this is the single biggest challenge we face – the almost maniacal hoarding of capital. Many DFIs do not have 'evergreen funds' which you, as an entrepreneur, know will stay with you as you grow and develop your business. They have 'term funds' where, at the end of five years, they shout at you 'Pay Back The Money!' because they want to cash out and move on.

Another issue which I want to raise briefly, is that our education system is just not producing the kind of people this economy needs. It is obsessed with employability, rather than the ability to create employment. I don't know what the solution is, I am not an expert. But I can say emphatically that our education system is missing the mark totally.

Finally, this is the challenge I want to pose to my fellow South African entrepreneurs in general, but my black brothers and sisters especially: we need to embrace Peter Thiel's principle of Zero to One. He says there are two ways of approaching a venture: taking that which is known and trying to improve it, or getting better at doing an old thing: that is one to N. Then there's a second way of moving from that which is known and creating something new, something wow! That is zero to one. We, as black entrepreneurs, now need to move to that space: zero to one, people!

SECTION 5

THE WAY FORWARD

Chapter Eleven

Born into black enterprise

Just a few years after apartheid became the official policy of the South African government, and apartheid laws were rolled out across the country with almost religious fervour by its architects, a strapping young man called Phillip Madi, like many others, left a desolate rural community in today's Mpumalanga area of Standerton to seek his fortune amidst the glittering lights of Johannesburg. The most attractive part of Johannesburg at that time was a vibrant area known as Sophiatown, a hipster's (and, indeed, even a gangster's) paradise. Underpinned by a multilingual, multi-ethnic, multi-racial character, it was a hotbed of fashion, culture and intellectualism, and all things chic. Its nonchalant, exuberant culture seemed to make it an island of racial normality within a vast sea of racial abnormality.

No sooner had Phillip arrived in Sophiatown, than he learnt that the area was about to be demolished to make way for a white residential suburb! Sophiatown was regarded as an eyesore by the then newly installed apartheid regime, and its very existence seemed to be sticking out a defiant tongue at the overzealous government. Everything about Sophiatown – from its urbane fashionistas of all races and hues, its budding intellectuals and idealists, its cosmopolitan music (mostly influenced by jazz from the US), its irreverent gangsters with their flashy cars – was incongruous with the apartheid tsunami heading its way. So it happened, almost inevitably, that all too soon its residents were forcibly removed into a newly constructed township known as Meadowlands, about 30 km away, while Sophiatown itself was renamed Triomf [Afrikaans for Triumph] in celebration of the success of the forced removal.

This was a major blow to an ambitious young man who had come all the way from Standerton to make his fortune in the city of gold. The very area which he had been told was a hotbed of opportunities, was suddenly being demolished. More importantly, he had promised his siblings back in Standerton that as soon as he was settled and established, he would be calling on them to join him in this vibrant community. At the drop of a hat, the apartheid government had virtually annihilated his dreams. But, nonetheless, like many other residents of Sophiatown, after initial resistance under the slogan "*ons dak nie, ons phola hier*" [we won't move, we'll remain here], on February 9, 1955, 2 000 policemen armed with handguns, rifles and truncheons forcefully moved the former residents to Meadowlands in Soweto. Sadly, the highly animated and resistant spirit of the residents of Sophiatown proved to be no match for the brutality of the apartheid forces. With apartheid beginning to insinuate itself into the fabric of society, the then newly installed NP leadership had decided that Sophiatown was just too close to white communities in Johannesburg – it had to go. But, more importantly, the old suburb was multi-ethnic and multiracial, which was the antithesis of the government's segregationist policies. The area also happened to be the only part of urban South Africa where blacks were entitled to obtain fully fledged freehold rights to their properties, and indeed a thriving black middle class of professionals and merchants was rising (indeed, even the serving President of the ANC at the time, Dr A.B. Xuma, lived in Sophiatown). Residents of Indian heritage were moved to Lenasia, and people of mixed race (coloured people) were moved to Eldorado Park.

No doubt, like many other residents of Sophiatown, Philip was bewildered and demoralised by this calamity. As the new residents of Meadowlands began to settle into their tiny newly constructed houses, Philip began to notice that because the area was without electricity, there was a desperate need for coal and firewood to cook with, warm homes and for other household uses. The entrepreneur in him began to innovate, realising that out of this rather traumatic and unfortunate situation there was an opportunity to make some kind of a living.

Philip hastily travelled back to his birthplace in Mpumalanga, around Witbank, where a number of coal mines were starting to spring up. He entered into agreements with a number of white coalminers who undertook to supply him with coal. Next, he identified a vacant and unused plot of land in Meadowlands, where his new supply of coal could be dumped (illegally, of course). That was the beginning of the Madi Coal Yards. Within the next three to five years, Philip became a major supplier of coal and firewood to not only Meadowlands, but also the emerging adjacent townships (later known as the South Western Townships or Soweto). These successes made Philip confident enough to invite his siblings (and later on, his parents too) to join him in Meadowlands and help him expand his enterprise. One of the siblings who relocated to Johannesburg was his youngest brother, Petrus, my father. The Madi Family Enterprises, as the business was known then, started expanding beyond the supply of coal and firewood into other business activities. My father, being the youngest, was assigned the responsibility of collecting dry-cleaning around the various townships on his bicycle, and soon their dry-cleaning business got off the ground. Later still they branched out into other enterprises, including the fledgling taxi industry. Although Philip's other siblings initially worked for him, they eventually spread their wings and became independent businesspeople in their own right – as did my father.

My father was extremely fortunate, because a few years later he met a young lady from the North West who turned out to be even more entrepreneurial than he was. My mother, Thulisile, established a catering business in Soweto that supplied school children with convenient, affordable food and beverages (bunny chow and soft drinks, amongst others). She became widely known around the schools in Soweto as 'Mom Teddy' because the most popular product she sold was a red lollipop in the shape of a teddy bear. Mom Teddy became a brand name which eventually completely dominated the schools catering industry in Soweto for close to a decade, and in the process my mother became wealthy in her own right. In 1975 the fledgling Soweto Chamber of Commerce voted her Businesswoman of the Year.

It would therefore be no exaggeration to say that I was born into enterprise. For me and my siblings this was an incredible learning experience in that, unlike many of our fellow citizens in Soweto at that time, we learnt and observed a great deal within this entrepreneurial setting. More importantly, we were learning that it was possible to live without any assistance from government, that we could be successful without being dependent on, or at the mercy of, a white person. (In fact, generally speaking, the government and whites were regarded with hostility in our world, where they were seen as the enemy!) My father used to boast in lighter moments that he may not have had much schooling, that he may not even speak English all that well, but that he could tell a white person to get lost if he wanted to. So, ironically, my siblings and I grew up in an environment where the notion of white superiority was not only irrelevant, but actually despised. All of us, including my cousins, were raised with the assumption was that as we grew older we would be working in one of the family enterprises. No one conceived of the notion of actually having to go and work for an outside firm, or having to work for a white person. In fact, working for a white person was regarded as a form of treason. I remember an incident where a cousin of mine decided to leave the family business to work for Avis, the car rental company. My poor cousin was actually viewed as a traitor and was ostracised. Eventually he rejoined the family business and all was forgiven!

I in particular was viewed as a bit of an oddball, because of my love of books. I recall numerous occasions where either my father or cousins would say sardonically: 'I wonder how that book is gonna feed him! He should be out there delivering coal or doing something like the rest of us, for God's sake!'

Of course all of us were in for the shock of our lives as we grew older and began to interact with the white world – from which we had been comfortably secluded – with its rampant apartheid brutality and its superiority complex. But the shock was even more brutal when in 1976, unrest flared up across Soweto as schoolchildren started revolting against the decision by the regime to impose the Afrikaans language as medium of instruction in black schools. Afrikaans, being the official language of the government in apartheid South Africa, was deeply resented in black communities, it being a symbol of subjugation. Its imposition in schools as a medium of instruction was therefore perceived as designed to humiliate black people. It turned out to be a step too far for the arrogant government, the proverbial final straw that broke the camel's back. So from June 16, 1976 there was widespread rioting in various parts of the township. Unfortunately, like many other forms of civil unrest, there was widespread destruction of property as well as looting. Ironically, black-owned enterprises were not necessarily exempt from such wilful damage, as my parents learnt all too painfully. Many well-established enterprises in the townships were ransacked and burnt to the ground by a criminal element which could not pass up on such a golden opportunity to loot and plunder.

My parents' enterprises did not escape this unfortunate fate. My father, being very suspicious of any activities or initiatives driven by the white establishment, did not believe in insuring his businesses or properties. Needless to say, there were no black-owned insurance companies, banks or financial institutions at that time. Black people preferred to establish their own informal alternative financial institutions like *stokvels*, burial societies, etc., that were cash based and obviously insecure. Dad's view was that insurance was essentially a scam by white people to find ways and means of milking black people of their hard-earned cash. Thus, when our family businesses were burnt to the ground and ransacked, along with those of many other businesspeople, my parents were ruined financially. They literally watched their life's work go up in flames. The same fate befell other members of our extended families who were also heavily engaged in various enterprises. This was the beginning of the end for the Madi business enterprises. Of course the irony in all of this is that it was the forward-thinking and relatively well-educated entrepreneurs in Soweto (like Richard Maponya) who were to survive these dramatic events, because they had insured their businesses and started establishing alliances with other white establishments. The defiant ones, like my parents and our extended family, met with financial ruin. My parents were subsequently reduced from business titans in Soweto to subsistence entrepreneurs – a situation which lasted pretty much for the rest of their lives.

Painful as it is to reflect on these events, there are all sorts of lessons to be learned from this, many of which are beyond the scope of this book. But for our current purposes, the key lesson is that entrepreneurship can become a culture (and, indeed, a religion) within either a family unit or even (as expanded later on in this book) a nation. We were brought up in an environment where we were taught that there was honour and glory in working for yourself and feeding your own family. Indeed, we learnt that there was deep dishonour in working for someone else (especially white people) and not being able to take care of your family. This form of cultural indoctrination was instilled in us from our infancy.

Chapter Twelve

Vuka Uzenzele! Creating and fostering an entrepreneurial culture

Many leading thinkers and entrepreneurs in South Africa have decried how, in their view, BEE has stifled the entrepreneurial culture within black communities: "BEE is killing entrepreneurship," decried business legend, Richard Maponya (*Destiny Magazine*, September 30, 2013); "Forget nationalisation and BEE, SA needs entrepreneurs," protested socio-economic commentator, Moeletsi Mbeki (*Mail & Guardian*, September 5, 2011).

The NDP

Any discussion on creating and fostering an entrepreneurial culture has to start with an acknowledgement of government's recently unveiled National Development Plan. However, it would be remiss not to recognise the fact that this is not the first such economic development plan to have emerged from the ANC government since it came to power in 1994: the RDP, under the administration of President Nelson Mandela, was more of a bottom-up approach designed to ensure community participation and leadership. It was premised on the idea that government would meet its citizenry halfway. The policy was based on mass mobilisation – at least conceptually. Needless to say, it fizzled out and was shelved, some say because of a lack of resources, others due to a lack of coordination between the respective government departments. The unfortunate legacy of the RDP programme is that it is now unfairly associated with inferior, low-cost housing projects across the country, with most homes being of such poor quality that they are literally crumbling.

In 1996, the RDP was superseded by the Growth Employment and Redistribution (Gear) (Visser, 2004) macroeconomic policy framework, which was closely associated with President Thabo Mbeki. Universally reviled by the left-wing alliance partners of the ANC, it was hailed as a triumph of neoliberal policies over the more socialistic approach of the RDP. Indeed, some argue that by sponsoring this policy framework, Mbeki made himself a mortal enemy of the left wing within the tripartite alliance.

Ten years later this policy spawned the Accelerated and Shared Growth Initiative for South Africa (Asgisa), which had as its custodian the then Deputy President, Ms Phumzile Mlambo-Ngcuka. The initiative was primarily designed to enhance the country's growth performance to an average of 4.5 per cent from 2006 to 2009, to six per cent from 2010 to 2014, and to halve unemployment and poverty by 2014. This initiative was unfortunately conceptualised and effected at the wrong time, however noble and viable its intentions may have been. The forces against President Mbeki had gathered enough momentum to eventually displace him two years later. In addition to being launched in a rather poisoned environment, the policy also seems to have suffered an identity crisis.

Indeed, critic Steven Friedman contended that it was not a policy at all but rather a list of projects designed to achieve stated objectives (*Business in Africa Magazine*, 2006).

In 2013, the ANC government under the leadership of President Jacob Zuma introduced the NDP to South Africa. Intended to be the galvanising point for stimulating growth and development in the country, the NDP began by envisioning what South Africa would look like in the year 2030. It was an elegantly crafted and well-thought-out plan that balanced soaring political ambition and poetic imagery with hard-core economic objectives. The document is punctuated by an inspiring preamble. It aims to fulfil its objectives of reducing poverty and inequality in South Africa by 2030 through job creation, a more equitable distribution of wealth, and improved education.

It is clear from the above that whatever the criticisms levelled against the South African government, failure to *produce policy* would certainly not be one. In fact, it is fairly commonplace to hear commentators stating that in South Africa the production of plans and policies is a national pastime. South Africa's business federation, Busa, even went so far as to state:

> There is a strong feeling in the business community that too many previous commitments to the well-intentioned policies such as RDP [Reconstruction and Development Programme], Gear [Growth, Employment and Redistribution], GDS [Growth and Development Summit], ASGISA and JIPSA (Joint Initiative on Priority Skills Acquisition) have led to too much talk and little action. (Busa, 2010)

What is interesting in respect of these policies, however, is that none of them placed entrepreneurship at the core. They generally proceeded from the premise that government would put together a policy or programme and would put resources at the disposal of various communities. The policies appeared to convey the message that government is the Alpha and Omega of development, and that is where, in my view, the challenge truly lies in resolving South Africa's major social and economic problems. The key challenge is this: How do we create a society brimming with entrepreneurial citizens and a government approach that almost dares its citizenry to stand up and be counted?

In a paper by Shankha Chakraborty, Jon C. Thompson and Etienne B. Yehoue (2015, p. 1), the authors argue that "differences in economic development across countries can be explained by a culture of entrepreneurship". They add that generally, in developing countries, people choose between risky entrepreneurship and low-risk employment. They identify a challenge that generally exists in societies that have been subjected to exploitative colonialism, where there tends to be a strong culture of anti-capitalism which can inhibit the development of an entrepreneurial culture. (Interestingly, our entrepreneur extraordinaire, Herman Mashaba, in his latest book, *Capitalist crusader* [2015]. argues that we as black people grew up equating apartheid with capitalism and believing both systems are designed to exploit the poor. We consequently continue to be suspicious, on a subconscious level, of capitalism as an adjunct of apartheid.)

That is why it is incumbent on our government to begin to preach the gospel of entrepreneurship, almost as Deng Xiaoping did in China when he assumed the presidency after the death of Chairman Mao. Indeed, he went so far as to say that to be rich is glorious, and that there is no nobility in poverty. With these comments he completely freed the Chinese people from the shackles of an anti-enterprise culture, and ushered in the vibrant and entrepreneurial culture we all see and admire today.

Furthermore, the role of government in encouraging and developing this culture is captured in a document published by Ernst & Young (EY), the *EYG20 Entrepreneurship Barometer* (2013). In that document, EY argue for the following three key activities to be led by government:

1 **Remove the stigma of failure**
   Business is inherently risky, and countries should therefore not allow values and practices that penalise risk-takers if they fail. Often, repeat entrepreneurs who have failed before, have higher rates of success

than first-time entrepreneurs. Cultures that show gratitude to failed entrepreneurs instead of condemnation, breed more entrepreneurs.

Even bankruptcy laws, therefore, must strike the right balance between protecting creditors' interests and offering entrepreneurs a second chance. Recent changes in South African and company law have to be commended because they have introduced such supportive mechanisms as business rescue, the equivalent of Chapter 11 bankruptcy filing in the US.

2   Open the door to excluded talent

This part becomes very interesting, because the various black advancement programmes that have been introduced in South Africa – be they AA or BEE – are all essentially designed to ensure that previously excluded talent is unleashed to foster growth and development in South Africa. The EY study continues: "Women, young people and immigrants can make a huge contribution, yet today they are often under-represented in the entrepreneurial community. Supporting these groups into entrepreneurship can broaden the entrepreneurial base and accelerate success." I would argue that as a country, we are woefully inadequate in so far as this aspect is concerned. Inherent in this limitation is the tendency – particularly amongst formerly advantaged South Africans – to view programmes designed to include previously excluded talent as a zero-sum game. The assumption is that it is impossible to speak of BEE which does not automatically lead to white economic disempowerment. This is a fallacious argument that almost defies logic, because it presupposes that the economic empowerment of blacks excludes white economic empowerment. Or, put differently, it assumes a stagnant economic pie which shows no signs of growth. Naturally, if the pie is not growing bigger, but is in effect shrinking, then the economic empowerment of one specific sector of our community will automatically lead to the disempowerment of another. Surely one must virtually be a morbid pessimist to conclude that South Africa's economy is destined to shrink in perpetuity. One can only assume that this is yet another example of the damage apartheid inflicted on our national psyche, in that it is almost impossible for us to conceive of a situation where there is empowerment for all.

3   Showcase successes

It is vital for government to encourage local role models to participate in events and campaigns that helps to inspire a new generation of entrepreneurial talent. Businesses should emphasise the social benefits of entrepreneurship – from job creation through to innovation and broader economic growth. For all intents and purposes, this becomes an evangelical exercise which entails preaching the gospel of enterprise almost in the same way as it was done in China post-Mao.

The EY study concludes by addressing entrepreneurs generally, as well as corporations:

> Entrepreneurs must (a) share their success story and (b) help the next generation of entrepreneurs;
> Corporations must (a) sponsor incubators and accelerators and (b) recognise the contributions and success of entrepreneurs.

The last point on corporations becomes even more significant if one considers the history of South Africa. Local corporations do not just have a responsibility to help enterprises so as to score points to meet their BBBEE targets, but they need to go the extra mile and become more proactive in helping budding entrepreneurs to succeed – especially those from disadvantaged communities. Mentorship programmes, collaboration, social capital and joint ventures are all avenues that can be pursued in this regard.

Vuka Uzenzele [Stand up and become enterprising!] The time for a national culture of entrepreneurship has come. As indicated earlier, the key learning gleaned since childhood, is that entrepreneurship can become a national culture if it spreads from an individual to a family unit. My contention is that it is possible for a government, for instance, to instil amongst its citizens a culture (almost a gospel) that confirms: Working for yourself is glorious. One can draw inspiration from China in this regard, a country where entrepreneurship is virtually a religion, spreading the message that individuals should 'stand up and do something for themselves'. Naturally this was a dramatic and fundamental departure from the preceding, staunch, state-driven gospel of communism and its hatred of free private enterprise. China's economic policy u-turn was even more dramatic than would be the case here in South Africa, given the fervour with which communism was preached to the Chinese. One could say this sea-change was almost akin to the Pope renouncing Christianity. It took a Herculean effort and great courage on the part of China's new leadership to make such a dramatic turnabout. This goes to prove, *beyond any doubt*, that it is possible for a government to change direction on its anti-enterprise stance and official policy, so as to unleash its people's creative spirit and vibrancy. And in the case of South Africa, it will not be that dramatic a change, as this country's espoused economic policy has never been anti-private enterprise – at least, on paper. It will simply be a matter of branching off in the right direction, rather than doing a complete u-turn. All that is required is for our politicians to have the courage of their convictions and begin to say to people: *Vuka Uzenzele!*, instead of preaching the same message of undertaking to create *x* million jobs (all targets which have been consistently missed anyway!), promising to build *x* number of houses, pressuring big business to hand over shares .... Such promises have created expectations and have instilled a culture where people sit around waiting for things to fall into their laps, instead of being enterprising themselves. When such promises are consistently not being met, people lose patience, and become angry and resentful. Our people are not stupid, they just need to be told the truth, rather than being appeased with flowery and hallucinatory promises and platitudes. The time has come for our leaders to look beyond the popularity polls, populist sloganeering, vacuous platitudes and the ambition to win the next election. To be continuously making promises that, possibly deep down in their hearts our leaders know will never be fulfilled, is like slowly fanning a fire that will one day consume us all.

That is why many critics of BEE in particular, people like the hugely successful and pioneering black cosmetics industrialist, Herman Mashaba (as you have read in his own words, earlier on in this book), find that it has been almost disempowering in its character, in that citizens expect an infusion of resources either from established business or from government. In this instance, BEE ironically becomes black economic disempowerment.

The time has come to change the message which is put out there.

Chapter Thirteen

From BEE to BEN

The new paradigm

At this point it may sound as if I am beginning to split hairs or play with words. However, this is probably the most crucial part of the book, as it seeks to shift the debate from its current impasse into a new, dynamic phase. The distinction between economic empowerment and economic enablement is critical both at a conceptual and an implementation level. It requires a paradigm shift.

Let us start by defining what empowerment means: empowerment is widely understood as the act of giving power or authority to someone; authorising a specific course of action by legal or official means. Virtually all dictionary definitions contain two words, almost without exception: 'authority' and 'official'. The irony in these two words is that they presuppose a situation in which a beneficiary of economic empowerment almost has to wait for official direction, that official nod or authorisation to proceed – obviously in addition to receiving the necessary resources. In a way, the beneficiary is almost disempowered until the aforementioned 'tools' or 'permissions' are put at his/her disposal. Empowerment (or any activity, for that matter) does not happen until there has been some authorisation from 'higher up' the chain of command. Many people argue that this has been the major flaw of BEE so far. Indeed, some would argue that the official programmes that have been implemented since the advent of democracy, that have been geared towards improving the lives of disadvantaged citizens (like the RDP, Gear, Jipsa, Asgisa), have all revolved around the principle that government would do something, and that the people would benefit from that which government did. So, all the citizens had to do was to sit and wait for official sanction and the official implementation of a programme from which they would – almost passively – reap the benefits. Even at private sector level, this has generally been the approach, especially in the initial phase of empowerment which was mainly ownership-focused. This explains why most transactions were vendor (i.e., company) financed or at least vendor-guaranteed, usually at prohibitive cost. On many occasions this led to the unravelling of transactions when markets turned, as they invariably do. One can therefore safely conclude that the traditional version of BEE has, in essence, been disempowering in nature.

That is why the time has come for a new approach to ensuring that blacks begin to participate fully in the economy of this country. The time has come for a new type of BEE: Black Economic Enablement. The *Oxford dictionary* defines enablement as: to give (someone) the ability or means to do something. It is further defined as: to make possible or easy. Most definitions of enablement do not carry the two phrases given in the above definition (i.e., 'official' and 'authority'), therefore it can be argued that black economic enablement will create an environment in which it is easy and possible for black people to participate in meaningful economic activity, without waiting for official authority or sanction. (For convenience, I refer to the traditional approach using the commonly used acronym BEE, while for this new approach I am espousing the use of the acronym BEN).

While traditional BEE has been a passive process in which blacks become objects of largess, BEN puts them on the active side of things. All that the authorities or private sector organisations need do is to make it possible or easy to engage in economic activity. The flip-side of this, of course, is that if an 'empowerment' transaction does not lead to beneficiaries being actively involved in value-adding economic activity (as has been the case with traditional BEE, on many occasions), then it does not cut it as a genuinely empowering initiative in terms of BEN.

Unlike the traditional BEE approach which says that 'this is what we have for you', 'we will help you get loans for this BEE deal' or 'we will build basic houses for you', the BEN approach is: 'What do you need to be economically active and self-sustainable so that you can, in the fullness of time, have the means to buy yourself a house or a tranche of shares, or whatever you require?' 'Instead of being a recipient of our [the state's] generosity, what can we do to make an entrepreneur out of you?'

It is important at this stage to refine what I mean by 'entrepreneur'. The tradition is to assume that the word implies a businessperson. If that becomes the accepted definition, then some could argue that not every South African has the desire or the aptitude to become a businessperson. But this is the narrow (and, dare I say, erroneous) definition of an entrepreneur. Once more, let's go back to the dictionary to extract the original meaning of the word. My interpretation of the *Oxford dictionary* definition is that an entrepreneur sets up a business (or several businesses) and takes on financial risks in the hope of turning a profit.

For me, this is where some confusion arises, namely in creating a context and paradigm that equate an entrepreneur with a for-profit motive and venture. And, correctly, not everyone has the stomach or the inclination to want to be in business. I am more comfortable with this definition of an entrepreneur from businessdictionary.com: someone who exercises initiative by organising a venture to benefit from an opportunity and, as the decision maker, decides what, how, and how much of a good or service will be produced.

As can be discerned from the above definition, there is no mention here of seeking to make a profit. A businessman or businesswoman does business [based] on what is possible, an entrepreneur on what is impossible, according to serial entrepreneur and former CEO of MySQL and Eucalyptus, Marten Mickos.

In my view, we need to migrate from the narrow definition of an entrepreneur to a broader one. I believe that anyone who stands up to do something, to solve a problem instead of sitting back and waiting for a solution from above, is an entrepreneur. That problem could be a leaking roof in his own (or a neighbour's) house, a collapsed fence at a local clinic or unreliable mail delivery. The motive may be profit, or it may not – it does not matter. What matters is that the individual stands up and tackles the challenge. It is true that many businesses are born this way, and many a staggering fortune has been built in the process. But it all starts with someone tackling his/her frustration with a persistent problem or challenge. After all, there is an old saying that necessity is the mother of invention. In my book, Louis Pasteur, Bill Gates, Aliko Dangote and Nelson Mandela are all entrepreneurs, because they stepped up to the plate and confronted challenging situations, instead of being overwhelmed by them.

According to economist, Joseph Alois Schumpeter (1883–1950), entrepreneurs are not necessarily motivated by profit, but regard it as a standard for measuring achievement or the success of their endeavour. In their studies, Backhaus and Schumpeter (2003) discovered that entrepreneurial individuals displayed the following traits:

- Self-reliance
- High levels of optimism (otherwise they would just sit down and moan and groan)
- They relish challenges, rather than being intimidated by them (Backhaus and Schumpeter, 2003, p. 356).

After all, what do we mean when we compliment someone by saying: 'That is very enterprising of you!' Certainly we are not saying: 'Wow, you've made yourself and all of us a boot-load of money!' What we mean is: 'You have resolutely and successfully overcome this particular challenge.' Ironically, the very same *Oxford dictionary* (http://www.oxforddictionaries.com/) that defines an entrepreneur as a businessperson, defines 'enterprising' as 'showing initiative and resourcefulness'!

For me, this is the perfect definition of an entrepreneur: someone who shows initiative and resourcefulness (thank you, *Oxford dictionary*, for correcting yourself!), and is not just a businessperson. And this is absolutely critical, because my advocating a migration from BEE to BEN is designed to facilitate the creation of an environment in which ordinary South Africans in general, and blacks in particular, can unleash their initiative and resourcefulness. In other words, they can be enterprising (without necessarily being entrepreneurs, as traditionally defined).

At a government policy level, within the paradigm of BEN, the idea would be to ensure that all regulations and resources are designed to ensure that it becomes both *easy and possible* for South Africans in general and black people in particular (given the numerous hurdles deliberately put in place by apartheid legislation, as explained in detail earlier) to enter into economic activity, at the level of their choice (be it industrial, retail or street level). Former trade unionist and member of the cabinet in the Mandela administration, Jay Naidoo, lamented what he calls "the demobilisation of the people" post-democracy. He noted that most of the programmes implemented in the new South Africa have had the effect of demobilising the masses and making people wait for programmes to trickle down from the authorities. This is in stark contrast to what happened during the anti-apartheid struggle, when people were galvanised and mobilised to take action. But, regrettably, the citizens of this country have generally been encouraged to sit and wait especially for lavish (and at times outlandish) election promises to materialise. And, of course, they are becoming restive and frustrated, fed up with waiting, and are instead resorting to violent street protests. "This is what sparks the fury, the anger that is driving much of the close to 13 000 service delivery protests each year" (Naidoo, 2014).

As indicated earlier, due to such unsavoury practices as 'tenderpreneurship', over the past few years BEE has assumed connotations of being given something for one's own benefit on the one hand, or being engaged in a corrupt and collusive effort as a result of one's political connections on the other. The implication is that some great benefit or gift is granted to an individual, usually without the recipient being deserving of such. Needless to say, the connotation of the word 'enablement' is very different. All that it implies is that an environment has been created for an individual to be able to use his/her own talent and initiative to improve their circumstances. Thus, whatever benefit that individual secures in the process, is fully deserved.

I therefore advocate that the national discourse – and, indeed, even the paradigm – shift from that of BEE to BEN. It is often said that there is great power in words, so if we continue to spread the gospel of empowerment, and people continue to wait for official sanction or authority, no growth or development will take place. Instead, it will lead to unmet expectations, anger and frustration. Ultimately, the situation will implode (see above for concerns about a Mzansi Spring). However, if we begin to spread the gospel of an environment in which people understand that they need to get up and do something, and that those with resources will help them to achieve their hopes and dreams, then it becomes a different ball game altogether.

The 80/20 principle

Another way of illustrating the essence of BEN, as contrasted to BEE, is as follows: no parents can argue that they conferred academic qualifications on their children. As parents, they simply provided the means, created a conducive environment and put in place support mechanisms for their children to secure those qualifications. In effect, the children themselves have had to do 80 per cent of the work, while the parents contributed the 20 per cent (by providing the necessary resources). Parents can claim credit for having seen to their children's educational 'enablement'. Once the children have secured those qualifications, *as a result of their own hard work*, how they utilise those qualifications in the course of their lives is, by and large, in their own hands. And that should apply to black economic enablement as well.

Regrettably, BEE is perceived as being the direct opposite of this situation, with the widely held belief that many beneficiaries are not deserving of their good fortune: 80 per cent of the work was done for them, and they only brought 20 per cent to the table, i.e., by having the 'correct' skin colour or by being politically connected. In the foreword to *Black economic empowerment in the new South Africa – the rights and wrongs*, Dr Reuel Khoza (1997, xii) states: "Often we bring no more to the table than the pedigree of our blackness and expect this to do the magic for us. History will tell you whether our brand of alchemy is more effective than of those that went before us."

In 2015, former Governor of the Reserve Bank, Tito Mboweni, went so far as to say that some established companies tend to bring in black partners as mere "door openers" for government contracts, i.e., they simply manage company relations with the powers-that-be, rather than participating meaningfully and equally as commercial partners. Mboweni stated: "I look at some of my black business people out there, they are actually not running businesses. You don't know how the mine is running, you are not involved, nothing. All you do is get a dividend. That's all and I think it's a disgrace" (*Financial Mail*, June 8, 2015, p. 1).

It can therefore be argued that some individuals have indeed paraded the colour of their skin (or their political connections) as a prime qualification for being empowered. Indeed, it has been the 80/20 principle in reverse; they only had to bring 20 per cent to the table (their blackness and, on certain occasions, political connections), while 80 per cent of the value came from their (white) partners. This is obviously unsustainable. That is why BEE on its own appears not to have generated much additional economic value for society as a whole, other than conferring staggering fortunes on a few select individuals. One would be hard pressed to point out new factories that have arisen or new jobs that have been created thanks to traditional BEE programmes.

The challenge that we now face as a nation is to create added value for the economy, as well as new jobs. BEE (or BEN, as I am now advocating) has to be an integral part of economic growth in this country. For as long as BEE does not generate new value for the economy or create job opportunities, we are stuck in a rut. This is what will distinguish BEN from BEE: enablement will generate and create greater value for the economy and begin to add value, while in the process creating much-needed jobs. How so? Because it will focus on fostering an enterprising spirit and culture, as stated earlier. We currently have a rather bizarre situation where BEE at times appears to work against economic growth and job creation. It appears to have, by and large, created rather strange breeds of entrepreneurs who do not add much value to the economic base, but in fact rather seem to be extracting value. We need to move beyond this. We need to reach a stage where the development of entrepreneurs (as I have defined them broadly) and the creation of an enterprising culture become the core principles of black economic advancement. *Vuka Uzenzele!* should be the rousing war cry of economic liberation for black people.

At the core of this principle is the age-old adage of teaching a man how to fish, instead of supplying him with fish. The trend thus far in traditional BEE transactions has been geared towards giving to people, instead of teaching them how to turn their aspirations into reality. BEN, on the other hand, will be based on the principle that there may not be much fish available at this stage to give to all and sundry, but that the skills, resources and support mechanisms will be made available for people to learn how to fish so that they can thus sustain themselves for the rest of their lives. Instead of those with the resources (be they government or the private sector) saying: 'We have plenty of fish in our bag', the new language will be: 'We don't have much fish in our bag, but we will impart the necessary skills to you. By the time we move on from here, you will have acquired all the skills and resources you need to be able to fish for yourself for the rest of your life.'

In essence, what I propose is that, using the current weighting of broad-based BEE scores, that what we regard as 'enterprise development' must now constitute 80 per cent of the entire scorecard that an organisation completes, period. The other elements must all be comprised of the remaining 20 per cent.

To again quote Dr Khoza (1997, p. xii): "Not enough attention is being paid to the planting of the acorns to grow the mighty oak trees of tomorrow. To think of oak trees is to forego immediate results and the instant gratification that comes with it in the form of income, status and power. To think of oak trees is to think of wealth creation; to cultivate businesses that will survive at least 3 to 4 generations from today."

Anthea Jeffery's Economic Empowerment for the Disadvantaged (EED)

In her recently published book, *BEE – helping or hurting?* (2014), Jeffery contends that traditional BEE has been racial in character. It was designed to help black people who are disadvantaged, and black people only. She therefore poses the question: What about disadvantaged people who are not black? Jeffery's suggestion is that BEE programmes must assume a non-racial character, in that the litmus test must be economic background. She proposes that if someone comes from an economically deprived background, regardless of whether they are black or white, they must qualify for an economic empowerment programme in one form or another. In this respect, Jeffery proposes EED as a BEE alternative. This innovative approach, of empowering the disadvantaged, indeed deserves serious consideration. Her contention (Jeffery, 2014) is that it will present the following advantages, namely

- make rapid economic growth, rather than redistribution, the overriding policy priority;

- re-orient labour laws to help the jobless gain access to employment;

- increase community control over schools, and give parents state-funded education vouchers.

- give school leavers state-funded vouchers for university or technical education at the institutions of their choice;

- sell off floundering SOEs to the private sector to help overcome the electricity crisis, for instance;

- promote entrepreneurship via a venture capital fund with monies from both the state and the private sector.

There is no doubt that Jeffery has carefully considered this subject, but her approach ignores the fundamental reality which obtains in South Africa today, namely that poverty has a distinct colour. On May 29, 1998, President Mbeki made a statement that deeply disturbed the country during a debate in parliament. He said:

> We therefore make bold to say that South Africa is a country of two nations. One of these nations is white, relatively prosperous, regardless of gender or geographic dispersal. It has ready access to a developed economic, physical, educational, communication and other infrastructure... The second and larger nation of South Africa is black and poor, with the worst affected being women in the rural areas, the black rural population in general and the disabled. This (black) nation lives under conditions of a grossly underdeveloped economic, physical, educational, communication and other infrastructure. It has virtually no possibility to exercise what in reality amounts to a theoretical right to equal opportunity, with that right being equal within this black nation only to the extent that it is equally incapable of realisation. (Mbeki, 1998)

If one studies current statistics, 17 years after this statement was made, it would appear that there has hardly been any meaningful change. In January 2013, Oxfam announced for the very first time that South Africa was the most unequal nation on earth (Oxfam media briefing, January 18, 2013). South Africa has largely retained this dubious honour ever since. At the time of writing, Oxfam had not only confirmed its position, but added the following:

> South Africa has one of the highest official unemployment rates in the world (25%) and is one of the most unequal countries, with a Gini coefficient of 0.69. The wealthiest 4% of households receive 32% of total income while 66% of households receive only 21% of all income.

Over half of South Africans live below the national poverty line and more than 10% live in extreme poverty, on less than $1.25 (R15.85) per day. (Oxfam, 2015)

Of course all the statistics retain a very strong racial character. In its March 2014 report on the 'State of poverty and its manifestation in the nine provinces of South Africa', the National Development Agency (NDA) presented this table that reflects the racial character of poverty in this country:

Table 2: Poverty by province and race in South Africa

Presenting poverty by race indicates that poverty still remains a racial issue in South Africa. Black South Africans account for the highest poverty in South Africa and among the poorest provinces. The coloureds have the second highest poverty in South Africa and among the poorest provinces. Poverty does not seem to be an issue among the Indians and whites.

	Poverty incidence				Poverty intensity				Poverty severity			
	Afr	col	Ind	Wh	Afr	col	Ind	wh	Afr	col	Ind	wh
KwaZulu Natal	0.33	0.13	0.01	0.00	0.11	0.04	0.00	0.00	0.05	0.02	0.00	0.00
Eastern Cape	0.32	0.19	0.00	0.00	0.11	0.05	0.00	0.00	0.05	0.02	0.00	0.00
Limpopo	0.32	0.33	0.00	0.01	0.12	0.10	0.00	0.00	0.06	0.03	0.00	0.00
Northern Cape	0.28	0.28	0.00	0.01	0.10	0.09	0.00	0.00	0.04	0.04	0.00	0.00
North West	0.27	0.23	0.00	0.01	0.09	0.08	0.00	0.00	0.04	0.04	0.00	0.00
National	**0.26**	**0.15**	**0.01**	**0.00**	**0.09**	**0.04**	**0.00**	**0.00**	**0.04**	**0.02**	**0.00**	**0.00**
Mpumalanga	0.25	0.00	0.10	0.00	0.08	0.00	0.05	0.00	0.04	0.00	0.02	0.00
Free State	0.21	0.14	0.00	0.00	0.07	0.04	0.00	0.00	0.03	0.02	0.00	0.00
Western Cape	0.13	0.11	0.00	0.00	0.03	0.03	0.00	0.00	0.01	0.01	0.00	0.00
Gauteng	0.13	0.03	0.00	0.00	0.04	0.01	0.00	0.00	0.02	0.00	0.00	0.00

KwaZulu-Natal has the highest poverty among blacks (33%), followed by Eastern Cape (32%) and Limpopo (32%). Northern Cape and North West also have significantly high populations of black poor (28% and 27%). Highest poverty among the coloureds is in Limpopo (33%). Compared to the national average of 15%, coloured poverty in Eastern Cape and KZN is not too high (19% and 13% respectively). Besides Limpopo, other provinces that exhibit high poverty among the coloureds are Northern Cape (28%) and North West (23%).

Source: NDA (March, 2014).

Going back therefore to Jeffery's proposal of a colour-blind EED programme, in my view this approach is fundamentally flawed, in that

1   one cannot seek to address the legacy of race-based, deliberate and legally enforced disempowerment by being colour blind. In any case, many studies (including the abovementioned) have proven that the majority of white people are born into an environment of economic privilege, while the average black person is born into an environment of economic disempowerment;

2   more importantly, Jeffery's approach is still one of 'empowerment', not enablement. The only difference this time around would be that, instead of those beneficiaries being exclusively black, white beneficiaries would be included. This approach, as I have stated earlier, does not adequately address the challenges facing our nation. In other words, people are still going to have things done for them.

And perceptions of widespread disparities in income, mainly based on race, are very strong throughout the country. Noting this, the editor of the mainly pro-business and usually conservative *Business Day*, Songezo Zibi, recently said:

> In a country in which race determined (and still does) your station in life, the colour of who makes money matters a great deal. It particularly does to those who do not make money or get involved in big business deals. Exclusion makes you note carefully who's having fun inside the tent.... In SA, those at the centre of the economic action are white men, with a smattering of black men, white women and virtually no black women. The colour of who makes money, of course, doesn't particularly matter to those enjoying the fruits of the action... (Business Day Live, 2015)

Ultimately, teaching people how to fish rather than delivering fish to them, regardless of the colour of their skin, will carry greater and longer-lasting prospects for success.

The roadmap to BEN

Migrating from the concept of empowerment to that of enablement is not just a play on words, as indicated earlier. It requires a change in approach, mindset, policy framework and outlook. Indeed, I argue that it is a complete paradigm shift. To illustrate this point further, and to clarify the key distinctions between the two approaches, Table 3 highlights the distinguishing features of each approach.

Table 3: The distinction between empowerment and enablement

EMPOWERMENT	ENABLEMENT
• There's a 'giver' and a 'taker' – unequal relationship	• The parties are 'sharers' of equal value – balanced relationship
• Creates rent-seekers	• Creates entrepreneurs
• It gives fish	• It enables people to be fishers themselves
• Perceived as punitive or penance	• Perceived as constructive and patriotic
• Charity guilt driven	• Opportunity-creation driven
• Reminiscent of the old relationship between Africa and the world – donors and receivers	• In line with the new relationship between Africa and the world – more *trade* less *aid*
• Likely to be an imposed relationship	• Relationship of 'willing partners'
• It is an event – BEE transaction, then wait for dividends	• It is a process – ongoing relationship of mutual learning and sharing
• May be opportunistic	• It is genuine and based on good faith
• Fosters a 'redistribution' mindset	• Fosters an entrepreneurial culture
• Prone to corruption and crony capitalism	• Broad-based and transparent
• Only engages the already successful and politically connected	• Likely to engage the unemployed and marginalised
• Has a distinct existence from job creation and economic growth	• Firmly located within the job creation and economic growth agenda
• Based on power dynamics, with the risk that 'power corrupts' those who have it	• Based on nation-building, mutual assistance mindset, not power dynamics
• BEE – perpetual inequality	• BEN – reverse inequality

Now that we have all met our new friend, BEN, it is time to discuss how to ensure that we have a meaningful working relationship with BEN. In other words, how do we get black economic enablement off the ground? What does such a roadmap look like? What is the plan of action? It is time to chart the way forward on how to go about implementing not only a culture, but also a programme of enablement, in our endeavour to include black people in serious economic activity in South Africa. It is crucial to point out that this approach is not just based on creating black moguls, but is designed to be as widely inclusive as possible, and to ensure that there is a broader sense of ownership of such a process – something which is different from the current scenario, where the perception is that BEE is useful and relevant only to a select few. Perhaps, more fundamentally, the key approach to enablement is that it is not a short-term 'overnight riches' kind of scenario. It entails a long, slow slog; it is a long-term process where ultimately the results may take longer to surface, but they will also have longer-lasting implications, which is fundamentally different from the hit-and-run approach of empowerment. Note that while this approach has a long-term focus, it will actually engage all the participants throughout its duration, unlike the traditional empowerment approach where parties rarely meet, and barely see each other unless there are board meetings or the black players are called upon to activate their political networks. Therefore, it is a process that, despite taking longer to show results, will keep all parties engaged throughout, by ensuring a state of continuous, mutual education and sharing.

The best way to capture the essence of ENABLEMENT as a distinct approach and process, is to convert the word itself into an acronym. Here goes:

- **E is for Enterprise (and entrepreneurial) development and for engagement!**

As stated earlier, there is really no empowerment that truly happens when, at the end of the process, absolutely no value has been added to the economy of the country. Such a process becomes extractive, rather than beneficial. And, unfortunately, that has been the case with traditional BEE. Going forward, we need to locate enterprise development and the creation of a new pool of entrepreneurs at the heart of the process.

An earlier section in this book outlines my views on what being an entrepreneur should entail, as well as the need to create an environment that not only enables enterprise, but preaches it as a virtue and glorifies it with the same fervour and enthusiasm as Deng Xiaoping did in China.

Once more, I argue that our approach should be that if an initiative does not have enterprise development as a key component, it does not constitute genuine empowerment. I argue further that from a BBBEE scoring point of view, 80 per cent of the credits should be allocated to enterprise development, with the other components making up the remaining 20 per cent. In any case, there are two globally accepted economic truisms that support this approach:

1. Since the 80s, employment has been generated by small, highly entrepreneurial fledgling operations, rather than established multinationals. In fact, over the past few decades, big companies have been consistent in one thing and one thing alone: they are almost always shedding jobs, while small entrepreneurial operations are almost always creating jobs (particularly if there is sufficient labour market flexibility. Current labour laws in South Africa are unfortunately almost hostile to small business development. Entrepreneur Herman Mashaba and the FMF have been vocal about this point, and the matter needs to be settled sooner rather than later).

2. Small, fledgling organisations need bigger established companies for initial support and sustainability. An apt analogy to use here, is that of a big shark (the big company) sustaining a shoal of small fish swimming alongside it. This model has been successful almost everywhere it has been followed, be it in Asia, the Western world or the Americas.

In conclusion, the priority pressure question to established big business should no longer be: 'What is the extent of your black shareholding?' (in accordance with the traditional BEE paradigm). Rather, it should be: 'What is the extent of your black enterprise development?'

Having observed the processes that are designed to ensure black economic advancement over the past two decades, from the days of the RDP, through Gear, Asgisa and Jipsa, I have always been dismayed by the low level of engagement between those parties with the resources, and the supposed beneficiaries of these processes. The approach traditionally has been from those with resources (be they government agencies or established corporates) that 'We have a plan for you. Sit down and listen to what we have to tell you.' Indeed, on many occasions a high degree of official arrogance on the part of those with the resources was evident, as if to say: 'Now that we have the resources and you don't, we have value to put on the table and you have nothing to bring to the table.' Unfortunately this has created a situation which saw many well-intentioned programmes eventually collapsing, because people on the ground were not fully engaged – they lacked a sense of ownership of the programme. Therefore, before an organisation in the private or public sector embarks on a programme designed to improve people's lives, economically speaking, it first has to engage with them, rather than swooping in and imposing directives on them.

Similarly, in private sector BEE tie-ups, the tendency (or the perception, at least) has been that these are forced marriages rather than voluntary collaborations. I know of many instances where a white corporate felt that the only way to secure a particular business deal, either from government or an SOE, was to link up with a particular group or an individual who would be politically acceptable to the powers-that-be. On the opposite end of the scale, I am also familiar with situations where an established white business proceeded to hastily dump its former partner, for no longer being 'politically palatable' to the powers-that-be.

In other words, instead of these relationships being happy ones, where the parties first 'got engaged' before eventually entering into 'a full marriage', there has been widespread enforced relations. Even Africa's richest man, the Nigerian businessman, Aliko Dangote, recently decried this tendency: "If I want to invest and then I am forced into a marriage with someone who does not have the same appetite as me, or who does not have the equity behind them, then we have a problem. I will move my capital elsewhere in the world" (Vecchiatto, 2013).

Therefore, to ensure the sustainability of any relationship between those who empower and those who are empowered, it is important that they not meet for the first time 'at the altar'. First establish a feeling of mutual respect and consent.

- **N is for Numbers**

What we mean here, is that the process of engagement (mentioned above) has to be as inclusive as possible. It has to include numbers. On many occasions these programmes have grinded to a halt because they were not as widely consultative as possible, only being confined to a very select few. In other words, they were pretty poor when it came to numbers. Naturally, the approach would not be to prioritise quantity over quality, but there have been many occasions where the process of consulting widely was seen by business (and, indeed, government) as cumbersome and complicated. The inclination then was to consult as few people as possible, before proceeding with implementation. What this approach does is to create the illusion of a speedy implementation of programmes, but it ends up excluding a large number of people who have to watch from a distance, disillusioned and dismayed at whatever is unfolding before their very eyes. Again, prudence would need to be exercised in determining the extent to which consultation has to happen and the number of stakeholders that need to be included in the process. However, the main point here is that if the engagement is confined to a select few, it is a recipe for medium- to long-term disaster.

Another dimension to this element is the need to worry about the fact that traditional BEE has really benefited only a select few. Uncomfortable and painful as it may be to admit, it is factually true. I would argue that one of the reasons why traditional BEE is at times viewed with scorn and hostility by many black communities, is because the beneficiaries have been the same faces over and over again. Indeed, certain high-profile individuals were starting to be seen as the 'owners' of this process, to the exclusion of multitudes of disadvantaged people. In my view, if BEE over the past two decades had created ten million 'thousandaires', instead of ten billionaires, it would have been widely hailed in South Africa. Unfortunately the opposite has been the case. This has led to the widening of the wealth gap in South Africa, giving us the dubious honour of being the most unequal society in the world. Even the high-profile economist, Thomas Piketty, on his recent visit to South Africa, labelled BEE as a major contributor to extreme inequality in our country, and all but called for its scrapping! We all need to become obsessed with numbers. We must let greater numbers of people benefit from these programmes. When an organisation, be it in the private or public sector, implements an 'empowerment' programme it must attempt, as far as possible, to ensure that as many people as possible benefit from it. There is an urgent need to cast the net of beneficiaries as widely as possible. The greater the number of people who benefit from 'empowerment' programmes, the greater the acceptance will be, on the part of the disadvantaged, of the genuineness of these processes, instead of BEE being viewed as yet another manifestation of crony-capitalism. I am aware that government has been moving towards trying to encourage less of a 'big-bus' approach to BEE, in an attempt to create individual black entrepreneurs. But the approach which presupposes that broad-based empowerment initiatives are mutually exclusive of black individual entrepreneurship is, in my view, based on the erroneous assumption that this is a zero-sum game. Assuming that black individual business triumph and broad-based economic advancement are mutually exclusive is a mistake. It is possible, certainly through the 'enablement' approach which I espouse in this book, to have both.

- **A is for Accountability**

The sure-fire way of guaranteeing that any programme will collapse, is to ensure that no one is accountable for its success or failure. Accountability here is used in relation to both those with resources as well as those without (i.e., the beneficiaries of the programme). It has been one of the tragedies of programmes designed to ensure black economic advancement that, on many occasions, lines of accountability are opaque. Some are even shrouded in mystery, leading to allegations that it is deliberately done because there is a whiff of corruption about the whole thing anyway.

From another angle, such a lack of accountability may manifest itself as lack of clarity about the value the beneficiaries will be bringing to the table, or how they plan to justify their involvement in the project. This was bemoaned by Khoza (1997, p. xii): "Often we bring no more to the table than the pedigree of blackness and expect this to do the magic for us."

Similarly, on the other hand there is a situation where an organisation that has entered into a supposedly broad-based empowerment transaction with a community, simply disappears following its conclusion, never to be heard from again. This leaves communities stranded, as they do not know who to hold accountable for whatever benefits they were told would be accruing to them at a later stage, when such benefits seem to have evaporated into thin air. Members of the communities that are supposed to benefit are left high and dry, and without obvious recourse. This, for instance, has been prevalent in the platinum belt, where communities remain disillusioned and stranded to this day, sometimes decades after a much-touted empowerment transaction was concluded with great pomp and fanfare. One case that stands out in this regard is the dispute between the Bakgatla ba Kgafela and Bapo ba Mogale in the platinum belt of the North-West Province. Here, local communities are at loggerheads with their chiefs and with mining companies. The common concern is that lavish empowerment promises were made when mining companies secured their mining licences, but these promises of community upliftment, jobs and other benefits have barely materialised. Instead, as the community leaders allege, their chiefs have become supremely wealthy while community members have been left in the lurch:

> Concerned citizens seeking to review the web of laws, regulations and multibillion-rand mining deals on these lands are shut out.... Traditional leaders, often by virtue of their position in councils, are being included in the distribution of equity and equity-based revenue such as dividends, with little or no guarantee that benefits will reach people on the ground. The recent conversion of the Bapo ba Mogale's royalty into a 3.3% Lonmin Plc equity holding guarantees ZAR6 100 million ($9.49 million) over five years is for the 'general management' of the community, but nothing for its development. In several cases, courts have issued crippling punitive cost orders against community leaders who have sought to challenge these exclusive arrangements. One such leader, community lawyer David Pheto, has been bankrupted by punitive cost orders. (Claassens & Boyle, 2015)

This is indeed a sad case of promises gone awry, of dreams deferred amidst very murky accountability lines.

- **B is for Black**

This may well turn out to be the most controversial part of the programme. I can almost hear shouts of 'Racism!' echoing. Referring to the statistics and schematics quoted in the section addressing Jeffery's motivation for her EED approach, it is clear that poverty is endemic in South Africa. Therefore, improving the lot of black people remains a priority. There is no other way of looking at it. Unfortunately, however, there is now a strong argument that the most consistent beneficiaries of empowerment transactions in the past have actually been corporate financial advisers, most of whom are white. They collect generous fees and then move on to the next empowerment transaction. Some years are ago, there was a joke which went like this: Five white guys walk into a presentation room and say: 'We are a black company!' While we may not be familiar with what exactly was at play in that situation, we can only assume the company was majority black owned, yet black participants were conspicuous by their absence. In other words, this may well have been the worst form of fronting. Therefore it is vital to ensure that when a transaction of this nature is implemented, there are clearly identified and confirmed black participants and beneficiaries – something that has, oddly enough, been overlooked and yet seems so obvious! Of course, we all now know which individuals in South Africa are defined as 'black' in terms of both the constitution, and empowerment and EE legislation in general. Therefore there will hopefully be no disingenuous protestations about how we define a black person. I can only hope we have moved beyond that by now.

- **L is for a Level playing field**

Needless to say, in initiatives of this nature the scales of power are out of balance: on the one hand there will be either a government agency or a private sector organisation with ample resources engaging with people who, on the other hand, have virtually no resources. This creates an imbalance in power relations. In the past, this led to situations where manipulation and even corruption thrived. Those with resources have to learn something which is fairly hard to come by these days: humility. Public or private sector organisations have to approach such engagements with less arrogance, greater humility and a less intimidating stance. In some of the engagements I witnessed while researching this book, one of the key complaints from the various communities (be they struggling entrepreneurs in the townships or just members of civil society generally), relates to the arrogance they have to contend with every time they try to engage with those stakeholders. The communities pick up undertones that are either contemptuous and intimidating, or, at worst, outright dismissive of whatever input they make. Therefore, this is a plea for government and private-sector organisations to learn to be humble and empathetic as they engage with the disempowered and the disadvantaged. An intimidating or know-it-all attitude does not lay the foundation for anything except eventual failure.

• E is for Enable

This should be the end goal of the process. The ultimate aim should be to leave beneficiaries stronger than they were at the start of the process: stronger in terms of their skills, their entrepreneurship, their resources and their character, so that they are ready to move forward successfully.

A private sector organisation or government entity eventually has to reach a stage where it effectively disengages, without relinquishing accountability. As those of us who are parents know, when you teach your child to ride a bike, at some stage you have to let go and let the child pedal on his/her own. But that does not mean that you can just walk away! You need to follow at a reasonable distance, so that when your child runs into difficulties or is on the brink of falling off the bike, you are there to hold it steady. In a way the litmus test for establishing whether this has been accomplished, is to determine whether people are able to run a project on their own – if not, it means they have not been enabled. They may have been 'empowered' (on paper at least), but they have not been enabled. This is therefore not a typical approach to BEE where people sit and wait to collect dividends at a future as-yet-undetermined date. They are engaged, they are full participants, and they are the masters of their own fate.

In conclusion, let me quote from an excellent article by Robert Barner (1994), entitled 'Enablement: The key to empowerment', which refers to employees as beneficiaries (although the concept is relevant to non-employees as well): "Employee empowerment is the transfer of power and authority from managers to lower-level employees. A better term might be 'enablement'. *Enablement involves helping people develop the necessary competencies to manage their own empowerment effectively. When enablement isn't part of an empowerment effort, the effort is likely to fail.*"

• M for Monitoring mechanisms

As is often said in management parlance, 'that which you cannot measure you cannot monitor, and that which you cannot monitor will not materialise'.

It is incumbent on organisations to satisfy themselves that all initiatives which form part of an enablement exercise are proceeding adequately, without undue delay or hindrance. The tendency in the past with regard to empowerment transactions was that once such a transaction had been launched with pomp and fanfare, all monitoring ceased. All parties went their separate ways, hoping for the day when they would reconvene to share the spoils.

Another dimension of a lack of monitoring tends to manifest itself in situations where boards of companies do not exercise diligent oversight over all their initiatives. Once a policy has been put in place or a transaction has been concluded and announced, the board at best assumes that everything is falling neatly into place or, at worst, heaves a sigh of relief that the company has finally dealt with government's rules and regulations, and thinks they can now get back to business. Vigilance is required all round. This includes beneficiaries of a programme, so that they do not sit back and hope everything will go well or that things will happen by themselves. Some argue that one of the reasons why things went badly in the platinum transactions mentioned above, is that the communities concerned were not vigilant enough from the get-go. They became complacent and allowed all sorts of malpractices to eventually creep in, only to wake up when taking corrective action was noticeably much more challenging.

- **E is for Employment**

In my view, the key tragedy with traditional empowerment programmes has been the absence of discourse around employment creation. It is almost as if the two concepts are irreconcilable. I would argue that BEE would be a much more popular endeavour with ordinary folk, if it led to the employment of many. It is important to realise that ultimately the key criterion for successful BEE is job creation. There cannot be economic empowerment in the midst of a dearth of jobs. To talk of BEE in the face of massive unemployment is like talking about a sumptuous meal when there is famine all round. It almost sounds cruel and cynical.

Without employment an individual is robbed of dignity, self-worth and a sense of purpose in life. Therefore it is unfortunate that BEE and job creation have been strange bedfellows thus far. It is my view that BEE would have been seen as relevant, useful, and uplifting by the average black South African, if job creation were at its core. That is why, going forward, initiatives of this nature must focus on creating employment opportunities. Priority (and indeed a higher rating on BEE scores) must be given to those empowerment programmes that demonstrably lead to job creation. And, conversely, poor ratings must be given to those empowerment initiatives that do not contain a plan and programme aimed at creating new jobs.

• N is for Nation building

This section is effectively a call for the revival of those programmes that were started by Aggrey Klaaste in the late 80s, for which he coined the phrase 'nation building'. It is a call not only to revive them, but to integrate them into present-day empowerment programmes. Let's refresh our memories about what the nation-building programme was, when it was first initiated by Dr Klaaste.

Dr Aggrey Zola Klaaste (6 January 1940 – 19 June 2004) was a highly respected black journalist, community activist and intellectual. He achieved national and international prominence at the time when he was editor of the Soweto-based anti-apartheid newspaper, *The Sowetan* (1988–2002). After observing the devastation (particularly on the black social and moral fabric) which the various black uprisings caused in the 70s and 80s, and the consequently brutal repression by the apartheid government, he felt that, although liberation had not yet dawned for black people, it was critical that a process of reconstructing the black family and community begin at once, lest liberation find a wasteland when it eventually dawned. This endeavour he called 'nation building'.

> According to Klaaste, institutions in the black community had to be rebuilt. In no time, business and society in general was giving Klaaste support and the African National Congress even gave its blessing to the campaign. (Mazwai, 2011)

While it would be an exaggeration to suggest that at present black South Africans are experiencing the same level of devastation as was the case during apartheid, it is nonetheless important to acknowledge that the high levels of inequality and unemployment in our country have had a devastating effect on the black psyche and black people's hope for the future, let alone on the family structure. Many argue that the high levels of violence in South African society, as manifested in minor crimes leading to the death or serious injury of the victims, various widely reported incidents of physical abuse in the home, or road rage incidents, are symptomatic of deep psychological scars in our society. It is widely known that there is no nation on earth that has had, persistently over a similar period of time, one in four people who is without work, as has been the case in South Africa. Therefore I would argue that we need to begin to not only confine ourselves to addressing the material conditions of our fellow citizens, but also to address 'soft' issues arising out of these challenging material conditions. And, in my view, there is no approach or programme better suited to deal with this challenge than Klaaste's nation-building project.

There would be no greater and more patriotic approach, in my view, than organisations integrating some nation-building initiative into their empowerment or enablement programmes. They will not only be helping to improve the physical conditions of beneficiaries, but they will also be 'growing' better and more balanced and responsible citizens. That can only set us up as a nation for greater stability and prosperity, going forward.

- **T is for Transformation**, a new version

Broadly speaking, in post-1994 South Africa the rather innocuous-sounding word, transformation, has been acquiring harsher and (some would say) more sinister connotations. I would wager that if I were to stand in the middle of Times Square in New York and shout: 'We want transformation!', passers-by would look at me with a smirk on their faces and conclude that I am in need of psychiatric help. But their attitude would either be that of mild amusement or muted sympathy. However, if I were to stand in Paul Kruger Square in Pretoria and shout the same phrase, the reaction would be entirely different. The word is not seen as entirely benign in South Africa. It will most likely either elicit shouts of: 'Hear hear!'; some may shout profanities at me or become aggressive. For South Africans, this is indeed a loaded term.

Exclusive of its benign global understandings, since the dawn of democracy in South Africa 'transformation' has, broadly speaking, acquired the following four connotations, largely dependent on whether one has left-wing (supposedly black) or right-wing (supposedly white) leanings:

1. Replace whites with blacks in institutions, organisations or sports teams;
2. Replace competency and operational efficiency with mismanagement and corruption;
3. Ensure that all institutions in the country, be they in the public or private sector, are representative of the demographics of the country;
4. Remove racial enclaves and ensure that we are a truly integrated rainbow nation, as envisaged by Mandela and other post-racial visionaries.

The above points indicate how emotive and highly charged the word has become. In the spirit of moving forward, it is my intention to coin my own interpretation of the word. In my view, transformation denotes those initiatives or processes that are designed to make it possible or easy for the previously excluded to access opportunities and resources in both the present and the future. Please mark my use of the two words, 'easy' and 'possible', as they are core to my definition of enablement, as defined earlier.

My definition, therefore, by its very nature, is more expansive than perhaps has traditionally been the case. Following this definition, I see the process of BEN as being the responsibility not just of the white Establishment (as has been the case in the recent past) – instead, the responsibility should be on those institutions or individuals with the necessary resources at their disposal to deploy towards accomplishing BEN, be they black or white institutions, black or white business moguls. In its simplest form, whether one is a white or a black billionaire, one has the moral and ethical (and indeed patriotic!) duty to deploy some resources towards BEN, not just in the form of charitable giveaways. Whether one is a leader of a JSE-listed entity or a leader of an SOE, that particular institution, because of the resources it has at its disposal, has the responsibility to deploy some of those resources towards BEN. Consequently, the colour or the character of the deployer of those resources becomes irrelevant. What becomes relevant is whether or not the individual or the institution has those resources.

In conclusion, it is therefore my hope that, going forward, pressure will not only be brought to bear on white institutions or white leaders to facilitate BEN, but that even black institutions and black business leaders will come under scrutiny and pressure to facilitate this process. It cannot be disputed that as things stand today, there are black institutions and businesses (or indeed black business leaders) with vast resources at their disposal. Why should they be exempt from pressure to facilitate BEN? We all have a responsibility to ensure that BEN happens, because ultimately there will be no peace, security or stability in this country unless and until the average South African has a stake in the success of the country.

CONCLUSION

At the beginning of this book there is a quote from Mark Barnes. True to my name, Phinda (which in Zulu translates to: say it again), I will repeat, using my own words, the meaning of Mr Barnes' words. The promise of a new South Africa, as politically negotiated in the early 90s by our founding fathers and mothers, will perpetually ring hollow until each and every South African has economically benefited from our democracy. Each one of us needs to be concerned about whether or not the lot of our fellow compatriots has improved.

If it hasn't, it is mission 'not yet accomplished'. But more importantly, as Barnes concludes, there will never be peace and stability in our land until the lot of the average South African has improved.

People cannot – and will never – sleep well in Sandton until the average Sowetan has food on the table. Therefore, it is in the interests of all those South Africans who have benefited from the democratic dividend, be they black or white, yellow or green, to concern themselves about whether or not a fellow citizen in Babanango or Barberton, Nkowankowa or Kimberley, Cape Town or KwaMhlanga, is living well. That, after all, was the vision of Nelson Rolihlahla Mandela.

REFERENCES

ANC. (2014). *Freedom Charter*. Retrieved from https://www.ancgauteng.org.za/index.php/documents/declaritions/19-the-freedom-charter/file [Last accessed September 7, 2015].

Appel, H. (1997). Voucher privatisation in Russia: Structural consequences and mass response in the second period of reform. *Europe-Asia Studies, 49*, 8, 1433–1449.

Backhaus, J., and Schumpeter, J. A. (2003). *Entrepreneurship, style and vision*. Illinois: University of Illinois at Urbana-Champaign.

Barner, R. (1994). Enablement: The key to empowerment. *Training & Development, 48*, 6, 33–36.

Barnes, M. (2013). Time to re-design black economic empowerment. *Business Day*, October 7. Retrieved from http://www.bdlive.co.za/opinion/columnists/2013/10/07/time-to-redesign-black-economic-empowerment [Last accessed September 7, 2015].

Barron, C. (2012). BEE killed self-reliance, says Richard Maponya. *Business Day*, December 9. Retrieved from http://www.bdlive.co.za/business/2012/12/09/bee-killed-self-reliance-says-richard-maponya [Last accessed October 5, 2015].

Black Economic Empowerment Commission (BEECom). (2001). *The BEECom report*. Johannesburg: Skotaville Press. Retrieved from https://www.westerncape.gov.za/text/2004/5/beecomreport.pdf [Last accessed September 8, 2015].

Browning, P. (1989). *Black economic empowerment: Shaping South African business for the 21st century*. Parklands: Fontein.

Bruce, P. (2015). *Thick end of the wedge: How the JSE can unite business in SA*. Business Day Live, May 22. Retrieved from http://www.bdlive.co.za/opinion/columnists/2015/05/22/thick-end-of-the-wedge-how-the-jse-can-unite-business-in-sa [Last accessed September 25, 2015].

Business Day. (2012, October 28). *Don't stress about us in South Africa*. Retrieved from http://www.bdlive.co.za/opinion/2012/10/28/dont-stress-about-us-in-sa [Last accessed September 7, 2015].

Business Day. (2013, October 7). *Time to redesign black economic empowerment*. Retrieved from http://www.bdlive.co.za/opinion/columnists/2013/10/07/time-to-redesign-black-economic-empowerment [Last accessed September 8, 2015].

Business Day. (2013, October 13). *Think big by growing smaller*. Retrieved from http://www.bdlive.co.za/business/2013/10/13/think-big-by-growing-smaller [Last accessed September 7, 2015].

Business Day. (2015, January 26). *Straight talk: Black industrialist move is timely*. Retrieved from http://www.bdlive.co.za/opinion/columnists/2015/07/06/straight-talk-black-industrialist-move-is-timely [Last accessed September 8, 2015].

Business Day. (2015, February 26). *Government-owned enterprises: State assets' problems 'result of governance failure'*. Retrieved from http://www.bdlive.co.za/business/2015/02/26/government-owned-enterprises-state-assets-problems-result-of-governance-failure [Last accessed September 8, 2015].

Business Day. (2015, March 17). *Motsepe accuses Eskom of 'letting SA down badly'*. Retrieved from http://www.bdlive.co.za/business/mining/2015/03/17/motsepe-accuses-eskom-of-letting-sa-down-badly [Last accessed September 7, 2015].

BusinessDictionary. (n.d.). Definition of 'entrepreneur'. Retrieved from http://www.businessdictionary.com/definition/entrepreneur.html [Last accessed September 8, 2015].

Business in Africa Magazine. (2006, June). What is Asgisa? Retrieved from http://com/ Economy/What-is-Asgisa-20060707 [Last accessed September 8, 2015].

Business Unity South Africa (Busa). (2010). *Perspectives on an inclusive job-rich growth path for South Africa by 2025.* Discussion document.

Butler, A. (2011). *Cyril Ramaphosa (Revised).* Auckland Park: Jacana Media.

Caldwell, D. (1989). *South Africa: The new revolution.* Saxonwold: The Free Market Foundation.

Chakraborty, S., Thompson, J. C., & Yehoue, E. B. (2015). Culture in development. *The World Bank Economic Review, 29,* 2. doi: 10.1093/wber/lhv018.

City Press. (2012, April 29.). *SA's black wealth accumulation crisis.* Retrieved from http://www.news24.com/archives/city-press/sas-black-wealth-accumulation-crisis-20150429 [Last accessed September 7, 2015].

Claassens, A., & Boyle, B. (2015). A promise betrayed: Policies and practice renew the rural dispossession of land, rights and prospects. *SAIA policy briefing* 124, January.

Destiny Magazine. (2013, September 30). *BEE killing entrepreneurship.* Retrieved from http://www.destinyconnect.com/2013/09/30/black-economic-empowerment-killing-entrepreneurship/ [Last accessed September 8, 2015].

Diaz, K. K. (2014). The myth of 100 black industrialists. *LinkedIn Pulse,* November 18. Retrieved from https://www.linkedin.com/pulse/20141118101516-92988875-the-myth-of-100-black-industrialists [Last accessed September 7, 2015].

Ellerman, D. (n.d.). *Lessons from Europe's voucher privatization.* http://cog.kent.edu/lib/ Ellerman5.htm [Last accessed September 20, 2015].

Ernst & Young (EY). (2012). *The power of three: Together, governments, entrepreneurs and corporations can spur growth across the G20.* Retrieved from http://www.ey.com/ Publication/vwLUAssets/The_power_of_three_-_SA/$FILE/EY%20G20%20 Entrepreneurship%20Barometer%202013%20Country%20Report%20-%20 South%20Africa_Low%20Res.pdf [Last accessed September 8, 2015].

EWN. (2011). *Skills shortage is SA's biggest challenge – Mboweni.* Retrieved from http://m. ewn.co.za/2011/08/19/Skills-shortage-is-SAs-biggest-challenge--Mboweni [Last accessed September 28, 2011].

Fin24. (2015). *Former Prasa CEO Lucky Montana: 'I'm innocent'.* Retrieved from http://www.fin24.com/BizNews/Former-Prasa-CEO-Lucky-Montana-Im-innocent-20150827 [Last accessed September 25, 2015].

Fin24 Archives. (2006-7). *What is Asgisa?* Retrieved from http://www.fin24 [Last accessed September 8, 2015].

Financial Mail. (2014, August 7). *Tito Mboweni and empowerment: Rude awakening.* Retrieved from http://www.financialmail.co.za/coverstory/2014/08/07/tito-mboweni-and-empowerment-rude-awakening [Last accessed September 25, 2015].

Gates, B. (2014). *Why inequality matters.* Retrieved from http://www.gatesnotes.com/ Books/Why-Inequality-Matters-Capital-in-21st-Century-Review (Last accessed October 2, 2015).

Human Capital Labour Reports. (2015). *South Africa.* Bryanston: KR Publishing.

Jacobs, S. (2002). *The ANC and black capitalism in South Africa.* Retrieved from http://ccs. ukzn.ac.za/files/southall.pdf [Last accessed September 25, 2015].

Jacobs, S. (2002). *About turn: The ANC and economic empowerment.* Retrieved from http:// www.nu.ac.za/indicator/Vol19No1/19.1htm [Last accessed September 25, 2015].

Jeffery, A. (2014). *BEE – helping or hurting?* Cape Town: NB Publishers.

Johnson, R. W. (2015). *How long will South Africa survive?* Cape Town: Jonathan Ball.

Khoza, R. (1997). Foreword. In P. M. Padi, *Black economic empowerment in South Africa – the rights and wrongs* (p. xii). Rosebank, South Africa: Knowledge Resources.

Macozoma, S. (2003). Address to the University of KZN: "From a theory of revolution to the management of the fragile state". In D. Everatt and V. Maphai (Eds.), *The real state of the nation: South Africa after 1990*. Development Update 4, 11–30. Also retrievable from http://ccs.ukzn.ac.za/files/theory%20of%20revolution.pdf

Madi, P. M. (1993). *Affirmative action in corporate South Africa – surviving in the jungle.* Kenwyn: Juta.

Madi, P. M. (1997). *Black economic empowerment in South Africa – the rights and the wrongs.* Rosebank: Knowledge Resources.

Mail & Guardian. (2011, September 5). *Forget nationalisation and BEE, SA needs entrepreneurs.* Retrieved from http://ht.ly/6lFjV?fb_ref=Default%2C%40Total [Last accessed September 8, 2015].

Mail & Guardian. (2015, March 6). *Govt supplier database a blow to corruption.* Retrieved from http://mg.co.za/article/2015-03-05-govt-supplier-database-a-blow-to-corruption [Last accessed September 8, 2015].

Mandela, N. 1994. *Long walk to freedom.* New York: Little, Brown & Company.

Mantashe, G. (2015). BEE not benefitting SA masses. SABC news bulletin, Friday, June 12.

Mashaba, H. (2015). *Capitalist crusader.* Blackheath: Bookstorm.

Masina, M., Deputy Minister of Trade and Industry. (2014). DTI media statement, August 14.

Mazwai, T. (2011). *Look to the proud legacy of Percy Qoboza and Aggrey Klaaste. Business Day*, August 24. Retrieved from http://www.bdlive.co.za/articles/2011/08/24/thami-mazwai-look-to-the-proud-legacy-of-qoboza-and-klaaste [Last accessed September 7, 2015].

Mbeki, M. (2009). *Why BEE should be abolished.* IOL Online, November, 29. Retrieved from http://www.iol.co.za/news/politics/why-bee-should-be-abolished-1.466121 [Last accessed September 25, 2015].

Mbeki, T. (1998). Address to Parliament, May 29.

Mbeki, T. (2000). Presidential keynote address. Retrieved from http://www.anc.org.za/show.php?id=2560 [Last accessed September 7, 2015].

Mbeki, T. (2015). *Mbeki: Apartheid legacy still hangs over SA.* EWN News, July 7. http://ewn.co.za/2015/07/07/Mbeki-Apartheid-legacy-still-hangs-over-SA [Last accessed September 25, 2015].

Mickos, M. (n.d). *What is the difference between a businessman and an entrepreneur?* Retrieved from https://www.quora.com/What-is-the-difference-between-a-businessman-and-an-entrepreneur [Last accessed September 25, 2015].

Molatlhwa, O. (2015). *Share the wealth or SA will suffer - Mashatile.* Times Live, September 16. Retrieved from http://www.timeslive.co.za/thetimes/2015/09/16/Share-the-wealth-or-SA-will-suffer--Mashatile [Last accessed October 10, 2015].

Motluoase, M. (1981). *Anthology of contemporary South African writings.* London: Heinemann.

Mu-hyun, C. (2015). *The chaebols: The rise of South Korea's mighty conglomerates.* CNet, April 6. Retrieved from http://www.cnet.com/news/the-chaebols-the-rise-of-south-koreas-mighty-conglomerates/ [Last accessed September 25, 2015].

Naidoo, J. (2014). The third annual Frederik van Zyl Slabbert (FVZS) honorary lecture at Stellenbosch University, South Africa, April.

Naki, E. (2012). Tenderpreneurs: The bad side of BEE. *The New Age*, February 22.

National Development Agency (NDA). (2014). *State of poverty and its manifestation in the nine provinces of South Africa*. Retrieved from http://www.nda.org.za/docs/Research%20Report%20-%20State%20of%20poverty%20in%209%20provinces%20of%20SA.PDF [Last accessed September 7, 2015].

National Planning Commission (NPC). (2011). *National Development Plan 2030: Our future – make it work*. Retrieved from http://www.statssa.gov.za/wp-content/uploads/2013/07/NDP-2030-Our-future-make-it-work.pdf [Last accessed September 7, 2015].

Ndebele, N. S. (2012). *Liberation betrayed by bloodshed. City Press*, August 26. Retrieved from http://www.news24.com/Archives/City-Press/Liberation-betrayed-by-bloodshed-20150430 [Last accessed September 8, 2015].

News24. (2015, January 7). *ANC to reclaim freedom charter – Mantashe*. Retrieved from http://www.news24.com/SouthAfrica/Politics/ANC-to-reclaim-freedom-charter-Mantashe-20150107-3 [Last accessed September 28, 2015].

Newton-King, N. (2013). *Black South Africans hold at least 23% of the Top 100 companies listed on the Johannesburg Stock Exchange*. Retrieved from https://www.jse.co.za/articles/black-south-africans-top-100-companies-listed-on-the-johannesburg-stock-exchange [Last accessed September 8, 2015].

O'Malley, P. (1990-1994). Nelson Mandela Centre of Memory, Chapter 7: Political violence in the era of negotiations and transition, 1990-1994. The report of the Truth and Reconciliation Commission, Volume 2. Retrieved from https://www.nelsonmandela.org/omalley/index.php/site/q/03lv02167/04lv02264/05lv02335/06lv02357/07lv02372/08lv02379.htm [Last accessed September 21, 2015].

Oxfam. (2013). Media briefing, January 18. Ref 02/2013.

Oxfam. (2015, June). *Is South Africa operating in a safe and just space?* Retrieved from http://www.scribd.com/doc/266668597/Is-South-Africa-Operating-in-a-Safe-and-Just-Space-Using-the-doughnut-model-to-explore-environmental-sustainability-and-social-justice#scribd [Last accessed September 8, 2015].

Oxford dictionary online. (n.d.). Retrieved from http://www.oxforddictionaries.com/ [Last accessed September 25, 2015].

Piketty, T. (2013). *Capital in the 21st century*. Trans A. Goldhammer. Cambridge, MA: Harvard University Press.

Piketty, T. (2014). *The economics of inequality*. Lecture delivered on January 7. Retrieved from http://piketty.pse.ens.fr/files/PikettyEcoIneg2013Lecture5.pdf [Last accessed October 2, 2015].

Plaut, M. (2012). *Behind the Marikana massacre. New Statesman*, August, 20. Retrieved from http://www.newstatesman.com/blogs/world-affairs/2012/08/behind-marikana-massacre [Last accessed September 25, 2015].

Rand Daily Mail. (2015, April 17). *Plan to create 100 black industrialists is doomed to fail. Here's why...* Retrieved from http://www.rdm.co.za/business/2015/04/17/plan-to-create-100-black-industrialists-is-doomed-to-fail.-here-s-why-... [Last accessed September 25, 2015].

South African History Online. (n.d.). *The Freedom Charter is adopted in Kliptown, Sunday, 26 June 1955*. Retrieved from http://www.sahistory.org.za/dated-event/freedom-charter-adopted-kliptown [Last accessed September 8, 2015].

South African History Online. (n.d.). *Boipatong massacre, 17 June 1992*. Retrieved from http://www.sahistory.org.za/topic/boipatong-massacre-17-june-1992 [Last accessed October 10, 2015].

South African History Online (n.d.). *Bantu Education Act, No. 47 of 1953*. Retrieved from http://www.sahistory.org.za/bantu-education-act-no-47-1953 [Last accessed September 21, 2015].

Southern African Institute of Race Relations (SAIRR). (2015). The rise and fall of Eskom and how to fix it. *SAIRR, 2,* 18.

Sparks, A. (2010). Discussion of 'first drafts'. Monday, June 28. Retrieved from http://www.booklounge.co.za/2010/06/28/Allister-Sparks-discussion-of-first-drafts/ [Last accessed September 8, 2015].

Stokes, G. (2012). Arab Spring (conference). Will the Arab Spring tear through South Africa? Retrieved from http://www.fanews.co.za/article/talked-about-features/25/the-stage/1145/will-the-arab-spring-tear-through-south-africa/12002 [Last accessed September 25, 2015].

Sunter, C. (2011). *Unfinished business*. News24, September 21. Retrieved from http://www.news24.com/Columnists/ClemSunter/Unfinished-business-20110921 [Last accessed September 8, 2015].

Sunter, C. (2012). *Is South Africa about to experience its own Arab Spring? The Leader Magazine*, September 29. Retrieved from http://www.leader.co.za/article.aspx?s=23&f=1&a=4011 [Last accessed September 8, 2015].

Suzman, H. (2009). *Key legislation in the formation of apartheid*. Retrieved from http://www.cortland.edu/cgis/suzman/apartheid.html [Last accessed September 7, 2015].

The South African. (2010, February 23). *How Malema made his millions*. Retrieved from http://www.thesouthafrican.com/how-malema-made-his-millions/ [Last accessed September 8, 2015].

The Sowetan. (2015, June 29). *Dirty money killing the ANC*. Retrieved from http://www.pressreader.com/south-africa/sowetan/20150629/281479275067251/TextView [Last accessed September 25, 2015].

Truth and Reconciliation Commission of South Africa Report. (1998). Volume Five. Retrieved from http://www.justice.gov.za/trc/report/finalreport/Volume5.pdf [Last accessed September 28, 2015].

Tutu, D., & Allen, J. (1994). *The rainbow people of God: The making of a peaceful revolution*. New York: Doubleday.

Vecchiatto, P. (2013). *Africa's richest man warns SA on "forced marriage" BEE. Business Day*, May 8. Retrieved from http://www.bdlive.co.za/business/2013/05/08/africas-richest-warns-sa-on-forced-marriage-bee [Last accessed September 8, 2015].

Visser, W. (2004). *Shifting RDP into Gear: The ANC government's dilemma in providing an equitable system of social security for the "new" South Africa*. Retrieved from http://sun025.sun.ac.za/portal/page/portal/Arts/Departemente1/geskiedenis/docs/rdp_into_gear.pdf [Last accessed September 25, 2015].

Vollgraaff, R. (2015). *Power crisis cripples investment, risks rating*. Fin24, April 8. Retrieved from http://www.fin24.com/Economy/Power-crisis-cripples-investment-risks-rating-20150408 [Last accessed September 21, 2015].

Wikipedia. (2015). *Tenderpreneur*. Retrieved from https://en.wikipedia.org/wiki/Tenderpreneur [Last accessed September 8, 2015].

Xiaoping, D. (1962). Speech at the Communist Youth League Conference, July. In *Chambers dictionary of quotations* (1993), p. 315.

Zibi, S. (2015). *Economic justice will help quiet the rage*. Business Day Live, September 21. Retrieved from http://www.bdlive.co.za/opinion/columnists/2015/09/21/ unembargoed-economic-justice-will-help-quiet-the-rage [Last accessed October 10, 2015].

Supplementary reading

On apartheid legislation, see https://www.nelsonmandela.org/omalley/index.php/site/ q/03lv01538/04lv01828/05lv01829/06lv01830.htm

On the pass laws, see http://www.sahistory.org.za/south-africa-1806-1899/pass-laws-south-africa-1800-1994

On the Sullivan principles, see https://en.wikipedia.org/wiki/Sullivan_principles

INDEX

Books by Phinda Madi

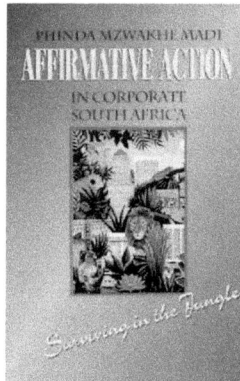

1993 Published by Juta & Company

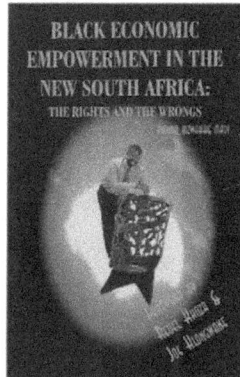

1997 Published by Knowledge Resources, Randburg

2002 Published by Knowledge Resources, Randburg

Books by Philida Madi